Personal
Financial Markets

**An examination of the evolving markets
for personal savings and financing
in the United Kingdom
and the United States**

edited by
R.L. CARTER
and
B. CHIPLIN
and
M.K. LEWIS
*Nottingham Institute of Financial Studies
University of Nottingham*

Philip Allan

First published 1986 by

PHILIP ALLAN PUBLISHERS LIMITED
MARKET PLACE
DEDDINGTON
OXFORD OX5 4SE

British Library Cataloguing in Publication Data

Personal financial markets.
  1. Financial institutions   2. Finance,
  Personal
  I. Carter, Robert L.   II. Chiplin, Brian
  III. Lewis, M.K.
  332.1   HG179

  ISBN 0-86003-540-9 ✓
  ISBN 0-86003-642-1 Pbk

Typeset by MHL Typesetting Ltd, Coventry
Printed in Great Britain by the Bocardo Press Ltd, Oxford

Personal
Financial Markets

Contents

Contributors

M.R. Binks, BA, PhD, Lecturer in Economics, University of Nottingham.

R.L. Carter, BSc (Econ), DPhil, FCII, Norwich Union Professor of Insurance Studies, University of Nottingham.

B. Chiplin, BA, Professor of Industrial Economics, University of Nottingham.

J. Coyne, BA, Lecturer in Industrial Economics and Finance, University of Nottingham.

S.R. Diacon, BSc, PhD, Lecturer with special reference to Insurance, University of Nottingham.

M.K. Lewis, BEc, PhD, Midland Bank Professor of Money and Banking, University of Nottingham.

T. Watkins, BA, Head of the Department of Business Management, Dorset Institute of Higher Education.

D.M. Wright, BA, MA, PhD, AIL, Lecturer with special reference to Accounting, University of Nottingham.

Preface

The financial services industry is one of the fastest growing sectors
of the British economy, and is undergoing rapid technological and
regulatory change. Forces of competition and structural adjustment
are sweeping away traditional barriers between different types of
financial services, blurring the lines between banks, building
societies, insurance companies, securities firms and other financial
institutions. New financial instruments and new market groupings
offer both opportunities and challenges to market participants and
to personal savers and borrowers.

The Nottingham Institute of Financial Studies was established
last year to coordinate research at the University of Nottingham into
financial markets. Members of the Institute have undertaken a
major review of the changes in the markets for personal financial
services, and that research forms the basis of this book.

As part of the review, members of the Institute visited and sent
questionnaires to leading executives of banks, building societies,
insurance companies and other financial institutions in the UK. We
consider that this survey provides a unique profile of the thinking
and attitudes of members of the financial industry, and the results
feature in most of the chapters which follow. Interviews were also
conducted with financial institutions in the United States, where
change has been so rapid that developments have been hailed as a
'personal financial services revolution'. Despite marked differences
in institutional structure, we find many similarities between recent
experiences in the US and the UK, and these comparisons feature in
a number of chapters.

The emphasis of the book is upon markets, rather than institutions, and the chapters in the first half of the book examine the

nature of financial markets, the contribution which they can make to the formation of national and personal wealth, the differences between financial services and other traded goods and services, the marketing and distribution of financial services, and the ways in which developments in information technology are transforming personal financial markets. People participate on both sides of financial and capital markets, and later chapters examine their supply of finance to the markets in the UK for short-term deposits and longer-term 'investments', and their demand for finance in the markets for housing finance and consumer credit. People can also place funds into new enterprises and themselves establish new firms, and one chapter is devoted to the demand for and supply of entrepreneurial finance. The concluding chapter looks at trends in market organisation and regulation, and the implications for the future of financial firms.

We are grateful to the institutions and people cooperating in the preparation of this study, and especially to those providing financial sponsorship. Heather Lockley and Helen Whalley assisted the authors in the preparation of the tables and figures, while Carole Hawthorne, Jill Wilson and Sue Grattage cheerfully typed the manuscript. Kay Lewis provided the book with an index.

University of Nottingham
August 1986

CHAPTER 1

Personal Saving and Finance

R.L. Carter, B. Chiplin and M.K. Lewis

1.1 Personal and National Wealth

On 31 December 1984 the personal sector[1] of the UK economy had a stock of physical assets valued at £666,900 million. Of the total, some 73 per cent (nearly £500,000 million) represented the value of houses and other dwellings and a further 15 per cent was held in the form of consumer durables. As well as these physical assets, the personal sector holds a large volume of financial assets including cash, bank and building society deposits, ordinary shares, unit trust units and life insurance and pension policies. The total estimated value of these financial assets stood at £569,613 million, some 85 per cent of the value of the physical assets. Financial liabilities are also incurred by the personal sector, mainly in the form of loans for house purchases and from banks and other sources for other purposes. At the end of 1984, these were estimated to be £173,525 million.

Net wealth is simply the total value of physical and financial assets minus the value of financial liabilities, and for the personal sector as a whole stood at over £1,000,000 million in December 1984. The personal sector is not, of course, the only sector in the economy, which also consists of the business, government and foreign sectors. Whilst figures for the wealth of some of these constituent parts are published on a regular basis, e.g. annually for the personal sector, data on total national wealth are not generally available. In fact, until 1980 there was no official estimate of such national wealth despite its obvious importance.[2] Figures were published in that year relating to the end of 1975 which are the latest figures currently available. At that time total national wealth was

1

estimated at £481,000 million or about £8,500 per head of population. Of this total, some 32 per cent was attributed to the personal sector, 28 per cent to the business sector and 39 per cent to the public sector.

In estimating the figure for total national wealth, the Central Statistical Office in effect undertook a stocktaking of the tangible assets then in the country. These were classified as follows:

	£ million
Agricultural and other land	11,300
Buildings and works	132,900
Dwellings	206,100
Cars, ships and aircraft	16,600
Plant and machinery	80,900
Producer stocks	35,000
Net claims on overseas	− 1,800

These assets enable the British people to satisfy some of their present and future needs and desires, in a number of ways. Some assets, like stocks of finished goods in retail shops, can be consumed directly. Others, such as durable goods like houses and motor vehicles, provide services which can be consumed over many years, and in some cases over several generations.

A considerable proportion of the wealth of a country consists of buildings, equipment and natural resources which need to be combined with human effort and skills to produce output. This fact immediately highlights one feature of the figures above − the missing items. Difficulties in measurement lead the statisticians to omit any calculation of the value of assets of national resources, such as coal and oil, which are still in the 'ground'. Also, one of the major assets of any country is the value of the skills and expertise embodied in the labour force. Such human capital is not included in the above table. Finally, since expenditure on consumer durables is counted as part of current consumers' expenditure in the national income accounts, the value of the stock of such durables is not included in this estimate of national wealth. At the end of 1975 the value of consumer durables was estimated to be £33,400 million.

Not all of these assets are located in the UK. UK citizens own property and structures abroad which can be sold off or used to obtain income and thus goods and services in future years. Foreigners own a part of the assets located in the UK, and the figure shown above indicates that the net value of claims held by Britons overseas was exceeded by that held by foreigners against the UK.

Ultimately virtually all of the wealth, whether allocated to the personal or business sectors, is owned by individuals. Furthermore, if we regard the state as simply representing the collective wishes of the inhabitants of the country, the ownership of *all* wealth can be seen as residing with individuals. Yet a person can be regarded as wealthy without holding any of the assets included by the Central Statistical Office when it summed the nation's wealth. Most British households own houses, cars and other consumer durables. Despite the present government's efforts to encourage new enterprise – examined in Chapter 9 – few are direct owners of buildings, equipment and stocks of producer goods. Instead, they hold claims which do not even rate a mention in the stocktaking above: currency, building society and bank deposits, national savings certificates, insurance policies, pension rights, and shares in corporations. These, as noted above, are financial assets which take the form of claims against other individuals, institutions, or governments.

Looked at in the aggregate, the contrast between the real and the financial assets could not be sharper. Most real assets, other than land and natural resources, are produced as part of the output of trading enterprises and governments either in one's own or other countries. They are physical, tangible goods, which derive their value from a capacity to yield a stream of goods and services in the future. A financial asset, by contrast, is simply a paper title or promise to payment at some time in the future. It arises when someone lends funds to another person, enterprise, government or public authority which wishes to borrow. Each financial asset necessarily has two dimensions to it: one is the entitlement to payment expected by the person or enterprise holding the asset; the other is the liability of the borrower who issued the asset to make this payment. It follows that every financial asset counted in one person's or organisation's wealth is at the same time a liability for some other person or organisation. With one's financial asset being another's debt, the financial claims wash out when aggregated. What remains are the tangible assets listed above, owned ultimately by individuals and households even if indirectly held by the government on their behalf.

From the viewpoint of the way the economy works, as opposed to national accounting, the financial claims are of the greatest

importance in enabling indirect ownership of the productive real
assets. Indirect ownership is perhaps the most distinctive feature of
modern capitalism. Individuals and households ultimately own the
real assets, but delegate control on a day-to-day, or even year-to-
year, basis to a network of intermediaries – firms, financial institutions and governments – which stand between them and the
ultimate constituents of wealth. This delegation occurs through
financial markets. Indeed, such delegation would not occur without
the existence of financial markets.

1.2 The Role of Financial Markets

Current Conservative Government policy places considerable
emphasis on entrepreneurship and 'personal capitalism' as distinct
from indirect ownership and delegation to intermediaries. Accordingly, people are being encouraged to establish and run their own
business enterprises. The extent to which UK households own corporate shares through unit trusts and insurance companies with the
corresponding delegation of responsibility to financial
intermediaries is often compared unfavourably with the position in
other countries, particularly the United States. Individuals are,
therefore, being urged to 'invest' in shares directly as exemplified,
for example, by the Government's attempt to encourage the personal ownership of British Telecom shares on its privatisation in
1985.

Such an argument is also behind the proposals for a personal
equity scheme introduced in the 1986 Budget. It ignores the fact that
there are marked institutional differences between countries. British
life insurers, for example, have long offered their policyholders
more imaginative and participatory 'investment' packages than
have their US counterparts (see Chapters 5 and 8). It also fails to
appreciate that financial markets are dynamic and subject to substantial change. There is some evidence, for example, of a marked
increase of direct ownership of shares in the UK in recent years.[3]

In addition, the argument ignores the variety of reasons which
prompt intermediation of wealth. Many of these reasons are common to intermediation through 'productive' firms as well as intermediation through the financial intermediaries. Indeed, in the next
chapter we explore the similarities – along with the differences –

between financial and non-financial products and the choices and opportunities open to financial and non-financial firms. But it is the financial intermediaries upon which we concentrate now.

Delegation to Intermediaries[4]

Control is delegated to financial intermediaries in part because, through specialisation, they are able to acquire and use information more efficiently than individuals and households. This information, at least in principle, enables the intermediaries to select better investments and monitor their performance at lower cost than would be the case if individuals themselves acquired the tangible assets and managed the investment. Intermediaries may also be more tax efficient and able to put together financial packages which defer liability for taxation partly through their superior knowledge. Of course, there are costs. The intermediary may not always act in the best interests of the household; there may be conflicts of interest between managers, shareholders, debtors and the parties to transactions. As we shall see, there are marked differences between the way such potential conflicts of interest are handled in the USA and Britain.

Delegation occurs also because the complex network of intermediation opens up choices to individuals and households which do not exist in the aggregate and because many real assets are indivisible. Intermediaries enable a large number of individuals to share in the ownership and returns from large-scale assets whilst economising on transaction costs. The textbook models of perfect competition or perfect contestability[5] view real assets as highly flexible in use with free entry and exit to and from markets. In practice there is a considerable degree of real asset specificity which serves to reduce the flexibility of asset use. Specificity may arise for a number of reasons; for example, because of high set up and relocation costs, the limited range of alternative uses for some assets, and because production facilities are often designed with particular customers in mind.[6]

Real and Financial Assets Contrasted

Assets with these specific characteristics can, of course, be sold to alternative owners, but the market will tend to be thinner the larger the size, the greater the indivisibility and the higher the degree of specificity. For example, capital can be withdrawn from shipping, at little cost, no more rapidly than the port facilities, dockyards and boats wear out. It can be transferred into roads no more quickly than trucks can be built and roadways constructed.

By contrast, an *individual* can generally shift from a relatively small holding of shares in shipping lines to those of road transport just as soon as a broker on the stock market can be contacted and the sale and purchase orders executed. Markets in which existing claims are traded enable the owners of the claims to sell their interest in them, so that someone other than the original supplier of the funds receives the interest, dividends, and other payments associated with the asset. Wealth held as cash, bank or building society deposits gives the holder generalised power with which to purchase any type of good or service.

An individual can also consume wealth much more quickly than can the nation as a whole. Cash or bank deposits can be realised readily. Ordinary shares or bonds can be sold off or used as backing for loans, enabling an individual to augment current income for consumption. Leaving aside external borrowings, these options do not exist for the nation, which can consume specific capital goods only by not devoting the resources needed over time for their maintenance or replacement. Yet the superstructure of financial markets enables entire generations to sell off or transfer their accumulated wealth to the next.

Liquidity

By enabling people to hold wealth in forms which can be changed at will and consumed readily, the network of financial markets creates an illusion. The capital assets which ultimately back up the financial assets issued do not generally have the same characteristics. One household's assets can be consumed or changed in character, with little loss in value, only so long as the great majority of other holders of wealth do not also seek to consume their holdings or alter the form of ownership. One small holder of ICI shares, for example, can liquidate his or her holdings with little loss, but all holders cannot do so. Similarly, one holder of a bank deposit can encash his or her balance, but not all depositors can do so at the same time. When acting in unison, the opportunities open to all wealthholders to consume their assets and change their form are no different from those of the nation as a whole.

The greater liquidity of individual as opposed to national wealth is in essence an illusion or 'act of magic' performed by financial markets, and is central to the process of wealth creation by permitting long-term investments to be financed by short-term funds. Each person buying shares in a company may have the intention of making the funds available only for a temporary period. Or, even if intending to provide the funds for a longer term, the person may wish to hold the option of withdrawing them at short notice. Nevertheless, from the viewpoint of the firm which issues the share capital – and in the eyes of society – the funds can be looked upon as a stable amount of long-term funds which can be invested in tangible, illiquid assets.

Banks transform funds entrusted to them for short periods of time into long-term loans to industry. Building societies take short-term deposit funds and transform them into 20-year loans for housing. These transformations are possible only so long as people have confidence in the institutions concerned, trust their stewardship and are prepared to continue delegating control of their funds to them. Without this confidence, the transformation would not be possible. In order to ensure that the transformation can continue without interruption, institutions group together in collective arrangements to protect depositors (and at the same time each other), and receive government support. Governments, of course, cannot alter the nature of the tangible, illiquid assets which lie at the end of the transformation process. It is merely that governments are better able to sustain the confidence necessary for the illusion to continue.

Portfolio Choices

Although the network of intermediation by financial institutions and markets underpinning modern capitalism is in many respects a fragile one, it permits a division of labour amongst households according to their differing wealth-holding requirements. Assets can be 'packaged' or 'tailormade' to the age, income, wealth, occupation, family responsibilities, tastes and outlook of the individual. Those who do not wish to, or cannot, specify too precisely when future spending needs will arise, and whose main concern is for funds to be readily available, can hold deposits or easily saleable securities. Those whose interest is in long-term appreciation of capital, perhaps at some risk, can be the owners of tangible assets and business enterprises.

For an individual, holding shares in a large public company constitutes a 'halfway house' between the rights and responsibilities of holding an enterprise's debt securities, such as bonds and debentures, on the one hand, and the rights and responsibilities of directly owning the assets of an enterprise and controlling the management of its affairs, on the other hand. Debtholders are entitled to (though there is a risk that they may not always receive) a specified money income along with ultimate repayments; the specified income being either a set nominal sum (as with fixed interest debt) or predetermined according to an agreed formula (as with variable rate loans or floating rate notes). Ordinary shares in public companies promise only a variable income, governed by the performance of the enterprise. Consequently, a share portfolio typically offers a higher expected return, a higher degree of risk and greater administrative and monitoring effort than a portfolio of fixed interest securities. Control of the enterprise itself brings greater rewards and risks. Hence a portfolio involving the direct holding of physical assets typically offers a higher expected return, a higher degree of risk and greater administrative effort than a comparable portfolio of non-controlling company shares. In this respect, encouragement to larger personal holdings of equity is no more than an intermediate step in a policy of personal 'entrepreneurship'.

Debt securities, company shares and the direct control of enterprise thus provide people with a clear hierarchy of portfolio choices about expected return, risk and efforts of administrating and monitoring assets. The job of market institutions at one level is to provide information, expertise and assistance in those choices. Investment specialists help individuals to select a portfolio of securities and manage them on the individual's behalf. Banks and other institutions help with finance and advice about the establishment of new enterprise and the acquisition of physical assets.

Financial Packages

At another level, market institutions are 'packagers' of financial services, offering a variety of financial products and bundling them together in forms convenient for people to buy. Which particular products are offered by any institution and what services are bundled up or prepackaged is an issue introduced in Chapter 2, and considered in subsequent chapters. Technology, marketing arrangements, preferences for risk-taking by institutions and people, and the economic environment, to mention some of the factors, alter the financial services which people want to consume jointly and those which it is economic to provide side by side or as a package.

As packagers of financial services, institutions augment considerably the hierarchy of financial options available by holding debt and equity of trading enterprises or physical assets. This encourages a more complete division of labour and specialisation of functions by savers and investors. Unit trusts, for example, buy shares, pool them to diversify risk, and then re-sell units or shares in the total, diversified portfolio. Substitution of a single contract with the trust for the individual shares enables diversification and professional investment guidance to be built-in, while a market can be established for the units themselves. People are thus provided with risk, liquidity and administrative choices which differ from those of the underlying shares.

Depository institutions and insurance companies go further. Life insurance companies package together savings via unit trusts with protection against premature death. In their insurance cover, the companies provide minimum guarantees as to the value of the portfolio. They conduct an internal capital market in the various trusts, typically offering policyholders the option to switch from one unit trust to another, without charge, one or two times per year. More explicit guarantees as to the value of the portfolio are given to those policyholders choosing to combine nominal savings plans, backed by bond holdings, with insurance cover.

Banks and other deposit-taking institutions package together access to various transactions media (cash, cheque payment, credit cards) with savings and loan vehicles. Like insurance companies, the depository institutions offer explicit guarantees as to the redemption value of the savings. In their case, they offer redemption at full face value, often at demand, despite holding portfolios of assets like mortgages and commercial loans which are individually risky and cannot be sold off to meet withdrawn deposits. This 'act of magic' greatly widens the financial choices open to individual savers. At the same time, it enables those investing in real assets to obtain the type of longer-term funding which they prefer.

Assistance to Saving

Just as there are marked differences between the individual and society as a whole in the ability to consume and rearrange wealth, there are also differences in the accumulation of wealth. Wealth is accumulated by both individuals and the nation primarily by saving, i.e. consuming less than income. Saving by individuals can take the form of acquiring a wide variety of assets. Some are claims against other individuals; others are purchases of financial assets or real assets from other individuals. These transfers do not change aggregate personal or national wealth. Borrowing and lending by the personal sector occur when new financial assets and liabilities are involved. Table 1.1 shows that in 1984 (as is usual) the personal sector was a net lender to other sectors, acquiring more financial assets than were created by its borrowing. This net lending enables the government and corporate sectors to undertake net investment in tangible assets, which we note are indirectly owned by persons through the network of intermediation.

Table 1.1   Sources and Uses of Funds of the Personal Sector, 1984

Sources	(£m)	(%)	Uses	(£m)	(%)
Saving	27,204	51	Investment in fixed assets	16,402	31
Capital transfers	2,955	5	Taxes on capital	1,446	3
Financial liabilities (borrowing)	23,511	44	Financial assets (lending)	35,670	66
	53,670	100		53,670	100

Source: Financial Statistics, February 1986, Table 9.2.

Personal saving over the past ten or so years has exhibited marked variations relative to its behaviour in earlier decades. Despite these variations, the way in which the personal sector has distributed its borrowings and acquisition of financial assets has shown some consistent patterns. These trends are examined in following sections.

1.3   Personal Savings in the UK

In the 1970s there was a sharp and rapid rise in the ratio of savings to income in the UK from an average of under 10 per cent in the 1960s to 13 per cent during 1973–84. This increase surprised many forecasters and commentators. Given this experience, it seems pertinent to ask whether the rise in the savings ratio is likely to be permanent or whether there is likely to be some reversal over the next decade. This section consequently seeks to lay out the facts as to what has happened to savings in the recent past.

In making a savings decision, individuals will tend to think of their total income in any one period, whether derived from wages and salaries, social security benefits, benefits from superannuation schemes or income in kind. From this income it is necessary to deduct income tax, contributions to national insurance and to superannuation schemes to arrive at personal disposable income. From the remaining income there will be some inescapable commitments in terms of mortgage repayments, rent, food, etc., but the remainder can be allocated between consumption or saving. This saving can itself imply future continued commitments or can be discretionary. Expenditure may, of course, be greater than disposable income, in which case a decision has to be made between drawing on past savings or borrowing. The reasons for saving can be grouped under four headings:

(i) The purchase of major consumer durables or other substantial items of expenditure, such as holidays, may be preceded by a period of savings. Because of the lumpiness and infrequency of such outlays relative to income, a period of saving is followed by dissaving as the expenditure occurs. Alternatively, it is possible to incur the expenditure first and make the 'saving' later through debt repayment. Which of these is preferred by households depends upon their access to borrowing, the cost of borrowings (interest rate plus associated charges), and their preferences between consumption now and consumption later.

(ii) Savings for retirement are generally considered the quantitatively most significant component of saving. This component is related to the concept of life-cycle behaviour. Like the first motive above, the basic reason arises from differences in the timing of receipts and consumption with a need to spread the latter out over the lifetime of the individual, given the fall in income which generally follows retirement. Thus the individual or household tends to accumulate wealth through saving during the pre-retirement phase by consuming less than disposable income during these years. Following retirement, wealth would be decreased to finance current consumption. Figure 1.1 illustrates this pattern.

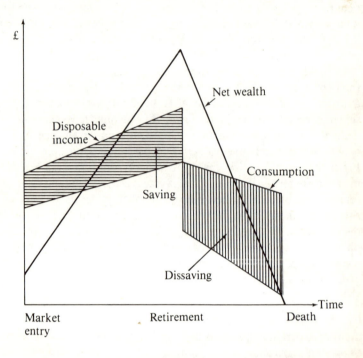

Figure 1.1   Saving and the Life Cycle

(iii) The life-cycle hypothesis implies that taken over the whole lifetime, savings of the individual household would average out at zero. (There could, however, be savings in the aggregate if a growing population puts more people into the working category and productivity growth means that new workers have higher real incomes than the retiring workers). But individuals and households accumulate wealth in excess of that needed to cover consumption in retirement in order to provide a bequest. Whilst it is true that substantial bequests are left and intergenerational transfers made, it is not clear whether these are the result of deliberate decisions or arise from an incorrect assessment of the date of death, with earlier than anticipated death leaving unspent the balances held for retirement.

(iv) This last point leads on to the final motive for saving discussed here. Future income, the interest rate in each period and the date of death are all uncertain. This uncertainty is likely to lead to precautionary saving. The greater the degree of uncertainty the higher will be the level of precautionary savings.

The Effects of Inflation

For most of the postwar period the rate of inflation was low and generally steady and hence was not considered to be of much significance for savings. The general presumption was that an increase in inflation would probably lead to a temporary reduction in the savings ratio as the expectation of price rises encouraged consumers to advance their consumption plans. With the acceleration of inflation in the 1970s, far from falling, the savings ratio actually increased in the UK. Thus an acceleration in the rate of inflation appeared to have the opposite effect to that expected. Alternative views of the effect of inflation on saving can broadly be summarised under three headings:

(i) Increased uncertainty coupled with the fear of unemployment led to a rise in demand for precautionary assets.

(ii) Consumers are not perfectly informed about price changes. If they underestimate the rate of inflation, then they will find prices raised by more than they expected and will interpret this observation as an increase in relative prices and will, therefore, tend to buy less. Thus, the incorrect expectation as to the actual rate of inflation will lead to lower consumption and consequently higher saving than if consumers had been well-informed. Obviously, for this explanation to have any long-term effect it is necessary that consumers continue consistently to underestimate the rate of change of prices.

(iii) The third argument stresses two effects of inflation on measured income and wealth. First, inflation tends to lead to higher nominal rates of interest, and the statistics on disposable income will include the money value of interest receipts, whereas what is of more relevance in determining saving behaviour is the real value. Second, some of the consumer's assets will be held in assets whose value is fixed in monetary terms. As inflation reduces the real value of these assets, increased saving will be required to preserve the real value of the consumer's wealth. Inflation will also reduce the real indebtedness of those repaying existing mortgages. Since the measure of income generally used to compute the savings ratio does not take account of capital gains and losses, the general effect in periods of accelerating inflation is to increase the measured savings ratio, although part of this is being used to maintain the real value of financial assets.

Behaviour of the Savings Ratio in the UK

The most readily available savings ratio is that for the personal sector as a whole. It is important to realise that the personal sector consists of more than just individuals; it also includes unincorporated businesses, sole traders, partnerships, non-profit-making bodies and trusts serving persons, e.g. universities, churches and charities. The published figures for personal saving are obtained as the difference between two very large aggregates: personal disposable income and consumers' expenditure. As such the figures are subject to errors in these two magnitudes and are subject to substantial revision between successive issues of the National Income Blue Book. The total of personal saving is made up of four elements:

(i) The difference between household current income and current expenditure – household saving.
(ii) Saving through life assurance and pension funds.
(iii) Stock appreciation and capital consumption of unincorporated businesses.
(iv) The current account balance of non-profit-making bodies serving persons.

It is worth looking at the precise treatment of life assurance and pension schemes in the national accounts for purposes of estimating savings. Transactions between persons and pension schemes are consolidated out in the personal sector accounts. Employers' contributions to occupational pension schemes are considered to be part of income from employment and are, therefore, part of personal income. Wages and salaries are included gross of employees' contributions. The investment incomes of the schemes are also regarded as personal income. Personal disposable income thus includes all the receipts of life assurance and pension funds on current account (excluding revaluations). These receipts are exactly equivalent to the sum of the benefits paid to policyholders or pensioners, any administrative costs charged to the schemes and a balance of saving.

A substantial part of the saving of the personal sector is not discretionary but can be regarded as committed. The precise distinction is rather difficult to make in practice but in principle saving is said to be committed where an initial decision results in regular transactions in that form in the future. Following an article in *Economic Trends* in November 1981, a table breaking down personal sector savings into its committed and discretionary elements has been included as a regular supplementary table in *Financial Statistics*. Committed saving includes net saving through life assurance and superannuation schemes; repayment of borrowing for house purchase; repayment of borrowing from retailers and finance houses; and SAYE deposits and building society subscription share deposits. There are some deficiencies in the series: in particular, repayments of borrowing from banks cannot be distinguished within the figures for net borrowing and are, therefore, placed within discretionary saving. Thus, the total for committed saving is underestimated and that for discretionary saving overestimated. When bank personal loans and loans for house purchase are important, this deficiency is obviously more marked.

Figure 1.2 traces out various savings ratios from 1974 to 1984. The ratio for the whole of the personal sector was under 10 per cent during the late 1960s and early 1970s and then rose during the mid- and late 1970s reaching a peak of 15 per cent in 1980. Since that time it has shown a sharp decline, falling by nearly 2 percentage points between 1980 and 1983.

Household saving comprises the bulk of the saving by the personal sector and the total household figure is shown as the second line on the chart. Since it is the major element it does, of course, follow a similar pattern to that of total personal sector saving and also reached a peak in 1980, since when it has fallen substantially.

As might be expected, committed saving by households shows a much steadier pattern and there has been a tendency for the ratio to increase during the 1980s.[7] Similarly, the ratio of saving in Life Assurance Funds which accounts for over half of household committed saving has shown a slight increase.

% of Personal disposable income

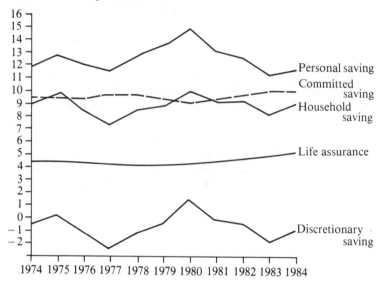

Figure 1.2   Savings Ratios, 1974 – 84

The ratio of household discretionary saving to personal disposable income has shown wide fluctuation and, after reaching a peak in 1980, has shown evidence of net discretionary dissaving by the household sector since 1981.

As mentioned earlier, data revisions have been substantial and their effect has been to make the observed rise in the ratio over the late 1970s much smaller than was at first thought. To some extent the problem of explaining why the savings ratio rose during a period of high inflation has disappeared as successive data revisions have reduced the magnitude of the increase. In the United States, which of course suffered lower inflation, the personal sector savings ratio remained pretty constant at around 6 per cent from 1977 to the present day. This represents a fall from a ratio of around 8 per cent in the early 1970s.

If inflation stays under reasonable control in the UK, a dramatic increase in the household savings ratio seems unlikely. Committed savings are expected to continue to increase in significance, and the household savings ratio is expected to return to around the 9 per cent level in 1990. Thus the growth in the total flow of saving will be determined largely by the rate of growth of personal disposable income.

1.4 The Pattern of Personal Financing

All wealth in a free enterprise economy is owned by persons, but indirect wealth-holding and intermediation of financial flows is the norm. Acquisition and management of most physical assets is delegated to trading enterprises. Allocation of savings to those enterprises is typically left to financial institutions.

Figure 1.3 sets out in schematic form the process of intermediation as it relates to the personal sector. On the left-hand side there are consumers and on the right, producers – the suppliers of personal financial services, principally banks, building societies, life insurance companies, insurance brokers, stockbrokers, pension funds and unit trusts. Savings by the personal sector represent the major source of the flow of funds to these producers. Although the proportions fluctuate from year to year, savings by the personal sector are around 44 per cent of total savings in any one year, whereas savings by industrial and commercial companies are around 40 per

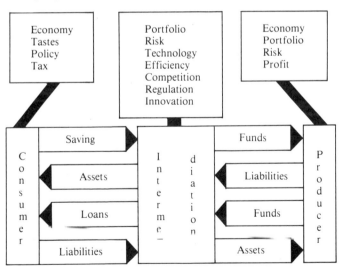

Figure 1.3 Financial Flows

cent. A high proportion of savings by industrial and commercial companies is reinvested within the firm. Over the last decade the personal sector has been the only one which has consistently been in financial surplus to the tune of an average of £8.8 billion a year. The savings by the personal sector are matched by liabilities generated by the institutions which comprise financial assets of the personal sector. The institutions also provide loans to the personal sector, which comprise financial liabilities of the personal sector and financial assets of the institutions. Since we are not concerned in this study with the corporate, public or foreign sectors, we have not included these in the chart, although they are, of course, an important part of the whole financial system.

The size of the various flows around the system is determined by a number of factors. On the consumer side the main ones are:

    (i)   the state of the economy and general economic conditions including forces affecting expectations;
  (ii)   the tastes and preferences of consumers;
 (iii)   government policy.

For producers the main determinants are:

    (i)   the state of the economy;
  (ii)   the portfolio strategies of the companies;
 (iii)   the attitude to risk of the companies;
 (iv)   profitability.

These variables are seen as affecting the total volume of the flow, both lending and borrowing, but this total volume will be divided up into different forms of intermediation and different types of financial instruments, financial assets and financial liabilities. There are some general factors which affect the process of intermediation itself, notably:

    (i)   portfolio behaviour;
  (ii)   attitude to risk;
 (iii)   technology;
 (iv)   efficiency;
  (v)   competition;
 (vi)   regulation;
(vii)   financial innovation.

Figure 1.3 makes clear that in terms of the total flow of funds for the personal sector, one also needs to take account of borrowing as well as savings, and the statistics for the personal sector as a whole are illustrated in Figure 1.4. Over the last five years there has been a marked increase in personal sector borrowing. Thus the decline in saving as a proportion of disposable income has been accompanied by a significant increase in borrowing which has meant that the total of saving plus borrowing has remained more or less constant at around 22 per cent of disposable income, although it did rise to 23 per cent in 1982 and fall to 21 per cent in 1983.

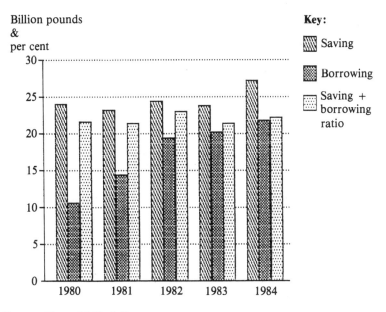

Billion pounds & per cent

Key:
▨ Saving
▩ Borrowing
▦ Saving + borrowing ratio

Source: Financial Statistics.

Figure 1.4 Personal Sector Saving and Borrowing

The distribution of personal financial assets is given in Figure 1.5. The marked feature of this chart is the rise in life insurance and pensions, both self-administered and through insurance companies, to account for 40 per cent of personal financial assets. These trends are examined in Chapter 8 which looks at the markets for personal 'investments'.

Personal Financial Markets

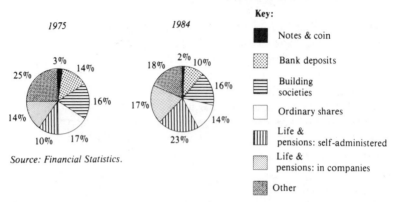

Figure 1.5   Financial Assets of the UK Personal Sector

Amongst the more 'liquid' assets, the progress made by the building societies relative to the monetary sector can be seen. This relative increase occurred despite a widening of the banking sector in 1980 as a consequence of the implementation of the Banking Act 1979. The market for liquid assets is examined in Chapter 6.

The position for liabilities is given in Figure 1.6. Here the noteworthy feature is the predominant importance of housing finance at 62 per cent of the total in 1984. Building societies remain predominant in this market with 48 per cent of total liabilities despite a rapid build up in the lending by banks. Some of the

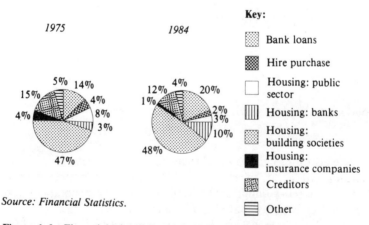

Figure 1.6   Financial Liabilities of the UK Personal Sector

building societies' housing finance is thought to be used by people for purposes other than the purchase of dwellings. Banks dominate the non-housing lending to the personal sector, involving consumer credit and credit-card lending. Chapter 7 looks at the market for housing finance and for consumer credit.

In conjunction with Chapter 9, examining the financial services relating to personal enterprise, these chapters are concerned with particular markets and developments in the UK.

1.5 A Financial Services Revolution?

Developments occurring in financial markets and the services and products they offer, not only in Britain but also in the United States and many other countries, are frequently characterised as a 'revolution in financial services'. Table 1.2 records some of the new financial products and practices in recent years. Whether or not the changes are better described as a 'revolution' or an 'evolution' is best left for later, but there is no doubt that a marked change has taken place in the competitive environment, one that is felt keenly by the producers of financial services.

Table 1.2 Major Financial Innovations in Personal Financial Markets

	Chapter
A. *PRODUCTS*	
Money market funds	5, 6
Money market accounts	5, 6
Cash management accounts	5
Sweep arrangements	6
Universal life insurance	5
Index-linked gilt-edged securities	8
Fixed-interest unit trusts	8
Savings plans investment trusts	8
Personal equity plans	8
Loan back on pensions	8
B. *PROCESSES*	
Automatic teller machines	4
Point of sale terminals	4
Electronic fund transfer	4
Electronic trading	4
Information technology	4
Automated clearing systems	4

Table 1.2 *continued*

C.	MARKET ARRANGEMENTS	
	Secondary mortgage markets	7
	Unlisted securities market (USM)	9
	Over-the-counter market (OTC)	9
	Business Expansion Scheme	9
	'Big Bang'	8, 10
	Joint ventures	2, 10
	Financial service centres	5
	Financial conglomerates	6, 10

As part of the research involved in the preparation of this work, the Nottingham Institute of Financial Studies conducted a survey in 1985 of nearly 500 financial institutions in Britain, involving banks, building societies, life insurance companies, non-life insurance companies, insurance brokers and stockbrokers. There was a general agreement by those responding (and the response rate of nearly 50 per cent was unusually high) of heightened competition and that competitive pressures would be by far the most important factor inhibiting their growth over the coming five years. Figure 1.7 summarises the result.

Competition in financial markets, as in those for other products, is multifaceted, and can come from other firms of that type, other financial firms and from new entrants to financial services. Figures 3.2, 3.5, and 3.8 in Chapter 3 summarise how banks, building societies and life insurance companies perceive their potential competitors. Banks see building societies and stockbrokers as strong competitors, but other banks pose the major threat. Building societies see the strongest competitors to be banks rather than other building societies. Life insurance companies see banks and building societies as a stronger threat than other insurers. These expectations are consistent with current trends elsewhere, especially in the United States, where there is, as in Britain, a blurring of the distinction between banks and savings institutions. Banks are diversifying into other financial services such as insurance, while stockbroking firms offer banking services.

A minority of those surveyed anticipated that growth would come from remaining in the same markets with the same products. Figure 1.8 sets out how firms saw that growth would occur. Most saw growth coming from the introduction of new products and entering

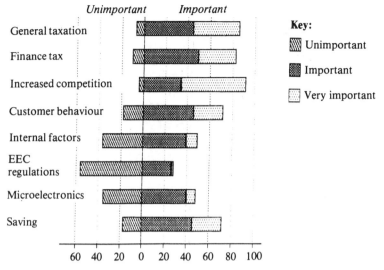

Source: NIFS survey.

Figure 1.7 Constraints on Growth

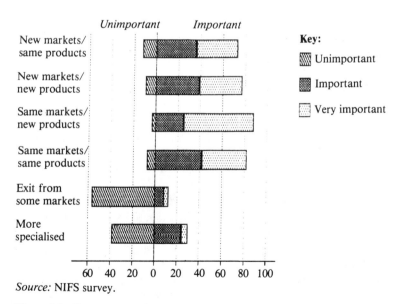

Source: NIFS survey.

Figure 1.8 Factors Increasing Growth

new markets. The results of this survey are discussed further in Chapter 3 which focuses on the marketing of financial services.

The process of change in the financial services industry, it would seem, is more one of the adaptation of existing firms than it is one of the birth of new ones. Reasons why this is the case are, we believe, inherent in the nature of the markets for financial services, indeed in the nature of financial services themselves. Chapter 2 looks into characteristics of markets for financial services, arguing that with the inherent substitutability of financial services and the short product cycles, competition can be expected to be fierce.

Competition in the 1980s has seen banks in both the US and UK lose their monopoly of the provision of transactions services to savings institutions and to securities firms. In the UK, building societies have lost their near monopoly of housing finance. Banks, in the run up to the so-called 'Big Bang' at the Stock Exchange, are preparing to enter securities broking, having established a strong presence in insurance, unit trust management and, in one instance, real estate. Retailers in the UK are following their US counterparts and experimenting with the provision of financial services.

Sources of Change

So strong have been the competitive forces in a number of countries in the 1980s that it is tempting to attribute much of the change to a spontaneous outbreak of competition. Certainly there has been a major alteration in attitudes to government controls and regulations across a number of countries and a number of activities which have seen privatisation and deregulation of airlines and transport as well as that of financial services. The Financial Services Bill which is going through Parliament in 1986 and the 'Big Bang' which occurs in October 1986 are prime examples.[8]

But decisions about deregulation do not occur in a vacuum. Deregulation both influences and is influenced by the economic and financial environment, and is responsive to pressures from firms in the regulated industries. It would also seem that many of the developments have been in anticipation of, rather than as the result of, deregulation, as illustrated by the moves by US banks into insurance and the attempts of building societies in the UK to enter other financial services. In Britain and America, and some other countries, the trend is for governments to remove, or at least relax, those regulations which primarily constrain competition between institutions, but to strengthen regulatory, including self-regulatory, controls aimed at protecting consumers. The proposals contained in the Financial Services Bill are a major step in that direction. New information technology is playing an important role, but often as facilitating desired changes rather than initiating them. There is no doubt that the financial services sector is undergoing a rapid technological transformation which is helping to break down traditional barriers between institutions and is leading to new and newly packaged products, and new marketing and distribution methods. Financial services are ideally suited for the application of computer technology, and further changes can be expected as institutions come to exploit fully the capabilities of the available technology. These possibilities are considered in Chapter 4.

Much of the talk of a financial services revolution comes from observing the pace of change in the United States. Without computer technology many of the innovations there would not have been possible. Information technology certainly provided the means but, nevertheless, the stimulus for change came from the efforts of individuals, businesses, financial institutions and markets to adapt to the historically high rates of inflation and interest rates in the late 1970s and early 1980s. With so many financial contracts fixed in nominal terms, lenders of funds sought to protect themselves from the erosion of their principal by seeking higher nominal rates of interest, a process which both created fundamental problems for some institutions and presented new opportunities for others. In particular, the readiness with which lenders turned from traditional repositories for savings to new financial instruments offered by securities firms has meant that those marketing financial services no longer talk of 'savers' but of 'investors'.

As Chapter 5 makes clear, developments in the US have occurred within a distinctive institutional framework. Because of years when change was retarded, the process of transition recently has been all the more rapid. Some adjustments which have been spread out more gradually in the UK have been telescoped within the space of a few years. For this reason, the process of structural change in the US appears to have taken on almost a life of its own. Experimentation is extensive and there are many ideas being tried out there which are a portent of future developments in the UK and other countries.

Notes

1. The figures are from *Financial Statistics*. The personal sector includes unincorporated businesses, sole traders and partnerships, and non-profit-making bodies such as universities, churches and charities as well as individuals.
2. See Pettigrew (1980).
3. See *The Times*, 24 April 1986.
4. A more detailed examination of the reasons for financial intermediation can be found in Lewis and Davis (forthcoming, 1987).
5. For a brief exposition of contestable markets, see Button (1985).
6. See, for example, Williamson (1985).
7. For a detailed discussion, see Kennally (1985).
8. For further discussion of these, see Redwood (1986) and Terry (1985).

References

Button, K.J. (1985) 'New approaches to the regulation of industry', *Royal Bank of Scotland Review*, December, pp. 18–34.

Kennally, G. (1985) 'Committee and discretionary saving of households', *National Institute Economic Review*, May.

Lewis, M.K. and Davis, K.T. (forthcoming, 1987) *Domestic and International Banking*, Philip Allan.

Pettigrew, C.W. (1980) 'National and sector balance sheets for the United Kingdom', *Economic Trends*, November.

Redwood, J. (1986) 'How to protect the investor', *Lloyds Bank Review*, April, pp. 21–35.

Terry, N.G. (1985) 'The "Big Bang" at the Stock Exchange', *Lloyds Bank Review*, April, pp. 16–30.

Williamson, O.E. (1985) *Economic Institutions of Capitalism*, The Free Press.

CHAPTER 2

Characteristics of Markets for Personal Financial Services

M.K. Lewis and B. Chiplin

2.1 Introduction

In this chapter we consider the nature of the markets for personal financial services. The traditional approach to the financial system has emphasised the institutions concerned, e.g. banks, building societies, insurance companies, stockbrokers, etc., rather than the underlying market framework. Increasingly these institutional boundaries are becoming less relevant as competition increases and financial innovations cross traditional lines. An understanding of the basic nature of the competitive process in financial markets is essential for any sensible analysis of the pressures and changes which are being experienced.

Central to such an analysis of financial markets is the following question: 'what characteristics of financial products distinguish them from other traded goods and services?' Our starting point, however, is in terms of the similarities rather than the differences, for the same fundamental choices of inputs, outputs and strategy are as relevant to the financial as to the non-financial firm. Thus, as noted in the classic paper by Ronald Coase (1937), the very existence of the firm itself, and its size and nature, in any activity depends upon a complex interaction of production and transaction costs.

We argue that market characteristics should be seen as a continuum, with financial services likely to be marked by a preponderance of certain features at one spectrum rather than differences in kind. In economic theory it is usual to define markets according to geography and product. Even here the attitudes of people to a range of factors are important, so that the geographic boundaries will differ for housing finance as compared with life insurance, while for other consumers convenience is paramount and for them clusters of products may be relevant. But there are many other dimensions, and financial markets represent those which are perhaps most conditioned by time, information characteristics, confidence and trust. Nevertheless, while recognising these special factors, the common principles relating to all market transactions must not be forgotten.

All products fulfil needs, and our analysis of personal financial markets begins with an examination of the nature of personal financial needs. We then look in turn at the 'service' and 'financial' aspects. These discussions form the basis of an analysis of the organisational framework of financial markets and the nature of the financial firm.

2.2 Personal Financial Needs

There is a vast array of personal financial services presently on offer. But most are directed, in one way or another, towards satisfying three basic financial needs of persons. These are:

(1) Transactions services, i.e. providing means of paying for and acquiring goods and services.
(2) Wealth accumulation, enabling individuals to rearrange the holding of wealth over time by means of saving and borrowing.
(3) Financial security, ensuring the continuance of consumption in the face of changed economic circumstances.

Transactions services generate a desire for financial instruments which serve three functions. One is to enable people to obtain goods – the 'means of exchange' function. A second is to effect payment for the goods which have been acquired, i.e. a means of payment. The third function comes about because purchases of goods are not perfectly synchronised with inflows of income. In the interim, people will accumulate or rundown transactions balances, which serve as a temporary store of purchasing power. Since the 'something' that serves payments needs acts also as a way of holding wealth, there is a necessary overlap between the 'market' for transactions services and that for wealth accumulation.

All three transactions functions may be satisfied by the holding of a current account with a bank and, indeed, such an account has been a traditional means of financing transactions for many people. But these functions can also be 'unbundled' and carried out by separate means. Thus a credit card issued, for example, by Access, Barclaycard or Marks and Spencer may enable the individual to obtain the goods; a bank current account may still be used for the actual payment. A building society savings account or a money market account with a unit trust may serve as the temporary abode of purchasing power in between receipt of income and payment for the goods.

In both the US and the UK the potential to unbundle a sequence of transactions has led the banks to introduce new payments instruments. In the US, the development of money market mutual funds (see Chapter 5) provided consumers with an attractive alternative to conventional chequeing and savings deposits for the temporary holding of wealth. Introduction of money market accounts by unit trust managers in the UK, followed by building societies, had the same effect. In both cases, the banks were forced by competitive pressures to introduce new accounts which combined higher interest rates with limited cheque-writing facilities. These new types of account provide higher interest but with some degree of liquidity and hence make them possible substitutes for the longer-term investment vehicles provided by life insurance companies.

Saving and borrowing enable people to rearrange their consumption spending over time. Saving enables people to shift consumption to future periods, and can take a variety of forms ranging from bank notes under the mattress, at one end of the spectrum, to the direct holding of real assets, at the other. In between, financial markets provide an array of different savings vehicles, such as bank and building society deposits, the holding of shares and securities, life insurance savings schemes, unit trusts and so on, conditioned by the preferences of the individual and the time horizon of the anticipated financial need. Borrowing enables consumption of goods and assets to be shifted forward in time, as with the consumption of housing services made possible by home purchases financed by housing loans, and consumer durables by personal loans.

Financial security can be obtained in two basic ways. One is by self-insurance, i.e. undertaking savings or having accumulated past savings and investments available in forms which can be drawn upon readily to sustain consumption in the face of economic losses. The other way of obtaining financial security is to transfer the risk of financial loss by buying insurance against premature death, robbery, fire, accidents, injury, unemployment and ill-health, and by transferring the risks associated with exchange-rate variations, interest-rate fluctuations, commodity price movements, through forward and other hedging contracts.

Figure 2.1 summarises the three basic financial needs and, for the purpose of illustration, identifies some major financial product lines with these needs. Most financial institutions offer a range of products which encompass at least two of these three needs. Banks

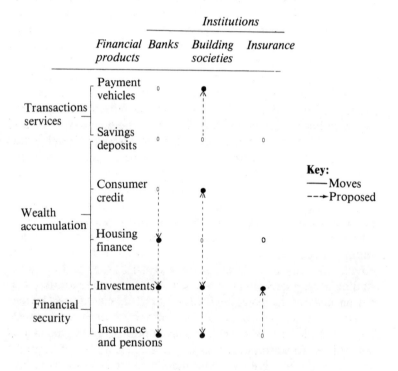

Figure 2.1   Personal Financial Markets

for the 'basic product' lines combine facilities for payment services (e.g. a cheque account); facilities for borrowing and lending (e.g. personal loans); and also means of holding wealth against changing events, albeit in liquid form (e.g. deposit and savings accounts). It seems quite natural that when offering bank deposits as a means of saving, they should offer their customers unit trusts and insurance-linked savings vehicles. It seems sensible to provide customers with insurance against various risks along with wealth-holding facilities which also give a measure of financial security. This is what has happened with the British banks.

Insurers bundle together insurance cover and vehicles for savings. Life offices could offer financial security solely by means of one-year term insurance (or temporary life insurance) contracts, with annual premiums rising sharply in line with the age of the life covered. But this is not the usual way. Under the standard form of term life insurance, a contract period of a number of years' duration is specified and a constant annual premium is determined. Under whole-of-life insurance the contract period is the remaining lifetime of the person. For one whose lifetime exactly matches the relevant mean expectation, payment by the insurer of the sum insured boils down to a simple refunding of premiums, augmented by investment income net of expenses, and the policy has acted as a vehicle for saving. In this way the policy is fulfilling a dual function of providing both death cover and an avenue for savings. Over the life of the contract, a stream of constant annual premiums is handed over to the insurance company, which holds and invests these funds on behalf of the insured. There is close affinity with a self-disciplined 'target saver' building up deposits in a time or savings account and, eventually, closing the account.

A feature of developments in the UK over the last one or two decades has been a broadening of the range of financial products offered by institutional groups. Life insurance offices have broadened their insurance plus savings deposit-type package into a variety of investment products based around unit trusts and managed portfolios. These are examined in Chapter 8. Banks have moved into life insurance and other protection products. They sell unit trusts and since 1984 have provided deposits which are better vehicles for longer-term savings. Since 1981, banks have moved into the provision of housing finance. Building societies are seeking to offer a broader range of insurance products to their customers and to expand lending into consumer finance. These developments are examined in Chapters 6 and 7.

Some of the reasons why financial institutions package together a number of financial products become apparent when we look into the service nature of the industry.

2.3   The Characteristics of a Service

Firms operating in personal financial markets produce services rather than goods. The essence of a service is that it is performed on a particular person's behalf: it brings about a change in the condition of an individual or organisation or of that of a good belonging to an individual or organisation.[1] Given the fundamental nature of a service, it cannot be regarded as existing until it is exchanged and, consequently, it cannot be produced in advance and stored on the shelf awaiting sale. Nor can services be ordered from stocks kept elsewhere. Thus, a service is basically intangible and non-storable whereas physical products have tangibility and can be stored and inventoried. A service does not exist until it is consumed. For personal services there is, by definition, an inherently close communication between a supplier of the service and the potential customer.

To a considerable extent this simple dichotomy between goods and services is misleading; after all, goods are not required for their own sake but for the services they render and the needs they satisfy. The provision of many services, including financial services, requires considerable investment in plant, buildings, computer equipment, staff, etc., in the same way as production of a loaf of bread necessitates investment in the bakery, oven and delivery trucks as well as the inputs of flour, yeast, etc. These investments are undertaken on the anticipation of future demand. The final act of 'production' of a service, which is necessarily simultaneous with its exchange, may be achieved at small additional cost. The firm which places a physical product in stock is regarded as purchasing the item from itself; for a service there is, admittedly, no tangible product in store, but the significant cost involved in having facilities in place to supply the service on demand implies that the difference is essentially one of degree. Consequently, it is more satisfactory to regard all goods and services as falling within a continuum stretching across the range of 'physical' and 'service' attributes.

Within this continuum, the affinity between a good and a financial service is closer when the financial service can be packaged and sold off-the-shelf. A simple example is a block of units in a unit trust currently held by the fund manager but available for immediate resale to the public. Similar considerations apply to many secondary markets which are likely to become of increasing significance in the future. New developments in such markets are represented by a financial institution acquiring a group of mortgages which it then partitions into bundles and resells. It can also be argued that off-the-shelf financial contracts which are accepted on demand are very close to the concept of a simple manufactured product. Standard insurance contracts and deposit accounts are examples. Indeed, developments in technology involving greater automatic acceptance of contracts will tend to make the similarity even clearer.

Hence, in many respects the supply of personal financial services has closer affinities with the production of goods than is often recognised. For both types of product the delivery to the final consumer is crucial. Traditionally producers of personal financial services have tended to be more vertically integrated forward to the retail stage than manufacturing companies as evidenced by the widescale self-owned branch networks of the banks and building societies. But there are specific factors to explain this feature just as the ownership of public houses, hotels and off-licences by brewers is amenable to such analysis. It does not follow that all or even a majority of personal financial services *necessarily* require such vertical integration and direct contact with customers. Again, the balance of advantage is being altered by technology and changing consumer habits.

Recognition of the similarities between the production of goods and the production of financial services, rather than a stressing of the differences, leads to the important point that the means and possible direction of expansion of the firm are essentially the same in the two cases. Thus, there are four types of growth available to all firms, financial or otherwise:

(i) The simplest case, corresponding to traditional ideas of large-scale operations or horizontal integration, is where more of the same activities are conducted from the same location in a concentration of activities in a large-scale plant.

(ii) In the second method of expansion, the services are provided from the same location to a new market (e.g. the building societies attracting wholesale deposits).

(iii) A third mode of expansion involves the establishment of activities in multiple locations, thus 'bringing the service to the customer'. By establishing branches and geographic outlets, the firm reduces the 'external costs' (search, transport, time, effort) incurred by the customer in obtaining services. Location increases in importance as the frequency of transactions rises and the average size of transactions decreases, with day-to-day payment functions falling into this category. However, as discussed in Chapter 4, changes in technology and the growth of Automatic Teller Machines, point-of-sale terminals and home banking will have important implications for the need to maintain a branch network.

(iv) A fourth form of expansion involves the extension of the range of services provided (or activities conducted) by the firm. Diversification may arise because customers demand a 'cluster of services' so that the relevant commodity is the group of services which are purchased jointly and at less cost and inconvenience than using separate suppliers.

Allowing, in addition, for economies of joint production or 'scope' (see Chapter 4), we have in (iv) the basis of banks' provision of agencies for insurance, and building societies' willingness to enter this business. Skills developed in providing particular services may be well suited to use in other activities, e.g. insurance companies using their investment skills to manage unit trusts. Also, non-financial firms like retailers may seek to tie financial services, such as access to short-term credit, to the sale of goods.

Diversification can take a variety of forms. One is internal expansion within the firm, as in 'universal banking', practised in Germany or Switzerland but less commonly elsewhere. Or there may be multifirm activities, as in the 'holding company' form of organisation, favoured by many financial firms in Britain and Australia. A number of financial services are combined outside of the individual firms, but within the group. Cross-selling of group product lines can occur, without the firms sacrificing their separate cultural and remuneration characteristics. Finally, there may be cooperative arrangements and ventures among firms to provide services, considered later in this chapter.

2.4 Financial Characteristics

In this section we examine the particular characteristics of financial products which distinguish them from many other goods and services. These essential characteristics may be classified as follows:

(1) the customer–firm interaction inherent in services;
(2) the two-way process of information flows;
(3) the safety sought after because exchanges take place over time;
(4) the trust needed because of delegated monitoring;
(5) the basic substitutability of financial services;
(6) the inability to patent services.

The importance of the interaction between the consumer and the firm has been discussed in the previous section. Since apparently diverse financial services are directed towards the three basic needs discussed in Section 2.2, it is clear that inherently there is considerable substitutability between financial products. We develop this point in a number of the following chapters. The inability to patent services has important implications for the innovation process and the length of time for which the innovator is ahead of the field. The issue is taken up later in this chapter. In the present section we concentrate on aspects of information, safety and trust which are inextricably linked to the intertemporal nature of financial contracts.

As noted in the previous section, whilst financial firms provide services, they also undertake a manufacturing process which qualitatively alters the characteristics of the securities in which they deal. Financial intermediaries stand between borrowers and lenders of funds, substituting claims against themselves which have greater liquidity and lower perceived and actual risk than lenders could obtain for themselves. It is the nature of this transformation which gives financial markets many of their special characteristics. By acting on behalf of many customers, they offer the potential of economies in transaction costs and in the process of information.

Information

As with the production of any other good, the 'manufacture' of financial products requires the use of labour, capital and materials. However, in contrast with many commodity market transactions which involve a contemporaneous two-way exchange of commodity and means of payments, with no obligation for a future transaction, and in which the identity of the transactors is often irrelevant, financial contracts are often crucially dependent on the characteristics of the transactors.

Information assumes significance when there is a separation of savings from the accumulation of wealth, and underlies the distinction which Keynes (1936) made between borrowing risks and lending risks:

> ... *entrepreneur's or borrower's risk* ... arises out of doubts in his own mind as to the probability of his actually earning the prospective yield for which he hopes. If a man is venturing his own money, this is the only risk which is relevant.
>
> But where a system of borrowing and lending exists, by which I mean the granting of loans with a margin of real or personal security, a second type of risk is relevant which we may call the *lender's risk*. This may be due either to *moral hazard*, i.e. voluntary default or other means of escape, possibly lawful, from the fulfilment of the obligation, or to the possible insufficiency of the margin of security, i.e. involuntary default due to the disappointment of expectation.
>
> Now the first type of risk is, in a sense, a real social cost, though susceptible to diminution by averaging as well as by an increased accuracy of foresight. The second, however, is a pure addition to the cost of investment which would not exist if the borrower and lender were the same person. (*Our emphasis*)

The addition referred to here, as noted by Stigler (1967), comes about because of information costs — costs of acquiring knowledge about borrowers and overseeing their performance during the course of the loan.

Financial institutions exist largely because they possess a comparative advantage over individuals in the acquisition, storage and use of information. Lending by most financial institutions is highly information specific. Loans from intermediaries are not normally bought 'off-the-rack' and are most often not characterised by the kind of anonymity and arm's length dealings that typify other competitive markets.

The information process involves a two-way flow which is not common for many consumer goods. When engaging in a transaction for a financial service, the customer is frequently required to provide a considerable degree of information relating to his or her personal, family and employment characteristics. Further, as with a bank account, for example, the bank acquires direct information about the economic habits, spending patterns and income of the customer as a direct byproduct of the normal operation of the service. The manufacturer of consumer goods, on the other hand, does not generally obtain any information about the attributes of his customers without engaging in direct market research.

Thus, banks and savings institutions, in particular, are able to utilise information gained from monitoring and conducting the savings and transactions accounts of their customers. They are in frequent contact with customers: the average UK customer makes one personal visit to the bank in a week. Contact through other means, such as the use of Automatic Teller machines, similarly provides the bank with information. The repeated contacts and use of the service means that over time banks are able to build up a profile of the person's suitability to obtain credit and ability to service the loan. This private information enhances the institutions' ability to make low-risk loans at little cost.

At the same time, this flow of information provides an incentive for potential borrowers to become depositors. By becoming depositors, future borrowers provide institutions with the information needed to sort out good from bad risks, so reducing the likelihood of being refused access to credit when needed. There is an implicit intertemporal contract whereby reliability as a depositor qualifies the customer for priority when seeking future loans and services.

Credit cards have not only reinforced the informational links between deposit and lending activities, but have revolutionised the information-gathering process. For a customer without a card, provision of financial services occurs via a succession of transactions and interactions between the firm and the customer over time, accompanied by the gathering of information about creditworthiness. With a credit card, a single act of judgment is made as to the customer's credit standing. The information so obtained is then used for generating transactions relating to purchases of goods along with instant access to credit.

Such information spillovers explain why banks and other

depository institutions bundle together transactions services, savings facilities and lending vehicles. Use of information to identify good loan risks assists depository institutions to offer full redemption of deposits at face value despite holding a portfolio of assets of potentially high individual risk. Because many loans are based on private information, they have traditionally had low marketability.

Safety

The fact that much of the information concerning the true risk of the asset portfolio is private to the financial institutions makes it almost impossible for individual depositors to reach an informed assessment of the institution's current and future financial viability. Yet the need for such assessment is apparent from the intertemporal character of financial contracts, whether explicit or implicit, for the institutions are trading future obligations against current receipts.

What is being purchased with an insurance contract or a bank deposit is a set of promises. The value of a 'set' of promises to the purchaser depends partly on what it is that is promised and partly on the likelihood that the promises will, when they fall due, be fulfilled. On both scores, the purchaser will be looking to buy some guarantee of quality. As far as the former is concerned, the purchaser is usually expected to be the best person to make the appropriate evaluation, so long as he or she is provided with relatively full and accurate information, and provided that there are inexpensive comebacks available when this is not the case.

But in so far as the likelihood of future delivery is concerned, it is difficult for the purchaser to make an accurate assessment. The further it is in the future that the promises are expected to fall due, the more difficult the task, yet the purchaser may not always get a second chance. Since the costs to the individual of a mistaken assessment are very high, and if the costs to society of arranging for collective assessment are not high, we can readily appreciate why governments have provided purchasers with some assurance that the promises to pay become actual payments. Regulation of life insurance has this objective.

Confidence

As was explained in Chapter 1, the whole superstructure of financial intermediation rests on confidence and trust. Without confidence the constituents of personal wealth would be no more liquid than the tangible assets upon which the financial claims are made. Somehow financial markets must reconcile the fluidity of personal wealth with the fixity and indivisibility of national wealth; the generality of many claims held by people with the specific nature of items of national wealth; and consumability of individual holdings with the inability to consume national assets readily.

A special problem exists in the case of banks and other depository institutions because the contrast between their liabilities (which have immediate and guaranteed encashability) and their assets (with high potential individual risk and low realisability) is the sharpest. Accordingly, collective arrangements have been introduced in most countries to ensure that the operation of the payments mechanism is unimpeded by worries about the safety of the institutions which are counterparties to the transactions.

In the absence of full information, people will use crude information to establish whether future promises made by intermediaries are reasonable and likely to be delivered. One indicator might be the size of the institution, on the grounds of 'safety in numbers' and that an institution which is large enough will attract public support. Another is longevity, since past survival might be seen as a guide to future prospects. Certainly, the largest financial institutions are long-lived. But the concentrations of financial power which result may be seen to be unwelcome both for their own sake or because, in comparison with alternative arrangements, they are inimical to competition and individual participation in the allocation of national savings to national investment. For example, the more generous public safety net in the US may allow many more small depository institutions to be viable than is the case in Britain.

Trust

Without trust, delegation – which is the essence of intermediation – cannot proceed far. Purchase of unit trusts, insurance policies, pension funds and asset management schemes involves an act of considerable faith in the stewardship of the institutions concerned. Establishment of an intertemporal relationship with a bank or savings institution rests on trust. Trust is an important lubricant of the financial system. Financial contracting is greatly simplified when one does not have to read the small print and can rely upon the other's behaviour. Experience in the US shows clearly the problems which can arise when there is incomplete trust. Much of the continued difficulties of the savings institutions can be traced to one feature: Americans do not trust their institutions sufficiently to give them the full discretionary power over interest rates which Britons sign over so readily to banks and building societies.

The importance of trust may introduce inertia into customer–firm relationships in Britain. Experience gained and information acquired to assess an institution's reliability has a considerable capital cost element, since it represents an irreversible investment of time and effort. Once an individual has found a firm to be trustworthy, he or she will want to stay with it, simply because it is cheaper to monitor its continuing performance than it is to check out a new supplier. The corollary from the firm's viewpoint is that it is often easier to sell additional products to the existing customer base than it is to acquire new customers. Movements in the population through birth and death do provide opportunities for change which is perhaps why the banks have concentrated considerable marketing efforts on children and students. Moreover, information acquired by customers is likely to be passed on to future generations.

Branding

Consequently, once trust is established, a firm may seek to trade on its good name by 'branding' tied suppliers. The entry of Lloyds Bank into the broking of real estate provides a case in point. Purchase of a house is the single most important financial decision which most people make, and a housing loan is usually the largest financial commitment into which they enter. Homebuyers want more than the finance; they are seeking access to conveyancing, legal services and insurance, along with reassurance about the wisdom of the purchase through the lender's valuation. Real estate agents are a vital – and often the first – link in the decision process, yet were perceived by Lloyds Bank to be geographically fragmented, suppliers of services of mediocre quality and, most importantly in view of their pivotal role in house purchases and sales, poorly regarded by the public.[2]

Through acquisition, Lloyds now have a chain of nearly 200 estate offices across the country branded with the Black Horse symbol giving them the 'credibility and reputation of the parent bank'.[3]

In place of the disaggregated process by which people obtain services in turn from real estate agent, surveyor, lawyer, bank or building society, finance company, insurance company, and retail furnishing store, the idea is for virtually every aspect of the home purchase to be made available through the offices – estate broking, surveys, valuations, conveyancing, mortgages, consumer credit, and insurance, through to pre-packaged interior designer furnishing schemes. Lloyds even intend to buy for later resale houses which hold up the chains of several transactors which can develop, a path pioneered by the Prudential Insurance Company.

Consumer Protection

The characteristics of financial products that we have discussed would seem, in general, to suggest that the key distinguishing factors in pesonal financial markets relate to the inherent intertemporal nature of dealings between the financial firm and its customers and the importance of particular types of information for the operation of these markets. Mistakes and wrong choices by consumers can have serious ramifications for their financial and economic circumstances. The question of consumer protection is, therefore, often fundamental to the regulatory framework which governs the operation of financial markets.

As financial institutions branch out into new fields, difficult questions are raised for financial regulation. These involve conflicts of interest, tied-in sales, confidentiality of information on computer files and how the safety of the basic financial functions of borrowing and lending can be isolated, if at all, from the new risks which are being undertaken: questions for which there are no easy answers.

There are some similarities and also marked differences between approaches in the US and UK to these matters. In both countries, the safety net provided for those institutions which operate the payments system ('banks') has been widened in line with the blurring which has occurred between banks and other depository institutions. In the US, back-up liquidity support from the Federal Reserve has been extended from a relatively 'select' group of 6,000-odd member banks to the 40,000-odd institutions now providing transactions services (member and other banks, savings institutions and credit unions). In the UK, savings banks and a large number of financiers have been swept up into the banking system under the requirement that all institutions accepting deposits from members of the public be treated as banks (building societies and insurance companies are covered by separate legislation). But the public safety net, formally at least, embraces just domestic 'banking' and not the other activities undertaken via the holding company umbrella. This is despite public perceptions, which may see bank-affiliated institutions as safer. Since British banks now offer a range of financial services as wide as any in the world, there is the question of whether bank-associated companies gain a competitive advantage over non-affiliated companies.

Protection of UK consumers from potential abuses of trust and self-dealing by suppliers of financial services is to be left under the Financial Services Bill of 1986 to self-regulatory bodies in particular industries. These are seen by their proponents as better able to identify and root out delinquents, and subject them to social ostracism. To these bodies falls the job of interpreting the general principles of business conduct laid out in the Financial Services Bill to fit the characteristics of particular markets and different categories of customers. While there are many points of detail to be resolved in the new self-regulatory framework, there are many commentators who doubt its adequacy, pointing to the abuses which the self-regulation of Lloyd's insurance syndicates has failed to prevent. Chapter 8 considers these points in more detail. Here we note that there are also two 'ultimate' arbiters in the British system. One is competition. A firm which seeks to bully a customer into buying a tied service is disciplined by competition from independent suppliers offering an unbundled service without strings attached to the purchase. The other is what Kenneth Arrow (1974) called the 'invisible institutions' of the principles of ethics and morality, self-discipline and social responsibility. British financial regulation, like policing in the community generally, has traditionally rested heavily upon such attitudes; but reliance on such strictures is increasingly being called into question.

A different philosophy has permeated thinking in the United States. Limitations are placed upon the range of services that firms under the public safety net and their holding companies can undertake. Banks there are not permitted to sell insurance and unit trusts. Their subsidiaries are not allowed to buy real estate and houses. In effect, the idea is to prevent problems and temptations for abuse from arising in the first place. But that formal regulatory approach is also under pressure as competition breaks down the previously watertight compartments dividing institutional groupings and activities.

2.5 Increased Competition in Financial Markets

Market boundaries can be broadened (or narrowed) by technology, attitudes of consumers, regulatory developments and the breadth of the public safety net. A conjunction of such events has served to bring about a more competitive environment in the 1980s. Many features have appeared which might be expected in any industry suddenly opened to greater competition. Certain packaged and product bundles introduced in earlier circumstances have broken down as the new entrants have picked off the most profitable lines of business. There has been much experimentation as firms seek the magical mix of services and products which will triumph over that offered by competitors. Since firms do not know in advance which combinations of products and mix of services will succeed, they have sought to establish a market presence in all experiments, each following the other so as to avoid missing out altogether on a possibly profitable avenue of business.

'Copy-catting' is particularly pronounced amongst financial institutions because the advantages of being first are likely to be short-lived. Successful innovations in finance cannot be patented, nor can the knowledge be bundled up and sold for royalties. As with other service industries (the self-service supermarket concept, for example), it is difficult to prevent imitation. For the leading innovators there is the kudos of having the reputation of a market leader and there are the profits when innovation results in gaining a march on rivals. In some cases the prime mover can sustain the advantage for a considerable time. Merrill Lynch's cash management account, arguably the most innovative invention of the past two decades, has not been successfully imitated by others.

A certain inertia is induced by customer–firm interaction over time. By staying with a firm, a customer buys goodwill, preferential access to borrowing and premature encashment of contracts in different circumstances. On the firm's part, it must show to customers that, by staying with it, they will not lose out to any great extent.

Successful innovations in products and investment must be copied, without a long lag. Firms need to keep abreast of successful strategies.

A good deal of marketing effort has gone into ascertaining what bundle of services is sought-after by consumers of financial services, and what is the primary relationship which will most generate customer–firm links. Both our investigations at the Nottingham Institute of Financial Studies and research in the US suggest that banks have the strongest base for expansion. But in interpreting these results we recall the longstanding distinction in retailing between so-called 'shopping goods' and 'convenience goods'. The former are those of high value, which are probably bought infrequently and for which a certain expenditure on search to ascertain prices and qualities of various products is worthwhile. Convenience goods, on the other hand, are those which tend to be of less value, probably bought frequently and which are also possibly less complex in character. When examining changes in financial markets, there are clearly different factors at work for the two types of goods.

Computer technology and innovations have enabled specific parts of financial packages, even in the case of convenience goods, to be supplied more efficiently on a stand alone basis. Consumers' 'do-it-yourself' unbundling of financial packages has prompted firms to repackage. For shopping goods the consumer is likely to require some form of expert advice and wish to compare the products offered by different suppliers. Such goods are not so likely to be sold off the 'supermarket' shelf. An important question is to what extent financial innovation is bringing more financial instruments within the realm of convenience goods and to what extent it is making them more complex and sophisticated.

Even if the combination of financial products in packages is becoming more important, it does not, of course, follow that the financial firm needs to produce each of these products in-house. In supplying a range of products, the firm always faces a make or buy decision. For example, whilst retail distributors such as Marks and Spencer and Sainsburys offer an extensive range of products sold under their own label, they have virtually no manufacturing capacity. These own-brand products are supplied under contract by independent manufacturers.

One similar route, which is proving popular for the financial firm, is the joint venture.

Joint Ventures

Developments in market organisation and information technology have dramatically altered the ability of small retail-based firms to obtain the benefits of diversification; some developments may have been induced by a desire for diversification. Futures and options markets of various kinds enable small institutions to shift financial exposures onto specialised risk bearers. Markets in which mortgage and other loans are bundled up and marketable securities issued against them enable a small firm to acquire participations in a wide range of financial assets. Computer technology allows depository institutions to locate ATMs in department stores, supermarkets, shopping centres and places of work. Terminals selling insurance and unit trusts (mutual funds) can be made available in the lobbies of banks and savings institutions.

In the United States, networking amongst firms involving credit cards, cash dispensing and travellers' cheques is beginning to be as important for financial services as franchising has been for the retailing of food. Many of the innovative financial products which have prompted reference to a financial services revolution in the United States, of which the cash management account is the leading example, are based around joint ventures between financial institutions. Joint ventures have been used extensively by the building societies and smaller banks in the UK. For example, there have been tie-ups between building societies and Scottish banks, unit trusts and merchant banks, which have enabled those groups to offer transactions services in competition with the clearing banks.

Cooperation in the provision of financial services is no new development. Provision of payment services by banks relies upon correspondent arrangements and interbank cooperation through the clearing house. In any market system, some form of interpersonal organisation is needed to secure the gains which come from individuals' different talents and the improvements in efficiency which come from specialisation in economic tasks. However, some writers (e.g. Leveson 1982) see in the growth of networking and joint ventures a revolution in 'integrative services' made possible by developments in information technology. Integrative services 'interconnect firms, units of firms or industries in different stages of the production process or in different locations' (*ibid*). The analogy with a transport system for goods is obvious. Networking allows firms to supplement their capabilities to achieve geographical spread, to share in any benefits from a diverse product line, and to reap economies of marketing while keeping to traditional patterns of specialisation. It means that a small firm does not have to try to do everything by itself, yet has the opportunity to distribute its skills quickly to larger numbers of customers.

The growth of joint ventures has introduced a distinction common in retailing, but less so in financial services, in terms of suppliers of intermediate products and final producers. In the past, suppliers of financial services to persons have participated at all levels, providing a vertically integrated operation. Savings institutions, for example, have initiated contact with the customer, made the housing loans, collected repayments and carried the asset. Joint ventures in Britain now permit foreign banks to make loans initiated by insurance firms and brokers. Secondary mortgage markets enable the functions to be separated further. In some packages in the US, origination is separated from the lending of funds, other parties insure the loans, still others do loan packaging, with different firms holding the loans as trustees for the securities issue.

As non-financial firms enter the finance industry, existing firms act as true 'wholesalers' supplying back-up support for the set-up of credit operations, as the Bank of Scotland has done for Marks and Spencer and Midland Bank for Tesco. As financial firms diversify horizontally by broadening their product range, they are making decisions about whether to act as agencies for specialist suppliers, put their own brand name on a product devised by someone else, or design and organise their own. Again, this is not a novel development; unit trust managers have long 'wholesaled' trusts to insurance companies. What is new is the pace of change and the extent of experimentation. We take up the issues for marketing which are raised by these developments in the next chapter.

Notes

1. For a detailed discussion of the main issues involved, see Hill (1977).
2. See comments by Fred Crawley, Chief General Manager, Lloyds Bank plc in *Retail Banker International Yearbook 1985–86*, pp. 70–4.
3. *Ibid.*

References

Arrow, K.J. (1974) *The Limits of Organization*, Norton.
Coase, R.H. (1937) 'The nature of the firm', *Economica*, New Series, Vol. IV, pp. 386–405.
Hill, T.P. (1977) 'On goods and services', *Review of Income and Wealth*, Vol. 23, No. 4, December, pp. 315–38.
Keynes, J.M. (1936) *General Theory of Employment, Interest and Money*, Macmillan.
Leveson, I.F. (1982) *The Economic Future of the United States*, Westview Press.
Stigler, G. (1967) 'Imperfections in the general market', *Journal of Political Economy*, June, pp. 287–92.

CHAPTER 3

The Marketing of Personal Financial Services

T. Watkins

3.1 Introduction

Many of the changes now occurring in the personal financial services industry have important implications for marketing by financial companies. This chapter examines current trends in the UK, taking account of experience in the United States. Marketing involves developing a strategy for meeting corporate objectives through the satisfaction of customers. We begin, therefore, with strategies and a consideration of consumer behaviour, and continue with an examination of marketing research and market segmentation. Finally, we investigate the three most important components of marketing strategy (distribution, promotion and advertising) and product range with particular reference to the major types of personal financial service.

3.2 Types of Marketing Strategies

Figure 3.1 summarises the role of marketing in personal financial services. Immediately at question is whether the marketing of financial services differs from the marketing of ordinary products. In the previous chapter it was argued that while there were important differences − factors relating to the significance of confidence, trust, safety and information flows for financial services, which cannot be ignored in marketing − they are differences of degree rather than

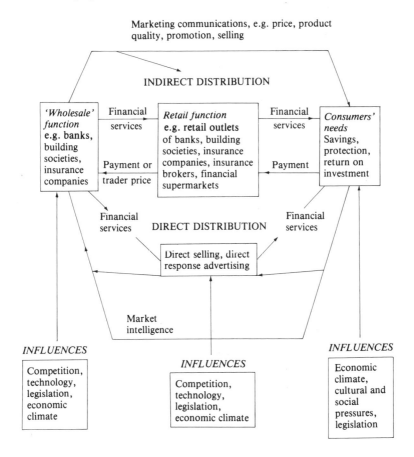

Figure 3.1   The Role of Marketing in Personal Financial
Services Provision

of kind. Indeed, because of the importance of customer–firm interactions in services, the role of marketing is paramount.
Consequently, the broad principles of marketing strategy (Porter
1985) can be applied to financial services. Firms may adopt one of
three main approaches:

(1) *Cost leadership:* the firm seeks to become *the* low-cost producer
across a broad range of products and services. In financial services

this may be achieved through standardisation and the sale of products or services 'off-the-peg' in ready-made form without any fashioning to the needs of individual customers. This low-cost strategy is best suited to mass markets with large homogeneous needs which are sensitive to price but not so concerned with quality of service. To be competitive the product must, of course, meet the criteria demanded by consumers and must possess comparable attributes to the products of other suppliers. The standardised range of services offered enables savings in administrative expenses and staff costs to be made, since neither highly trained staff nor professional intermediaries are really necessary to sell the products.

Ideally, standardised products should be easy to understand and simple to sell. Given the need to obtain ready access to a mass market, some financial services firms have attempted to liaise with organisations that possess high-street premises (department stores, building societies, post offices, estate agents, etc.), while others have attempted their own mass marketing (via newspaper and television advertisements, direct mail from acquired mailing lists, etc.). Alternatively, other firms with existing access to mass markets have used this advantage to diversify into financial services. Since standardised products are essentially low-price, high-volume ones, they may be unsuitable for distribution outlets remunerated by commission.

(2) *Differentiation:* the firm seeks to be unique in respect of one or more of the characteristics which are valued by customers. Such differentiation can be achieved through, for example, the nature of the product itself or its distribution system. In financial services, with the inherent close customer–firm interaction, it could be reflected in the provision of bespoke products which are tailored to individual customer needs with a correspondingly large degree of flexibility.

Customisation, or product-differentiated marketing, is designed to offer variety to buyers rather than to appeal to different market segments. The strategy will appeal to buyers who are concerned with personalised individual service, albeit at a higher price. Products are essentially high-price, low-volume ones since they are more complex to understand and difficult to sell. Distribution of such financial services products may be by brokers or highly trained direct salesmen, but some firms in the US have fashioned themselves into 'financial boutiques' catering for high net worth individuals (Chapter 5).

(3) *Focus:* the firm identifies specialist market segments which it seeks to supply to the exclusion of others. As in the general case, it can seek either a cost or a differentiation advantage. Such specialised or target marketing requires the seller to distinguish among many market segments, select one or more of these segments (market targeting) and develop products and marketing mixes tailored to each segment (product positioning). Markets may be segmented in a number of ways, e.g. by geographic location or demographic characteristics or by social or behavioural characteristics. The market for financial services is usually segmented by wealth or by occupation or affinity grouping, by social class and by price responsiveness. Whether a direct or indirect distribution system is employed will depend very much on the most effective way of contacting the particular segments.

In general it can be argued that the firm needs to choose one or other of these strategies and a 'stuck in the middle' position is unlikely to lead to success since each is a fundamentally different approach to creating and sustaining a competitive advantage (Porter 1985). Development of an appropriate strategy along these lines rests on identifying consumers' needs and their marketing characteristics.

3.3 Consumers' Characteristics and Behaviour

Financial services satisfy three basic needs of consumers: the making of monetary payments and transactions; wealth accumulation by means of savings, borrowings, and 'investments'; and financial security and protection. These needs are the building blocks for financial services (Chapter 2). However, the intensity with which these needs are demanded and the ways in which the services are sought after will differ between households according to some identifiable characteristics.

Consumer Sophistication

A widening of educational opportunities, improvements in transport and communications, and the switch from secondary to tertiary employment have undoubtedly led to increased consumer sophistication. Accompanying this, the range of possible outlets for consumer savings and sources for borrowing is expanding. Traditional simple products such as bank accounts, building society accounts, endowment mortgages and ordinary shares are being extended by an increasing number of packaged products involving previously separate elements such as unit-linked insurance, high-interest chequing accounts and money market funds.

Evidence from the US in a survey by the Federal Reserve Bank of Atlanta (Bennett 1984) suggests that households are looking for more information and advice. Half of those surveyed considered that being able to obtain information and advice regarding financial decisions is highly important; a quarter considered it crucial. However, whether rational or otherwise, traditionally consumers have been unwilling to pay directly for such services. One-third of those surveyed said they did not know how to choose financial products and services; more than half said they never obtain information about differences in financial products; and two-thirds said they never sought advice as to which financial products were best suited to their needs. Some other results of the Atlanta survey are reported in Chapter 5.

As the variety and sophistication of financial products increases, the associated possible demand for information and advice represents a clear strategic opportunity for financial institutions and intermediaries. As the boundaries between traditional financial sectors continue to dissolve, sellers must concern themselves more with developing and maintaining a distinct image in the market place. Reputation, trust, confidence and safety are necessary requirements for financial products (see Chapter 2 for a fuller discussion).

One way of measuring consumer sophistication is through the concept of the repertoire. The repertoire is the short-list of alternatives from which a consumer makes the final choice. It can be hypothesised that a consumer seeking a 'shopping good' will consider more alternatives than one seeking a 'convenience' product. The information which it is worth collecting for the latter is much less. There are important marketing implications in terms of Porter's (1985) strategies from this crucial distinction.

Income

High-income households in the US use a wider variety of financial institutions than do low-income households, which may reflect the

importance of 'shopping goods' characteristics. A 1982 study by Electronic Banking Inc. found that less than 2 per cent of all respondent households dealt with only one financial institution; 39 per cent dealt with a bank and one other; 42 per cent a bank and two others; and 17 per cent a bank and three or more other institutions. The likelihood of a high-income household (more than $50,000 per annum) using four or more financial institutions was twice the norm.

The penetration of US households by various types of financial institution by income group is shown in Table 3.1. Such penetration appears income-elastic for a number of categories, especially money market mutual funds and full-service brokerage facilities, both supplied by securities firms. The implications, if this trend occurs in the UK, are that high-quality products with high returns will be valued by high-income consumers but the difficulty of gaining extra business will become intense, thus indicating a need to broaden the appeal of the product to other groups. The reduction of transactions costs through improved information technology (see Chapter 4) together with regulatory changes such as the 'Big Bang' (see Chapters 8 and 10) is likely to aid this objective.

Age and Social Grouping

Market penetration of personal financial services in the UK by age and social grouping is shown in Tables 3.2 and 3.3 respectively. Social ranking, being occupation based, is highly correlated with income and, as is consistent with the US evidence, penetration is generally higher for the higher-income groups. The figures do indicate room for expansion of existing services, particularly amongst the DE and C2 groups. The Trustee Savings Bank group has already found a ready market for unit trusts and insurance from amongst its traditional customer base. Market penetration by age (Table 3.3) shows a fairly even spread within each service for those over 21 and less than 65 years old, although there is considerable variation between them. Reputation and accumulated experience tend to introduce considerable inertia and brand loyalty into financial markets (see Chapter 2). Thus, it is not surprising that many suppliers have targeted their efforts towards the young age groups, particularly amongst the banks with their emphasis on students in both schools and higher education.

Table 3.1 US Household Penetration of Financial Services by Income
Level (%)

		Income		
Service	*Total*	*Under $25,000*	*$25–40,000*	*$40–60,000*	*Over $60,000*
Regular checking account	66.1	71.2	64.1	61.7	71.2
Money market mutual funds	16.2	10.4	14.8	22.3	34.8
Full service brokerage	12.7	5.9	10.6	23.8	31.8
Term life insurance	31.4	25.0	30.8	45.1	35.0
Whole life insurance	43.9	34.9	49.5	52.9	50.0
Universal life insurance	6.9	4.5	9.2	8.3	6.1

Source: Payments Systems Inc., 1983.

Table 3.2 UK Market Penetration of Personal Financial Services by Social
Grouping (%)

Social group	*% size of segment in GB*	*Bank current account*	*Building society account (any type)*	*Bank deposit account*	*Bank credit card*	*Shop credit card*	*Life assurance*	*Other insurance**
AB	17	89	66	40	51	4	65	76
C1	22	79	61	35	38	3	67	73
C2	31	62	52	35	24	2	69	64
DE	30	38	35	32	12	1	61	56

Sources: (1) NOP *Financial Research Survey*, October 1983–March 1984, all except:
(2) Life assurance and insurance figures – AGB Index, June 1982
* Other insurance includes house, house contents, personal possessions, motor, etc.

When market penetration is low, the marketing campaign can be directed primarily at expanding the total market and there is still considerable room for such expansion in the UK. However, as the market matures, a change in emphasis is required which is directed at encouraging brand loyalty. Because of search and information costs, it is easier to sell additional products to existing customers than to acquire new ones.

Table 3.3 UK Market Penetration of Personal Financial Services by Age Grouping (%)

Age group	Size of segment in GB	Bank current account	Building society account (any type)	Bank deposit account	Bank credit card	Shop credit card	Life assurance	Other insurance*
16−20	10	38	48	30	9	1 ⎫	38	29
21−24	8	65	56	31	24	3 ⎭		
25−34	18	75	61	31	36	4	72	71
35−44	15	76	55	37	40	4	76	73
45−54	15	72	51	38	36	3	71	68
55−64	14	63	52	37	29	2	77	75
65+	19	48	40	37	16	1	61	80

Sources (1) NOP *Financial Research Survey*, October 1983–March 1984, all except;
(2) Life assurance and insurance figures – AGB Index, June 1982.
* Other insurance includes house, house contents, personal possessions, motor, etc.

Family Life Cycle

As well as age, a market segmentation strategy can also be based on family life-cycle characteristics and indeed, as noted in Chapter 1, such life-cycle behaviour is a fundamental determinant of saving itself. A study by Lansing and Morgan (1955) categorised the life cycle of families as follows:

(1) Bachelor stage: young single people
(2) Newly married couples: young, no children
(3) The full nest 1: young, married couples with dependent children
(4) The full nest 2: older, married couples with dependent children
(5) The empty nest: older, married couples with no children living with them
(6) The solitary survivor: older, single people

Such life-cycle categories can be used as a means of identifying target markets for personal financial services. Family needs and circumstances change as careers develop and wealth is accumulated. This characteristic is linked to age but not precisely, and financial services can be targeted to specific segments such as saving plans for school fees, pension provision and other lump-sum investment products.

Personality

Personality factors may be important as consumer characteristics in the choice of personal financial services. As noted above, one important dimension is in terms of the need for advice, but the type of advice required varies between consumers. Advice built into financial products will in future be monitored by self-regulatory agencies, as well as subject to assessment via high credibility sources such as *Money Which?* and media advice programmes/pages which are increasing in coverage and frequency. In-home interactive communication systems based on Prestel could improve availability of advice still further so that the sophisticated consumer is more able to make an informed choice.

Although, in principle, personality variables such as 'independence' could be used as a means of segmenting the market, in practice the isolation of personality types is difficult. It can be argued that advertising appeals can be constructed so as to appeal to particular personality types. This psychographics or lifestyle approach is gaining popularity in marketing practice in other fields in the UK. The technique is discussed by Engel and Blackwell (1982).

Summary

This section has examined various consumer characteristics which form important dimensions in the construction of a marketing strategy for financial services firms. The implications of these variables will now be discussed in a brief consideration of the marketing strategy of each of the major types of financial institutions: banks, building societies and insurance companies. The major elements of the marketing strategy considered will be advertising, distribution and product range.

3.4   Marketing Strategies of Major Sectors

The Banks

The survey undertaken by the Nottingham Institute of Financial Studies in early 1985, methodological details of which are appended, investigates bank competitive and marketing strategy intentions.

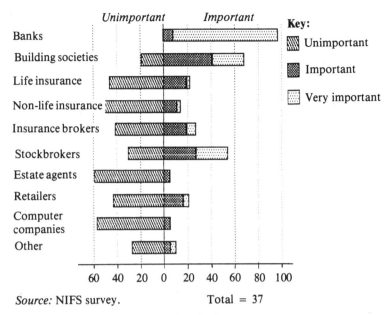

Source: NIFS survey.   Total = 37

Figure 3.2   Sources of Competition for Banks

Figure 3.2 shows the perceived competitive threats. These responses clearly show the importance of the expected threat from building societies and from stockbrokers, but little apparent concern about insurance companies over the next five years. Figure 3.3 shows the strategic growth intentions of the bank respondents. The development of new products is seen as a major factor for both new and existing markets. There is some evidence of inertia by some respondents. Figure 3.4 shows intentions which banks hold for competitive and marketing strategic action to attain growth. Internal growth and direct marketing are perceived as major influences by over 50% of respondents from the banking sector.

These findings indicate a competitive scenario in which marketing variables are important, particularly product range, advertising and other forms of promotion and distribution. The major banks are well advanced in the development of a wide range of personal financial products covering money transmission, saving and protection provision when links with insurance companies are included.

In terms of advertising, Table 3.4 shows that the 1984 MEAL

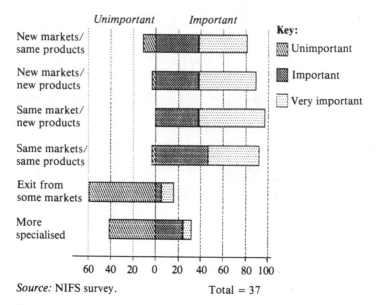

Figure 3.3   Factors Influencing Asset Growth of Banks

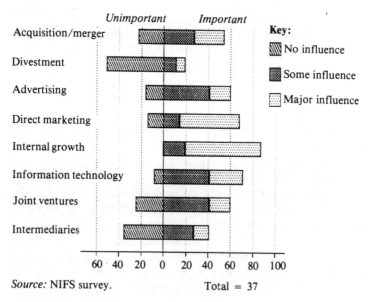

Figure 3.4   Strategies for Bank Asset Growth

Table 3.4 Advertising Expenditures of Banks and Building Societies, 1984 (£000)

Source	Total expenditure	TV	Press
Joint-stock banks	51,963	30,179	217,834
Merchant banks	312	–	312
Foreign banks and travel cheques	9,442	3,179	6,263
Credit cards	11,590	8,090	3,500
Building societies	60,197	23,128	37,069

expenditures in mass media by the banking sector exceeded those of the building societies. It is anticipated that the expenditure by banks on media advertising will continue to grow rapidly. Content analysis of the TV campaigns used by the joint-stock banks since 1984 indicates that the banks are directing much of this marketing effort at countering the competition from the building societies. The services advertised, such as Saturday opening, free banking, higher-interest accounts and special offers to students, are ones in which the large building societies have appealed to customers.

Building Societies

From the NIFS survey, Figure 3.5 shows, for the 82 building society respondents, the expected importance of various sources of competition. Banks are clearly viewed as a very important source of competition over the five years to 1990. The future marketing strategy of building societies will be closely influenced by the Building Societies Act, discussed in Chapter 6. This legislation is expected to allow the building societies to offer a much wider range of services than at present. Figure 3.6 shows that for building societies, like banks, the development of new products in both existing and new markets is seen as an important factor affecting their growth. Figure 3.7 shows that advertising is seen as the most important strategy for achieving this growth, with direct marketing, internal growth, information technology and the use of intermediaries also being major elements.

The level of advertising of building societies was shown in Table 3.4. The building societies have been taking an increasing share of

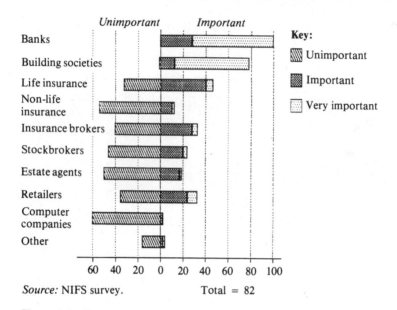

Figure 3.5 Sources of Competition for Building Societies

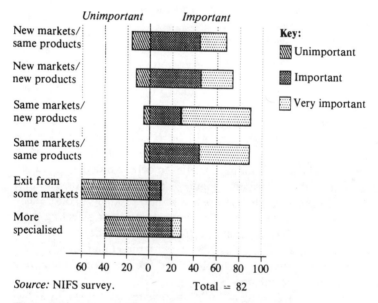

Figure 3.6 Factors Affecting Growth of Building Societies

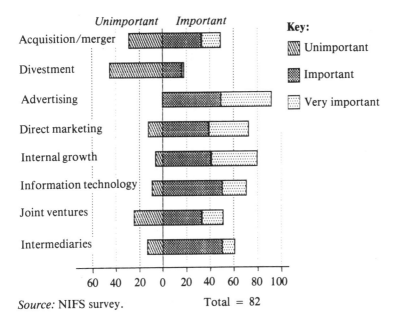

Source: NIFS survey.

Total = 82

Figure 3.7 Strategies for Building Societies Growth

financial advertising expenditures for several years. Table 3.5 shows
the proportions of mass media advertising expenditure over the
period 1977–84. The share taken by the building societies rose from
31 per cent in 1977 to 40 per cent in 1983 but fell back to 36 per cent
in 1984 as the joint-stock banks increased their levels of expenditure. Total expenditure has increased over sixfold in the eight years
reviewed, and is expected to continue to grow rapidly.

Since the building societies cartel on interest-rate setting broke
down, there has been increased price competition, but the majority
of marketing activity is still centred on non-price competition as the
different societies seek to establish a distinctive personality in the
perception of actual and potential consumers.

Press advertising by building societies is increasingly encouraging
direct response by readers using higher interest-rate offers to entice
new account opening. New services can also be used in this context.
A prime example is the Abbey National 'Cheque-Save' account
which uses press advertising to stress the 'banking' features of this
account under the headline 'free banking'.

Table 3.5   Share of Press and TV Advertising by Financial Institutions, 1977–84

Year	Insurance companies (%)	Building societies (%)	Banks (%)	Unit trusts (%)	National savings (%)	Total expenditure (£m)
1977	24	31	32	7	5	29.7
1978	27	33	27	9	4	29.2
1979	22	36	27	9	4	40.0
1980	21	36	30	5	6	59.5
1981	21	37	26	6	8	86.1
1982	22	40	28	5	4	111.0
1983	24	40	27	6	3	146.8
1984	23	36	31	6	4	197.5

Source: MEAL.

Both building societies and banks commonly send regular account statements to customers and there are opportunities for the use of direct mail offers. The offer of related services such as loans or mortgages can be promoted in this way, often using personalisation of the copy. Some building societies which have on-line facilities to branches are dispensing with the issuing of mailed statements, with interest credited to accounts automatically and entered into passbooks when the client next visits the branch.

In terms of retail presence, it is claimed that building society branches are much 'friendlier' than are those of banks (Walden 1984) and, given the increased competition between banks and building societies with product ranges with high levels of overlap, this may give building societies the edge in attracting customer usage. High-street premises are expensive and it is anticipated that the number of branches will fall over the next five years. The innovative move by Nottingham Building Society which introduced the 'Homelink' service using Prestel had the aim of extending the geographical range of the society nationwide by electronic in-home means rather than by establishing extra branches.

Building society branch staff have traditionally been 'clerical' rather than 'sales' orientated. The need for management marketing and sales training is likely to add expense to the developing role of the societies. Additionally, new services can only be offered by trained staff. The building societies may need to recruit insurance professionals to offer these services on a wide scale, for example. These human factors add costs to an already expensive set-up. There will be a need to add value to the services offered or a need to reduce the number of branches and to concentrate on fewer branches with a wider range of services provided by experts. But this will then reduce the convenience of access offered to consumers.

Further evidence on the importance of convenience from the consumers' perspective is provided by a survey carried out by the Nottingham Evening Post Market Research Department in October 1984. It found that choice of bank branch was determined primarily by location – convenience to home and/or workplace – with over half of the 599 adult respondents specifying this reason. It found that 29 per cent of building society savings account holders chose their building society because it had a 'convenient branch', this being the most popular reason.

Thus the likely competitive and marketing strategy of building societies is not without problems and there is a major management challenge to be faced.

Insurance Companies

The long tradition of the insurance institutions can be seen as both a strength and a weakness in the development of marketing strategy in the new competitive climate. It is a strength because of the large customer base, often very long established and loyal. It is a weakness because in many cases this has led to blinkered thinking and management domination by a 'production orientation' in which actuarial considerations are of paramount importance. Life offices surveyed by NIFS clearly take a parochial view and expect the bulk of future competition to come from within the industry (Figure 3.8).

The industry has been dominated by tradition, so much so that when innovative approaches were tried they were often spectacularly successful as in the case of Mark Weinberg and Hambro (now Allied Dunbar) and Abbey Life. The traditional approach was exacerbated by a tendency to promote from within and not to recruit from outside the industry. This is gradually changing and the types of outside professionals recruited have been primarily DP specialists and marketing managers.

Figure 3.9 shows that whilst life insurance companies see operating in the same markets with the same products as important

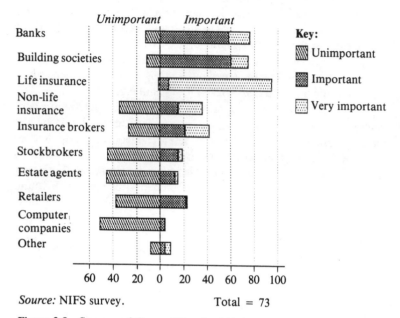

Source: NIFS survey.   Total = 73

Figure 3.8 Sources of Competition for Life Insurance

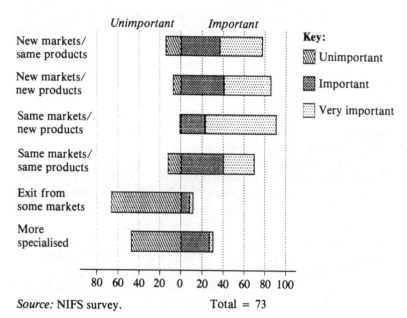

Source: NIFS survey.   Total = 73

Figure 3.9 Factors Affecting Growth of Life Insurance

for their growth, their emphasis on this aspect is less than for either banks or building societies. New products, either in the same or new markets, are seen as being important by over 80 per cent of the respondents. In examining the strategies by which growth is expected to be achieved (Figure 3.10) the life insurance companies see direct marketing as being of greater importance, and merger or acquisition less so, than the respondents from the banks and building societies.

As shown in Table 3.6, the insurance companies have increased their advertising expenditures in line with the market, and there is a trend for increased use of the mass media. The period since 1980 has shown a rapid growth, with press advertising expenditure showing a particularly marked increase. The use of TV advertising has tended to be spasmodic, with relatively few companies using this outlet.

Insurance companies use a plethora of distribution systems, both direct and indirect in nature. Traditionally the home service agent, employed on a salary plus commission basis by the company, has sold and serviced personal financial products direct to the customers who are often on a low-income level. This role has already been

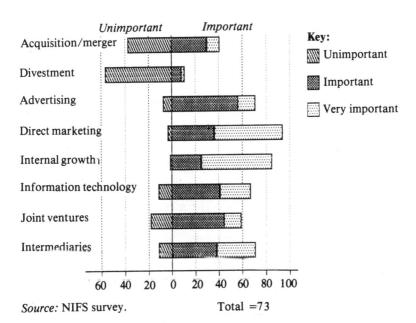

Source: NIFS survey.   Total = 73

Figure 3.10 Strategies for Life Insurance Growth

Table 3.6   Insurance Advertising in the Press and TV, 1968–84
              (£000)

	TV	Press	Total TV and press
1968	254	2,093	2,348
1969	20	2,931	2,951
1970	94	2,757	2,852
1971	49	2,993	3,042
1972	64	4,053	4,116
1973	320	4,467	4,787
1974	1,254	4,069	5,323
1975	806	3,467	4,273
1976	1,568	4,225	5,793
1977	1,859	5,273	7,132
1978	1,481	6,408	7,889
1979	975	7,823	8,798
1980	3,570	8,924	12,494
1981	4,886	13,203	18,089
1982	8,241	16,170	24,411
1983	11,169	24,054	35,223
1984	9,856	28,106	37,962

Source: MEAL.
Notes: (1) Excludes investment and growth bonds.
         (2) ITV strike of eleven weeks in 1979.

discussed earlier in this chapter. The use of commission-only, self-employed sales forces has grown rapidly since the 1960s and these have been aimed primarily at higher-income households. This route is characterised by a high rate of staff turnover and a subsequently high recruitment and training cost. It has tended to involve a 'hard sell' approach, at variance with the trend to better-informed and more sophisticated consumers. The more recent approach, which began in the commission-only sector and has spread into the home service sector, is to offer a personal financial planning service to clients covering a much wider range of services. This personal financial planning service focuses on a review of the individual's or family's needs and then updating the services provided.

The other direct routes are impersonal, using direct mail or direct-response media advertising. These save the cost of the salesforce and still enable the insurance company to retain control of the distribution effort. Response levels are notoriously poor but costs are potentially lower than using other delivery routes. As in all marketing, 'back room' operations are needed. It is difficult and costly to provide a back-up service for any queries generated by the promotion. The additional benefit is that the company generates a moving list from responses which can be used to sell other services. If done properly, mailing can be highly successful, as some US insurers targeting interest groups such as servicemen and teachers have found.

Indirect delivery routes centre on the use of brokers and other intermediaries who are owned independently of the insurance company and who usually carry a wide range of competitive products. Customers are meant to be advised impartially by these intermediaries as to the best product for their need. Inevitably there is a need for regulatory control since the advice may not be independent of the brokers' remuneration. The Register of Life Assurance Commissions (ROLAC) and the Gower Report are attempts to control this sector of activity (Chapter 8).

It is increasingly likely that the retailing of insurance products will become available in a very wide variety of outlets besides insurance brokers and the part-time agents, such as solicitors and accountants, traditionally used. Both banks and building societies are already heavily involved in such developments and several experiments involving major retailers as outlets for personal financial services are underway. The possibility of own-label retailer brands of personal financial services remains.

3.5 Developing a Marketing Strategy for Financial Services

The major decisions which suppliers have to make in devising a marketing strategy centred on customer needs in target market segments involve the product range, the type of delivery system to use and the size and allocation of the promotional budget. This chapter has examined some of the major trends in these variables across the industry and has considered the implications for each of the three major types of institutions.

In the aftermath of the many changes which are affecting the industry, the most successful competitors are likely to be the ones which most nearly meet consumer needs. Perhaps the most obvious requirement is for an effective marketing information system which carefully tracks developing consumer trends as an output to strategic marketing decisions. The key is in effective coordination of information flows. Financial institutions in general are provided with a flow of accurate information about their customers by the very nature of the product (Chapter 2). These data could be marshalled and built up by a continuous process of market intelligence gathering using such services as:

- Government publications on demographic, economic, and social trends.
- Industry statistics from trade associations.
- In-company data particularly relating to sales trends, e.g. rates of growth of account holding, average balances, sums assured. Also, customer data can be collected when new accounts are opened.
- Market research surveys, either continuous panel studies or *ad hoc* investigations in specific markets.

These can be integrated into a marketing information system which is a centralised resource available to assist in marketing decision making. The marketing plan for a financial services institution will involve setting the levels of marketing activity in a number of interrelated areas. These include:

(a) *Marketing communications* – the allocation of the promotional budget between personal selling, public relations, media advertising and other forms of promotion such as sponsorship and sales literature.

(b) *Determination of the product range* – the institution must decide on the width and depth of the product range to be offered to the market. In addition, the quality settings for this product range must be determined in conjunction with the needs in the market segments targeted.

(c) *Price setting* – in financial services there is a complex interaction between price and product quality and this is the focus for much competitive pressure.

(d) *Distribution strategy* – will the institution provide its own retail outlets or deal with independent intermediaries or direct with clients?

As an example, Figure 3.11 shows in schematic form a marketing information system for an insurance company based on the use of information from the proposal form and from other sources. The on-line database could be supported by an off-line library input when necessary. The system could issue summary data on a regular basis which would have the advantage of keeping all managers aware of marketing performance and customer profiles. Other market research services could be tapped to augment this basic system. Examples could include the AGB index service and the Taylor–Nelson Monitor service (broker attitudes). A major application is in market segmentation, especially using direct marketing. In an article in the *Banker* (April 1984) Crossdale-Appleby suggests a number of bases for financial services marketing segmentation:

(i) demographics (age groups) – of specific relevance to life insurance;

(ii) product usage rate (by size of existing life policy) – it may be easier to make existing policyholders add to their policy sum assured than to gain first time buyers;

(iii) behaviour and attitudes – why do people save, for rate of return or for protection? What is the trade-off between the two?

(iv) life style – the ways in which people live and the purchasing decisions they make, the types of product they buy;

(v) individual values – are individual consumers rational, future orientated, leisure orientated, do they live by traditional values, quality products, try new things, etc.?

To these segments could be added the other stratifying variables discussed earlier such as income, age and life-cycle stage.

At the current stage in marketing developments in the financial sector, very few companies have developed marketing information systems. There is some evidence of the use of computer-based sales aids. For example, insurance companies such as Allied Dunbar and Abbey Life use an interactive computer system to obain a personalised life assurance quotation for a sales prospect. There is little

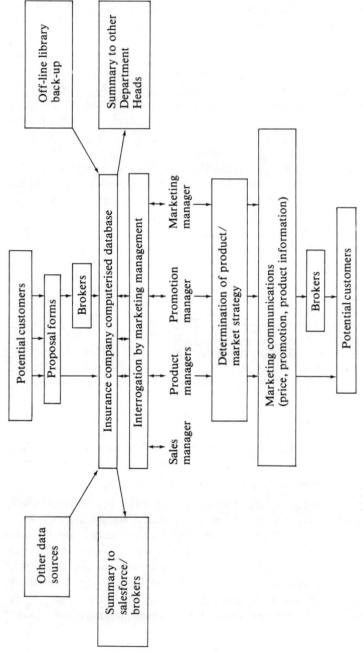

Figure 3.11 A Marketing Information System in Insurance

or no evidence of extensive use of a computerised data base of customer information being drawn on as an input to strategic marketing decisions.

3.6 Future Developments in Marketing Research

As competition for a larger share of consumers' personal savings increases and they are offered a wider range of alternatives, the way in which these services are presented to them will become more important. Consumers' choices must be monitored and effective marketing communications developed. Marketing intelligence is expected to grow and there is likely to be greater emphasis on the final consumer, including the use of qualitative research. The sophistication of marketing segmentation will also increase as such companies become aware of the facilities for targeting and refining their marketing appeals to specific customer groups.

Also, market research can be used to test promotional copy on consumers and to probe the value of branding of products. The simplification of products and the way in which they are presented to consumers is one answer to increasing convenience for consumers. It may be possible to probe consumer reactions to links with other organisations to offer joint products or joint or tied distribution. This would involve investigation of the consumers' perceptions of corporate images which could affect their reactions to linked products.

It is expected that the use of marketing information systems in financial services will develop as their potential is realised and the cost falls. An improved system of management was the major expected influence of micro-electronic technology in the survey conducted by the Nottingham Institute of Financial Studies with just over 50 per cent of respondents classing it as 'very important' and a further 42 per cent classing it as 'important'. Developments in information technology are examined in the following chapter.

References

Bennett, A. (1984) 'Consumer demand for product deregulation', *Federal Reserve Bank of Atlanta Economic Review*, May, pp. 28–40.

Crossdale-Appleby, D. (1984) 'Target marketing of financial services', *The Banker*, April, pp. 51–9.

Engel, J.F. and Blackwell, R.D. (1982) *Consumer Behavior*, 4th edn, Dryden Press.

Lansing, J.B. and Morgan, J.N. (1955) 'Consumer finances over the life cycle', in L.H. Clark (ed) *Consumer Behavior*, New York University Press.

Porter, M.E. (1985) *Competitive Advantage: Creating and Sustaining Superior Performance*, The Free Press.

Walden, H. (1984) 'How building societies see their role in the financial services revolution', *The Banker*, March, pp. 33–8.

APPENDIX A
The Nottingham Institute of Financial Studies Survey of Trends in Personal Financial Services

(1) Aims of Survey

During the literature searches and face-to-face interviews which were carried out as part of this research project, certain issues emerged which it was felt important to quantify. In particular, a large amount of anecdotal evidence on the current and expected trends in competition and growth of the personal financial services market was obtained. In order to provide some evidence on these trends, it was decided to administer a mailed questionnaire survey to the major sectors of this industry.

(2) Methodology

The sample used for the survey consisted of institutions in the following areas:

- Banks (all those listed in *The Banker's Almanac and Year Book* [1984])

- Building Societies (all those listed in *Building Societies Year Book* 1983)
- Life Insurance and Pensions (all those listed in *The Insurance Directory and Yearbook* 1983/4 supplemented by *Financial Times International*)
- Non-Life Insurance (all those listed in the *Insurance Directory and Yearbook* 1982/3 supplemented by *Financial Times International*)
- Insurance Brokers (sample of larger brokers from *Financial Times International Yearbook* 1982/3)

plus a random 10 per cent of Stockbrokers (from *The Stock Exchange Official Yearbook* 1984/5).

In total 487 institutions were mailed a copy of the questionnaire during December 1984, with a follow-up mailed questionnaire being sent in January 1985.

The overall response rate obtained was as follows:

	Number	*(%)*
Returned fully completed and usable	212	43.5
Notified refusals	24	4.9
No reply	251	51.6
Total	487	100.0

This response rate may be considered as highly encouraging given that this type of questionnaire usually attracts a response rate of 25–35 per cent. The greater than expected rate probably indicates a high level of interest in the subject matter.

The split of response between different types of institutions is shown below for the major sectors:

	Number of questionnaires sent	*Number of usable returns*	*Response rate (%)*
Insurance companies (life, non-life and brokers)	173	80	46.2
Building societies	157	80	51.0
Banks	115	37	32.2
Stockbrokers	42	15	35.7

The most frequently occurring job titles of respondents, where known, are shown in the following table for the three main sectors:

Job title	Banks	Building societies	Insurance companies
Chief Executive	–	3	4
Chief/General Manager	4	17	12
Assistant General Manager	–	11	2
Director	12	2	6
Managing Director	1	6	6
Marketing Manager	1	4	13
Company Secretary	4	8	4
Actuary	–	–	8
Financial Director/ Accountant	1	2	5

Respondents' job titles

In addition, there was a wide variety of one-off responses such as Corporate Planning Manager, Deputy Managing Director, Senior Planning Officer, Development Manager, Economist, Agency Manager, Research and Development Manager, UK Sales Manager and Head of Group Planning. For stockbrokers, respondents included two Senior Partners and eight Partners and one Director.

Clearly, the calibre of respondent in organisational terms is very high. Again, this can be taken to indicate a high level of interest in the subject of the enquiry.

CHAPTER 4

Information Technology and Personal Financial Services

B. Chiplin

4.1 Introduction

Most financial markets have been transformed in recent years by the pace of innovation (Silber 1983). Financial innovation can be in the form of a new product, or a new process for supplying or delivering an existing product. Examples of product innovations in personal financial markets are cash management schemes, and new flexible life and pension policies. Process innovation, first evident in the 'back office', has increasingly moved 'out front' with the emergence of automatic teller machines (ATMs), point-of-sale terminals and home banking. At the same time, these process changes have so altered the nature and characteristics of the service provided that the distinction between process and product innovation has become less relevant.

As well as technology itself, a number of influences have stimulated financial innovation, including volatile inflation, interest rates and exchange rates, changes in the regulatory and tax system, and the general level of economic activity. Intermediation is central to the operation of financial markets and financial innovation can be seen as a response to profit opportunities which arise from inefficiencies in financial intermediation and/or incompleteness in financial markets (Van Horne 1985).

Rapid developments in information technology have been one of the major forces facilitating change in the markets for personal financial services in response to such profit opportunities. Information technology has radically altered the competitive environment; broken down barriers between traditional institutional sectors; and set in motion changes in the structure of the industry and the way that transactions are conducted which could have far-reaching consequences.

We can define information technology as the integrated use of computing, micro-electronics and telecommunications technologies. As applied to financial services it has three main elements:

   (i) The rapid storage, processing and retrieval of information about customer accounts, share prices, interest rates and foreign exchange rates through the use of low-cost electronics.

  (ii) The direct control of systems for processing accounts and other data and the automation of routine functions such as order-processing, cheque-clearing and the balancing of accounts.

 (iii) The rapid communication of information to customers and agents by electronic means.

These technological changes are having a profound effect on the way financial companies conduct their business and on the way financial services are provided to customers. The former is examined later, but first the stages of technological development within a typical financial services company are considered.

4.2   The Stages of Technological Development

The development of information technology within the financial services sector has been an evolutionary process falling into a number of stages.[1] These stages can be seen as beginning with batch-processing mainframe computers, progressing through on-line systems; distributed processing; and the integration of text and data. Batch processing occurs when the data to be analysed are accumulated and the computer deals with them as a group; in interactive processing, on the other hand, the data are entered as available, immediately processed and the results displayed. In an on-line system the device which is being used for interactive processing is connected directly to the computer. In distributed processing, both the handling and storage of data are located near where the information arises or is used and communications links are established to and from other storage and processing facilities as appropriate.

Progress has been dependent on changes in both the computing equipment itself (hardware) as well as the programs which allow the equipment to be used (software). Figure 4.1 illustrates the evolutionary process for a financial firm in terms of six stages:

(i) Installation of a central (mainframe) computer at head office using batch processing with all work carried out on the computer.

(ii) The head office computer goes on-line with interactive processing. Terminals are installed at head office for data input and enquiry.

(iii) The head office computer goes on-line to remote sites and is accessed via local terminals. This development enables the remote offices to perform the same functions as the head office.

(iv) Distributed processing is introduced and computing facilities are extended by the installation of mini-computers handling much of the routine administration in each of the remote offices whilst retaining links to the central computer at head office.

(v) Word-processing facilities are provided which are typically small mini- or micro-computers with video display units and letter quality printers. These can be stand-alone devices, shared networks or terminals and software connected to the main computer. During this stage, word-processing facilities alone are provided and there is no access to, or processing of, the business database.

(vi) The processes offered by stages (i) through to (v) are consolidated and the various systems fully integrated. At the same time their capabilities are extended to cover features such as terminals installed in agents' offices to give direct access to the company's computer systems for rate quotations, direct entering of policy or loan application details, etc.; the integration of word, data and graphics processing; and the use of computer systems and terminals for job training.

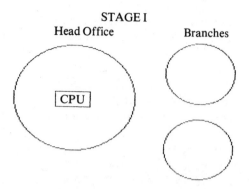

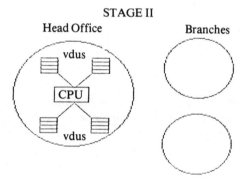

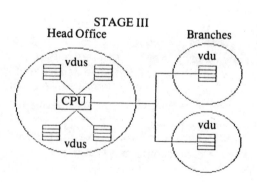

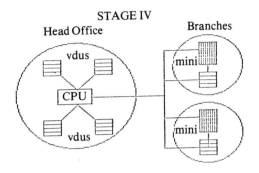

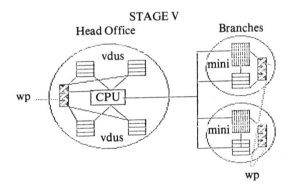

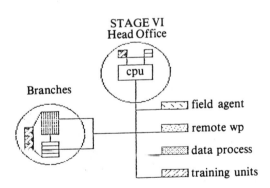

Figure 4.1

The culmination of these stages (as presently envisaged) is the 'paperless office' which applies electronics to all functions within the office, including at least the following capabilities:

(i) The ability to put documents, whether typed, handwritten or graphic, into electronic form and transmit and reproduce them.

(ii) Electronic storage of data replacing current paper-based systems and providing terminal access for the creation, storage, searching, sorting, updating and retrieving of files.

(iii) The provision of electronic mail (i.e. messages transmitted across terminals) for intra-company correspondence.

The evolutionary process begins, therefore, with the introduction of a mainframe computer and is characterised by the extension of on-line facilities within the head office, to remote sites and ultimately to non-company offices such as brokers and agents. The increase in the number of different users is an important part of the process. The second major aspect of the development is the extension of computing capacity through the introduction of mini- and micro-computers ending with the idea of 'one per desk'.

What is the reality of progress to date in the UK? The study by Rajan allows the rough-and-ready classification of insurance companies in his sample by these stages of development. The results of this exercise are shown in Figure 4.2. According to this evidence, at the time of his study (1982–83), some 75 per cent of insurance companies were between stages III and V, with stage III being the most common, i.e. mainframe head office computer with remote terminals in branches. There remained, therefore, considerable room for development, and both Rajan and Barras and Swann expected stage V to have been completed for the majority of insurance companies by 1987/88. The more recent investigations by the Nottingham Institute of Financial Studies would tend to confirm this prediction. The development of computing power within financial services has been such that in 1985 some 10 per cent of the respondents to the questionnaire distributed by the Institute regarded computing as one of their important business activities.

Banking is the most automated of all the service industries and the manifestations of the technology are readily apparent through the network of ATMs. Building societies have tended to be rather

(%)

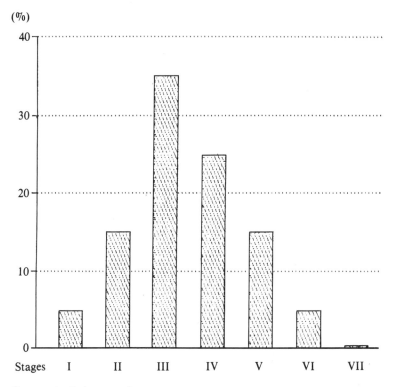

Source: A. Rajan *op. cit.*

Figure 4.2 Insurance Companies: Stages of Application of Technology (%)

slower to introduce the new technology, but their adoption of new processes has progressed rapidly in the mid-1980s. These developments have radically altered the nature and scope of information available and the speed with which it can be accessed. The processes through which financial services are handled have also been brought closer to the consumer in the sense that, for example, ATMs, home banking and in-branch terminals have enabled the consumer to access information on demand on the state of his or her account. In addition, the facilities for self-management of accounts and the transfer of funds have been improved.

In an important respect, therefore, technological innovation has offered a significant extension of the do-it-yourself concept so much in evidence through the growth of the ordinary supermarket. The speed and integration of computer-based services together with self-service offer the potential for considerable savings in transaction costs. Such transaction costs are a significant component of the costs of production of financial services and, indeed, themselves offer (as noted in Chapter 2) one rationale for the very existence of financial intermediaries.

One problem here (as noted in Chapter 6) is that people's behaviour changes and with self-service they can escalate overall costs even though per unit costs are much lower. For example, with current charging practices the cost to a customer of a cash withdrawal from an ATM is much cheaper than one over the counter, particularly in terms of time and convenience. Thus, there is some evidence (Vittas 1984) that bank customers may make two or three ATM transactions to withdraw a given sum of money in comparison with a single cheque cashed over the counter. Similarly, home banking might be expected to lead to a greater volume of transactions. It is critical, therefore, to price services correctly to realise the potential savings. The reduction in per unit transaction costs to both the financial institutions and the customers has become a key element in the competitive process. For services with the characteristics of convenience goods, the technological changes have reduced the need for personal contact and hence offered the potential of significant savings in labour costs.

The consolidation and integration of information systems, whilst appearing a relatively small change in technology, nevertheless has important implications for the conduct of financial business. For example, the speed of modern communications via computer links has reduced the need for physical market places where buyers and sellers meet on a face-to-face basis. The operation of the foreign exchange market where the dealing rooms of market traders are linked through an array of telephones and visual display units is a case in point. The picture is in marked contrast to the floor of the London Stock Exchange with its bustle of interpersonal contact. The electronic market place is likely to become far more prevalent across a wide range of financial services.

These technological changes are affecting the whole personal financial services sector and in the next section we investigate how they are affecting the market process.

4.3 Information Technology and the Market Process

Developments in information technology are seen as having three major effects:[2]

(i) A change in process technology with reduced transaction and other costs. This change leads to new distribution systems which can result in increased efficiency, greater competition and the generation of new customers and larger total markets than would otherwise be the case. The market share and size of market for any one company depends, of course, on its own competitive ability.

(ii) New product development allowing the introduction of innovatory and improved financial services. The introduction of new products expands the total market amongst existing customers and attracts new customers into the market.

(iii) Changes in the communication and interaction with customers.

These three effects are not mutually exclusive. Thus, for example, the effect of technology on costs may bring certain products into the range of commercial viability, such as those associated with increased flexibility in life insurance markets and cash management plans. The introduction of ATMs and home banking marks not only a change in the distribution system but also a change in the nature of the product. As noted in Chapter 2, new technology also makes possible the joint packaging of previously separate products.

In our questionnaire to financial institutions, including insurance companies, banks and building societies, the Nottingham Institute of Financial Studies asked respondents to consider the effect of micro-electronic technology on various aspects of their business over the next five years. The aspects were: communications with customers and distributors of financial services; the development of new products; the effect on costs; and questions relating to databases, office and information systems. Companies were also asked to consider the impact of information technology on their growth prospects. The replies are summarised in Figure 4.3 which records only those responses where the effects are seen to be important or very important. The following broad conclusions are suggested by these responses:

Personal Financial Markets

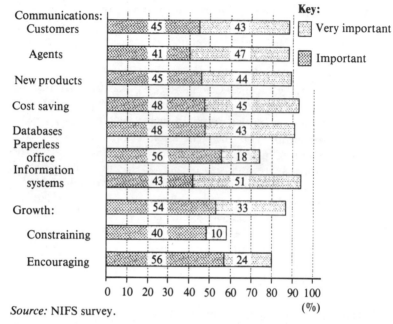

Figure 4.3 Effects of Micro-electronic Technology

Source: NIFS survey.

(i) Micro-electronic technology is expected to have an important influence on their business by the overwhelming majority of respondents even amongst those who do not envisage that it will be a major feature of their strategy for growth.

(ii) Micro-electronic technology is expected to have a major influence on the efficiency with which business is controlled and conducted. In particular, the item given the greatest weight by respondents is that relating to improved management information systems. These improvements in information systems have clear implications for marketing and were discussed in Chapter 3. Cost savings and improved communications links are also expected to be important by the vast majority of respondents.

(iii) The emergence of 'paperless' office systems is seen as far less significant in general, a view which is consistent with the implementation of information technology to date as outlined in the previous section.

(iv) A substantial proportion of companies see information technology as a major influence on achieving their growth plans. Somewhat surprisingly, over half the respondents see micro-electronic technology as being an important factor constraining their growth. The unease could be accounted for by at least two reasons: either the belief that technology and its acceptance by consumers will not keep pace with the plans of the company; or, and perhaps more likely, the fear that those companies left behind, or making the wrong choices, during a period of rapid change will suffer. On the other hand, some 80 per cent of respondents see micro-electronic technology as encouraging growth.

4.4 Technology and Market Structure

In this section the question is examined as to whether the changes in technology which are taking place are likely to have a significant effect on the structure of markets for financial services. In particular we shall be concerned with whether the changes favour the large organisation over the small; and whether smaller institutions are likely to find themselves in considerable difficulties on this account in future years.

In looking at the effect on the size of firm there are two important economic concepts which need to be distinguished:

(i) economies of scale.
(ii) economies of scope.

These two concepts will be considered separately.

Economies of Scale

Economies of scale occur when the average (per unit) cost of producing a given product declines as output increases and the firm moves to larger and larger sized plants. Such economies arise from various factors including indivisibilities in resources which imply a minimum optimum size of plant and the exploitation of the advantages of specialisation and the division of labour. Figure 4.4 illustrates the general principles. The long-run average cost curve is sketched as showing, first, declining average cost; then constant

86

Personal Financial Markets

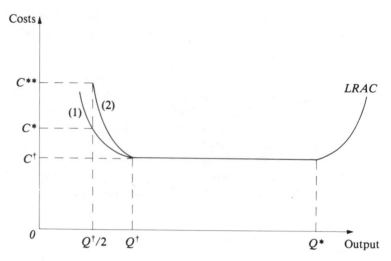

Figure 4.4 Economies of Scale

average cost; and finally increasing average cost. These three stages show economies of scale; constant returns to scale; and diseconomies of scale respectively. Output $Q\dagger$ represents the lowest output for which average costs are at a minimum — the minimum optimum size. Strictly speaking, this diagram relates to a single plant producing a homogeneous product. There may be further advantages of multiplant operation arising from finance, marketing and promotion, and so on.[3]

The minimum optimum size is clearly important since plants which are below this size will be at a disadvantage. The larger the minimum optimum size, the larger is the minimum size of firm required for production at least cost. The relationship between the minimum optimum size and the total market is also important since it determines the maximum number of firms that can operate efficiently in a market. If, for example, a firm of minimum optimum size would account for 50 per cent of a market, efficiency considerations alone would imply that no more than two firms can be justified. However, the slope of the average cost curve before $Q\dagger$ also needs to be considered. This slope determines how much of a disadvantage is suffered by smaller firms. For example, an output half the minimum optimum size is shown in Figure 4.4 and if the cost curve is as in (1), then the disadvantage suffered by such a firm as compared with the optimum (C^* – $C\dagger$) is clearly less than in the case of cost curve (2) – (C^{**} – $C\dagger$).

What are the facts for financial services? It has to be admitted that the measurement of cost curves in the financial services sector is extremely difficult because of the problem of measuring output. A number of studies[4] suggest that there are significant economies of scale at the plant level for small units, but these economies tend to be exhausted at a relatively low level. In addition, there is little evidence of substantial economies of multiplant operation. These conclusions need to be qualified: first, many of the results relate to experience in the US, but given the importance of regulation and the restriction of the activities of financial firms in the United States, it might be questioned whether the results of these American studies are generally applicable in other environments. There is some evidence for other countries, particularly in banking, that the minimum optimum size is perhaps rather larger than would be suggested by the American findings. Second, given the underlying difficulties of measurement, a number of alternative methods and approaches have been adopted in the literature which do produce differing results. Third, the empirical studies have mainly been conducted before the introduction of the latest electronic technology which may alter the balance of advantage. Finally, most of the evidence is in terms of resource costs which ignores the possible importance of pecuniary economies of scale to the individual firm.

Bearing these points in mind, however, a distillation of the empirical evidence would suggest that technical economies of scale themselves cannot be seen as a major factor leading to the emergence of giant financial firms. This finding is consistent with recent research into manufacturing industry which would tend to support similar conclusions, with the minimum optimum size of plant being at around 1 per cent of the market in nearly all sectors in the UK (Lyons 1980).

These results do put the argument about technology and the size of firm in some perspective. Information technology does not now necessarily favour the large organisation. In the early phases, computing equipment was bulky, expensive, and required substantial investment in software and systems design to be effective. Over time the emergence of time-sharing and computer bureaux has reduced the advantage of the large firm to a considerable extent. The introduction of micro-electronics brought down the cost of hardware and computing power by a very large factor, with desk-top computers now able to equal or even outperform the old generation mainframes. The growth in the market for business applications also brought with it the availability of high-quality off-the-shelf software which reduced the necessity for expensive in-house development work.

Telecommunications, data-communications networks (or the so-called Value Added Networks such as that being developed for the London financial market), public-access networks (such as the gateways on Prestel), and the growth of readily accessible computerised databases are equally available to the small as to the large firm. Much of the application of the new technology is, in fact, being pioneered by the smaller organisations, such as the Nottingham Building Society with Homelink and home banking by the Bank of Scotland. Those components of the technology which require considerable investment, such as the establishment of networks, or the installation of point-of-sale equipment, and which might imply economies of scale, can be alleviated by sharing through joint ventures (see Chapter 2, p. 45 above). Indeed, some of the investment in new technology needed for the infra-structure of new payments is so vast that it may even exceed the capabilities of large organisations acting alone. Again, the joint venture offers a way forward (Phillips 1982):

> Economies of scale in funds management, distribution, and in the electronic and mechanical aspects of clearing mean that many institutions will be unable independently to enter new markets with new products, or indeed, competitively to maintain their old services in their old markets ... In many respects, the sharing of product offerings, with compatible hardware and software and general customer recognition is highly pro-competitive. It keeps in the marketplace numbers of firms that would otherwise disappear; it also makes entry easier if pro-competitive, non-exclusionary participants are allowed.

Economies of Scope

Whereas economies of scale can be taken to relate to the production of a single product, economies of scope occur when there are gains from joint production of more than one product. Economies of scope exist if the total cost of producing two goods jointly, $C(X, Y)$, is lower than the combined cost, $Cx(X) + Cy(Y)$, of producing the same amounts of each good separately. Thus they can occur when two or more outputs share one or more inputs, either capital or labour, in the production process either directly or through networking.[5]

Economies of scope are likely to be of more significance in financial markets than economies of scale due to the wide applicability of much of the technology and the inherent substitutability of financial products (Chapter 2). These rest on the existence of an indivisible input which is not specific to a single product and, therefore, has alternative uses. A couple of examples should serve to illustrate the principles: an automatic teller machine or a point-of-sale terminal is an indivisible asset which does not have to be specific to any individual product or supplier; there may, therefore, be advantages to be gained from utilising them for various different products and/or suppliers. A branch network of a bank, building society or insurance company is likewise an expensive asset which has varied uses. As technology has increased the feasibility of links between products, it may make sense to use the branch for purposes other than its traditional one.

The concept of economies of scope is potentially of wide applicability and is fundamentally at the heart of the rationale for financial conglomerates. However, care must be taken: the rhetoric may well disguise the true facts. For economies of scope to be exploited there must be excess capacity once assets are selected at their minimum optimum size for a single product; and these assets must be non-specific. If micro-electronic technology substantially increases productivity, then it might create or expand excess capacity within, say, an existing branch network which could be exploited. But some assets in a branch will be specific, including perhaps the 'human capital' represented by the skills of the workforce. Bank tellers or employees of building societies do not, in general, have the necessary training to handle, for example, insurance broking. Additional investment in human skills will, therefore, be required and one has to question carefully the net gains that accrue from combining operations.

Many similar arguments were heard in the 1950s and 1960s about the benefits of large firms and industrial conglomerates, and in both the UK and the USA there was a substantial amount of merger activity. In retrospect, the effect of such mergers on profitability seems at best neutral and in a significant number of cases seems to have led to a worsening of the position. There also appear to be few clear gains to the owners of acquiring firms.[6] Indeed, the recent recession has caused many companies to reassess their strategy and divest themselves of some of the activities acquired during earlier periods.[7] The major problems which seem to have arisen include the failure to recognise the complexities of the new operation; a failure to appreciate the strengths of the primary business; and a failure to recognise the demands on management from the running of a conglomerate business.

4.5   Technology and the Development of Payments Systems[8]

Consumers may make a payment in settlement of a transaction using the following instruments:

(a) cash (paid over the counter or to an account);
(b) payment orders;
(c) cheques;
(d) giro, transferring funds from one account to another;
(e) plastic cards;
(f) electronic fund transfers.

(b), (c) and (d) are paper-based instruments; (e), the plastic card, was initially used as the basis of paper-based credit-card sytems and has now been developed as an essential component of electronic fund transfers. The credit card is also increasingly being used as a method of identification and as a means of providing information about the status of the customer. In addition, unlike the other five items, it is essentially an exchange instrument offering an automatic line of credit rather than a payment as such. Thus, the customer is obliged to make the payment in the future (plus interest) to the credit-card company rather than the retailer at the moment of exchange.

Payments can be subdivided into regular and irregular ones. The former may be for fixed amounts, such as mortgage payments and insurance premiums, or variable values such as wages, gas and electricity bills and so on. Irregular payments comprise casual purchases where settlement is made immediately and trade credit where payment is made later against an invoice.

The payments system as a whole represents a series of cooperative links between banks, their customers and different parts of the banking system. Developments in technology can be seen as introducing electronics to existing links and extending the system through the introduction of new links. Large customers and individual banks submit large volume payments to an Automated Clearing House for distribution to other members of the system. In recent years this clearing house system has moved from a paper-based to an electronic system in both London and New York where it is known as CHAPS and CHIPS respectively. As regards personal financial services, the most important innovations relate to the electronic links introduced in retail banking through automatic teller machines, point-of-sale systems and home banking.

Figure 4.5 traces the past and one view of the predicted future development of selected financial transactions. As can be seen, cash transactions of between £5 and £50 are likely to remain quantitatively the most significant. Cheques will continue to expand, but at a reduced rate after 1990 as other forms become more important. A possible path for Electronic Fund Transfers at point of sale (EFTPOS) shows them rising from virtually zero in 1986 to about 600 million in 1996. At that level they are expected to be only slightly less significant than credit-card transactions. Such forecasts are highly speculative. A more detailed discussion of EFTPOS will follow shortly, but first the development of automatic teller machines will be considered.

4.6   The Growth of Automatic Teller Machines

The recent growth of automatic teller machines (ATMs) in the UK is shown in Figure 4.6. By June 1985 the total number of ATMs in service at just over 7,200 was some 56 per cent higher than the number in operation in mid-1983. The numbers are expected to increase by a further 18 per cent by the end of 1986. The average number of cash transactions per machine is now around 1,000 per week with an average cash value of £32 per transaction. Other industrial countries have shown a similar increase in the number of ATMs, with around 90,000 being in service in the United States and 30,000 in Japan.

Reflecting the advantages mentioned earlier, there is an increasing tendency for the sharing of ATM networks. In the UK joint networks have been established by Nat-West/Midland, and that of Barclays/Lloyds is expected to be available towards the end of 1986.

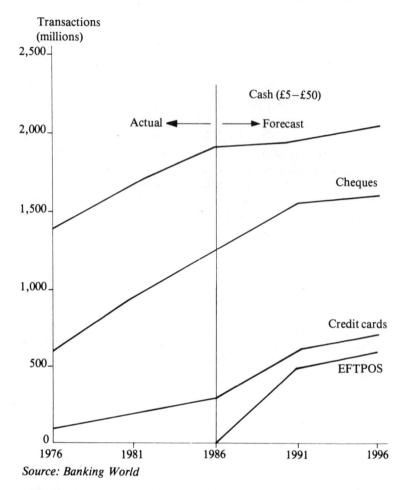

Source: Banking World

Figure 4.5   Transaction Methods in the UK

Other institutions are also combining facilities such as the Link group including Abbey National, National Girobank and Citibank; and the EFT group of seven building societies. In the United States, many small banks find the cost of establishing and running their own network prohibitive and the emphasis is on major shared networks. For example, the 'PLUS' system is the first national shared network and is scheduled to link some 10,000 machines over the next five years.

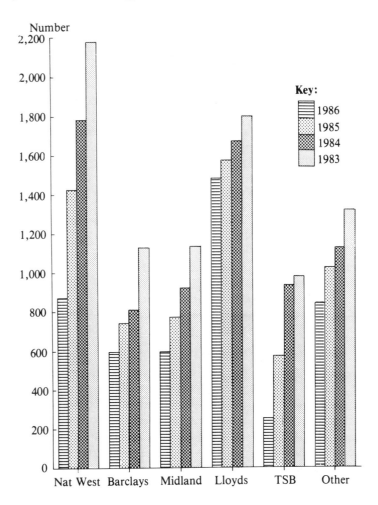

Figure 4.6 ATMs Installed: UK 1983–86

In the UK there is also a trend towards the installation of single function rapid cash dispensers in bank branches. ATMs were introduced to avoid the increasing per unit cost of money withdrawal through bank tellers. Lloyds began with in-bank cash dispensers, but the other banks concentrated on in-the-wall ATMs outside the branch offering 24-hour service. However, the potential marketing value of the bank lobby has been recognised (an economy of scope) where the customer can possibly be sold a range of banking products, and hence the switch to in-bank dispensers. This move is also linked to the return to Saturday opening in an increasing number of bank branches. In addition the cash dispensers are considerably cheaper to install, running at about a third of the cost of an ATM (£10,000 as compared with £30,000). A further development is the introduction of information terminals within branches which separates the information and transfer function from cash dispensing. Such terminals do not need the physical security measures associated with ATMs.

A full-service ATM has the ability to provide at least the following facilities:

   (i)   cash dispensing;
  (ii)   balance information;
 (iii)   the ordering of a new cheque book;
 (iv)   the ordering or displaying of statements;
  (v)   the deposit of cash and payment documents;
 (vi)   transfers from one account to another: either (a) of the same customer; or (b) between a customer and a third party.

Many ATMs operating in the UK do not currently offer this full range of services and, in particular, they do not generally provide the facility for account transfers. However, the machines themselves are becoming more sophisticated; software and hardware support is being introduced; and, perhaps above all, consumer acceptance of the concept is increasing. Correspondingly, the range of services being offered through ATMs is being enlarged and in some cases includes access to savings accounts. Further development of these facilities is expected by 1990 and is likely to include a further extension of the range of transactions and information which can be accessed. In particular, the application of 'expert systems' to financial transactions is likely to increase. Thus, consumer credit applications could be dealt with and decided on-line through a series of questions answered by the consumer at a terminal together with a check of the account database. Similarly, the underwriting of standard insurance policies could be conducted instantly either through terminals in branch and agents' offices or through public-access networks.

A recent report (Hanley, Cohn, D'Arista and Mitchell 1984)

highlights the cost savings which can be achieved through the introduction of ATMs in place of transactions handled by tellers:

> There are currently more than 14,000 banks in the United States with
> nearly 50,000 locations, including 36,000 bank branches. Tellers number
> more than 300,000 compared with 35,000 ATMs now installed in the
> United States. In most cases, a bank location will have one ATM and, on
> average, seven or eight teller positions. Tellers' salaries average more than
> $10,000 plus $2,500 in fringe benefits, and have been rising steadily
> because of inflation. The cost of an ATM ranges between
> $17,000–$100,000. In 1981, a typical teller transaction cost $0.63; this is
> forecast to rise to $1.61 by 1986. An ATM transaction cost $0.82 in 1980,
> less in 1981, and is expected to fall to $0.22 by 1986. In addition, machine
> 'down-time' is 5.5%, close to the teller absentee rate. Given the
> economies associated with ATM deployment, we expect the number of
> tellers to decrease.

These figures relate to per unit costs but, as discussed earlier,
there is likely to be an increase in the volume of transactions and
hence the impact on total costs will not be as dramatic as suggested
by the quotation. One particular New York bank estimates that an
electronically handled personal account costs an average of $120 a
year to service, whereas an account dealt with through branches
costs around $188 a year.

The new technology has had the important effect of shifting
business to the bank as a whole from the collection of units or
branches. Thus, because chequebooks have a branch on them,
customers tend to regard the account as being with a branch. In fact,
the account is with the bank and can be accessed in a variety of ways,
one of which is in 'the' branch. As the range of services offered by
ATMs, point-of-sale, and home banking extends, the tendency
towards centralisation is enhanced. Whilst there may be potential
cost savings, both per unit and total, from the use of ATMs, it has to
be recognised that in the longer term their importance may decline
as other forms of electronic payment become more significant.

4.7 The Development of EFTPOS

Electronic Fund Transfers at the point of sale (EFTPOS) represent
only one of the forms that can be undertaken by electronic fund
transfers. The various possibilities are:

   EFTPOS   electronic fund transfers at the point of sale;

EFTPOL   electronic fund transfers at the place of living (e.g.
          home banking);
EFTPOB   electronic fund transfers at the point of banking (e.g.
          ATMs and cash dispensers at branches);
EFTPOP   electronic fund transfers at the point of passing (e.g.
          ATMs in public places such as railway stations);
EFTPOW   electronic fund transfers at the place of work (e.g.
          ATMs in factories and offices).

Home banking will be discussed in the next section and the growth
of ATMs has already been considered; in this section, therefore,
attention will be focused on EFTPOS.[8]

There are various electronic functions which can be provided at
the point of sale. These include:

    (i) on-line credit authorisation, e.g. of Access and
      Barclaycard;
    (ii) on-line credit authorisation with electronic settlement;
    (iii) cheque verification;
    (iv) cheque guarantee;
    (v) ATMs at the point of sale;
    (vi) multiple-function, customer-operated point-of-sale equip-
      ment;
    (vii) checkout-operator-controlled direct debit;
    (viii) customer-operated direct debit, e.g. at petrol pumps.

The main focus of current interest is the development of direct
debit to pay for purchases. The development of such systems
depends on the ability of financial institutions to deal with the transactions, the participation of the retailer, and cost-effective communications systems.

Retailers introducing point-of-sale equipment onto their premises
clearly want to be able to deal with accounts from more than one
bank or credit-card company; at the same time they would be reluctant to have equipment from more than one bank in place. Consequently, if EFTPOS is to be successful it requires some form of
shared network. Major issues in such sharing include the determination of access to the system by different financial companies, and
how the cost of installation and running is to be shared between the
participants. The Committee of London Clearing Bankers and the
Retail Consortium have reached agreement on the introduction of a
nationwide EFTPOS system. The current proposals envisage a total
of 250,000 terminals linking the point of sale (retailer), the retailer's

bank and the customer's bank or credit-card company. Details of allocating the cost between the financial institutions and the retailers are critical but have yet to be decided.

A number of pilot schemes are already in existence or about to be introduced. These include the Clydesdale Bank Counterplus scheme in conjunction with BP and operating at a number of filling stations in Scotland; a Midland Bank network of 30 terminals in retail stores and petrol stations in Milton Keynes; a Nat-West network of 30 terminals in filling stations; and a joint venture between Access and Visa for 1,000 terminals in London and the South East. In addition, Barclaycard has already installed a number of self-ticketing machines at British Rail stations which provide self-selected rail tickets charged to the card account.

The economics of the EFTPOS system are by no means as clear cut as its proponents often maintain. It is helpful to consider some of the issues relating to the system from the point of view of the three main interested parties – consumers, retailers and financial institutions.

Consumers Given the present methods involved in charges for payments services, it appears that consumers may have little to gain. There may be a slightly lower risk of theft if they have to carry less cash, but if they are already paying by cheque for small transactions they will lose the 'float'.[9] For transactions settled by cheque, the 'float' is of the order of three days whereas payment by credit card generates an even longer float of at least 30 days. EFTPOS transactions imply immediate debit and unless charging systems for credit cards and current accounts change radically, it is difficult to see any substantial gain to the consumer from EFTPOS. In principle the issue is a question of pricing which can be resolved either by appropriate full marginal-cost charges on all banking services or by, for example, a reduction in the cost of EFTPOS sales relative to those made by other means such as a cheque. An alternative approach has been adopted in some American trials where the banks have introduced an artificial float in order to try and gain consumer acceptance.

Retailers EFTPOS would appear to offer few advantages in terms of inventory control over sophisticated electronic cash registers in which store groups have invested heavily. Retailers are, of course, concerned with the amount of time taken by a customer to settle a transaction at the checkout. EFTPOS has no advantage over cash except in relation to security, but will generally be quicker than cheque transactions. One possible argument is of a defensive nature: failure by one store group to offer the facility may result in lost business. Such an argument is far from convincing: first, as has just been argued, there seems little benefit to consumers and hence little incentive to switch stores for the reason of EFTPOS alone; and, second, consumers do not currently use debit cards for other forms of transaction, but rather there has been a significant spread of credit-card usage.

Banks EFTPOS offers the potential for a further reduction in expensive paper transfers, but the bankers involved in the proposed national network in the UK do not expect any reduction in paperwork for at least ten years after the introduction of the system. They may also hope to attract deposits that might have gone to other financial institutions which are not linked to EFTPOS. Such a strategy would only be successful if these other institutions could be excluded from the network which might raise problems of anticompetitive practices under UK competition policy. There would seem to be significant economies of scale and scope in the provision of EFTPOS facilities which imply that the viable size for a successful operation would need a significant proportion of transactions to be conducted by such means.

Given the reservations expressed in the preceding paragraphs, it is perhaps not surprising that surveys of consumers and retailers show rather mixed reactions. Thus, for example, in a recent survey of consumers conducted for ICL it appears that eight out of ten Britons are ignorant of EFTPOS and more than 60 per cent of those who did understand it were not in favour. Similarly, in a survey of retailers over 60 per cent thought that there was no consumer demand for EFTPOS but, on the other hand, 77 per cent saw it as an inevitable development.[10] Despite this evident lack of enthusiasm it seems likely that by the mid-1990s point-of-sale terminals will be commonplace in many of the larger retail establishments.

4.8 Home Banking

Home banking essentially began in the United States in the mid-1970s through the use of the 800 telephone number system for bill paying. The 800 number is a direct-dial free-phone service to the specified number from anywhere in the US. Such a type of service was only introduced in the UK in 1985. Savings and loans institutions (the US form of the UK's building societies) first introduced the service as a means of avoiding the restriction of paying interest on demand deposits, and the commercial banks soon followed. The banking service under this system permits the customer to give oral instructions over the phone for the performance of a variety of banking services. Deposits to accounts may be made through the mail. Automation was introduced through touch-tone telephones where the pressing of certain keys initialised various transactions. Many institutions operating such a system still retain a manned service, however, sometimes on a round-the-clock basis.

Such a system is one way of allowing financial transactions to be conducted from home. However, the more commonly understood form of home banking involves Viewdata. The pioneering system in the UK was that introduced by the Nottingham Building Society. This service is accessed via a gateway on Prestel and hence any user has to be registered with Prestel and meet the associated charges as well as the cost of the generally local phone call. The hardware requirements in the home are a keyboard/adaptor and a TV set or a suitable home computer and modem. For depositors with more than a particular balance, the keyboard/modem is provided free.

The following services are provided by the system:

(i) A Bank of Scotland chequebook account;
(ii) a Visa card;
(iii) account information;
(iv) electronic funds transfer between the building society account and the bank account;
(v) major bill payment such as rates, utilities and mortgage payments;
(vi) electronic mail;
(vii) a number of ancillary services such as shopping information, news and an electronic link with Thomas Cook for travel-agency services.

The system does offer a number of other services; for example, members were able to subscribe to the issue of British Telecom shares on its flotation in 1985. It is also noteworthy that the banking facilities were provided as a joint venture with the Bank of Scotland. The strategy behind the introduction of home banking by the Society was clear: it wished to widen its net of deposit-taking and the alternative to home banking would have been the opening of one additional branch. In the view of the Society the capital costs involved in a new branch would have been similar to those of the home banking system. Thus, the introduction of home banking was seen as a direct alternative to branching.

The Nottingham Building Society's system was followed in 1985 by the introduction of its own home banking service by the Bank of Scotland. One of the main factors behind this move was explained by the Bank's Chief Executive as follows (Patullo 1985):

> . . . a desire to expand our retail business beyond the boundaries of our traditional domestic business in Scotland. Corporate lending banking business can be readily serviced by a small number of regional offices, and arms-length banking, for a significant number of personal customers, can be serviced by correspondence to and from a specially established central banking services unit. In order to develop and improve the bank's marketing effectiveness in attracting personal business without the cost of a bricks-and-mortar infrastructure we decided to examine a new Prestel-based delivery system for banking services.

Mr. Patullo goes on to explain the attributes of the system:

> The service is the first of a family of remote delivery systems. It is aimed at home banking via the TV screen for personal customers, and has four broad features. First, provision of information on balances and transactions including immediate scrutiny of all statements, standing orders, direct debits, etc. Secondly, provided transfers between related accounts are effected before 5pm they will earn interest overnight. Thirdly, the payment of bills of varying amounts can be made on different dates up to 30 days ahead to regular payees: this requires the once-and-for-all insertion of the beneficiaries' bank accounts, references to be quoted, etc. Fourthly, a new high interest investment account enables profitable cash management by even small account holders.

One of the most obvious developments of such a system is in the field of cash management for small businesses which could have significant implications for the operation of their organisation. Such cash management applications are already widespread amongst larger corporations. As regards the personal customer one of the major developments will undoubtedly be the provision of 'sweeping' arrangements whereby excess cash balances are automatically placed on deposit for the customer. Such provisions are a major feature of many schemes in the United States and are being introduced in the UK.

The development of home banking in the UK has, therefore, largely been undertaken by smaller organisations. The major clearing banks are experimenting with similar systems. Banks in the United States are also engaged on similar projects of which Chemical Bank, Citibank and Chase Manhattan can perhaps be regarded as the leaders.

Home banking is very much in its infancy and many experts express considerable scepticism about its likely impact on the financial sector in the next decade at least. There is considerable doubt as to the likely size of any first-mover advantages in this area and many banks and financial institutions are prepared to await future developments and adapt as necessary. Professor Jack Revell has expressed the following view of the financial system of the future (Revell 1985):

> It consists of a number of different kinds of terminals, linked to the central computers of banks by a data network and enabling bank customers to carry out most of their transactions and obtain much of the information that they need without involving bank staff; it will be a largely do-it-yourself system. The terminals will be ATMs (probably reduced to the functions of dispensing cash and accepting deposits), EFTPOS terminals in retail shops and petrol stations, terminals connected to television sets or microcomputers in home and offices, and terminals on bank premises or in any other building to which the public has access serving as the call boxes of the system. Connected to the system will be facilities for carrying out all sorts of other financial transactions, such as the buying and selling of securities and the negotiation of insurance.

Progress towards such a future is, however, likely to be fairly slow and this view is shared by the majority of the respondents to our questionnaire survey. Figure 4.7 records the responses to the statement that in-home computerised information services (e.g. Prestel) will account for over 5 per cent of personal financial transactions in five years. Only 33 per cent agree or strongly agree with this statement, whereas 37 per cent disagree or strongly disagree and 30 per cent are neutral. The picture for the growth of ATMs shows rather higher penetration with 72 per cent of respondents agreeing or strongly agreeing with the view that ATMs will account for over 10 per cent of personal financial transactions in five years' time.

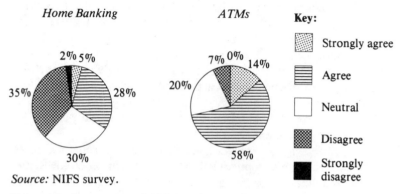

Source: NIFS survey.

Figure 4.7 Importance of ATMs and Home Banking

4.9 Conclusions

There is no doubt that the financial services sector is undergoing a rapid technological transformation. These technological changes are breaking down barriers between institutions and leading to increased competition between them and the generation of new and newly-packaged products.[11]

The main conclusions we would wish to stress are:

(1) The changes which are taking place in technology in financial markets do not necessarily favour the large organisation. There is considerable scope for joint ventures and the large financial conglomerate does not necessarily possess a comparative advantage.

(2) There will continue to be significant developments in payments systems, but cash and cheques will remain the major element until well into the 1990s at least.

(3) At the moment EFTPOS does not appear to offer significant advantages to either consumers or retailers. Added value or new charging arrangements will have to be introduced into the system if it is to be anywhere near the success its proponents claim.

(4) Home banking is not yet a service of any significance. It may, however, offer a valuable service to smaller businesses in cash management, and information terminals will become a more significant feature of bank lobbies.

(5) The most significant cost savings and benefits from microelectronics are likely to remain in 'back office' work, i.e. be

process rather than product oriented. Many financial companies still have a fair way to go in introducing integrated database and management information systems.

(6) The market for financial services will become more competitive based on both process and product technology. There will be some shakeout of those less able to adapt to changing circumstances.

(7) Marketing will become even more significant, especially linked to new financial products made feasible by the new technology and the more effective integration of the data available to financial institutions as a direct consequence of their integration with customers.

Notes

1. See, for example, the studies by Barras and Swann (1984) and Rajan (1984).
2. For some of the wider social issues see, for example, Hartley (1985) and Freeman (1982).
3. For a discussion of the economies of multiplant operation, see Scherer (1980).
4. See, for example, Benston, Hanweck and Humphrey (1982), Barnes (1985), and Praetz (1983).
5. For an application of the concept to financial services, see Kane (1984).
6. For a review of the literature in the US, see Jensen and Ruback (1983). For an interesting UK study, see Meeks (1977).
7. On the divestment issue, see Coyne and Wright (1986).
8. For excellent discussions of payment systems in general and the impact of electronics in particular, see Revell (1983) and Frazer and Vittas (1984).
9. The 'float' is the period between writing the cheque and the amount being deducted from the customer's bank account.
10. See, for example, the results of two surveys conducted for ICL and summarised in Gendall (1985).
11. For a detailed discussion of the possible impact of technology on competition and the implications for public policy towards monopoly and anti-competitive practices, see Solomon (1985).

References

Barnes, P.A. (1985) 'UK building societies — a study of the gains from merger', *Journal of Business and Financial Accounting*, Vol. 12, No. 1.
Barras, R. and Swann, J. (1984) *The Adoption and Impact of Information*

Technology in the UK Insurance Industry, The Technical Change Centre, May.

Benston, G.J., Hanweck, G.A., and Humphrey, D.B. (1982) 'Scale economies in banking: a restructuring and reassessment', *Journal of Money Credit and Banking*, Vol. 14, November, pp. 435–56.

Coyne, J. and Wright, M. (eds) (1986) *Divestment and Strategic Change*, Philip Allan.

Frazer, P. and Vittas, D. (1984) *Retail Banking*, Lafferty Publications, London.

Freeman, C. (1982) 'The economic implications of microelectronics', in C.D. Cohen (ed.), *Agenda for Britain 1: Micro Policy*, Philip Allan.

Gendall, S. (1985) 'No-go for EFTPOS', *Banking World*, September, pp. 23–5.

Hanley, T.H., Cohn, J.L., D'Arista, C.A., and Mitchell, N.A. (1984) 'Electronic banking: yesterday, today and tomorrow', Salomon Brothers, New York, April.

Hartley, K. (1985) 'Information technology and public policy', in P. Johnson and B. Thomas (eds), *Economic Perspectives on Key Issues*, Philip Allan.

Jensen, M.C. and Ruback, R.S. (1983) 'The market for corporate control: the scientific evidence', *Journal of Financial Economics*, Vol. 11, pp. 5–50.

Kane, E.J. (1984) 'Technological and regulatory forces in the developing fusion of financial services competition', *Journal of Finance*, Vol. XXXIX, No. 3, July, pp. 759–72.

Lyons, B.R. (1980) 'A new measure of minimum efficient plant size in UK manufacturing industry', *Economica*, Vol. 47, pp. 19–34.

Meeks, G. (1977) *Disappointing Marriage: A Study of the Gains from Merger*, Cambridge University Press.

Patullo, B. (1985) 'Pioneering Bank of Scotland', *Banking World*, July, pp. 24–6.

Phillips, A. (1982) 'Financial institutions in a revolutionary era', *Journal of Credit Union Management and Economics*, Vol. 2, Spring, p. 17.

Praetz, P.D. (1983) 'The effect of size and other economic factors on the expense rate behaviour of UK life insurance companies', *The Journal of the Institute of Actuaries*, Vol. 110, Part 2, No. 445, September, pp. 383–8.

Rajan, A. (1984) *New Technology and Employment in Insurance, Banking and Building Societies*, Gower Publishing.

Revell, J.R.S. (1983) *Banking and Electronic Fund Transfers*, OECD.

Revell, J.R.S. (1985) 'Progress with electronic banking', *The Irish Banking Review*, September, pp. 12–19.

Scherer, F.M. (1980) *Industrial Market Structure and Economic Performance*, second edition, Rand McNally, pp. 101–19.

Silber, William L. (1983) 'The process of financial innovation', *American Economic Review Papers and Proceedings*, Vol. 73, May, pp. 89–95.

Solomon, E.H. (1985) 'The dynamics of banking antitrust: the new technology and product realignment', *The Antitrust Bulletin*, Fall, pp. 537–81.

Van Horne, J.C. (1985) 'Of financial innovations and excesses', *The Journal of Finance*, Vol. XL, No. 3, July, pp. 621–31.

Vittas, D. (1984) 'Pricing policies for ATM transactions', Committee of London Clearing Bankers, paper presented to 6th EFMA Convention of the European Financial Marketing Association, Montreux, March.

CHAPTER 5

Financial Services in the United States

M.K. Lewis

5.1 Comparisons with the UK*

As noted in Chapter 2, intermediation is the hallmark of present-day
financial markets. This is as true of the US as it is of the UK.
Perhaps nearly 20 per cent of persons in the US are direct holders of
shares (as compared with at most 14 per cent of the UK population).
And those people hold about 30 per cent of the outstanding shares
and other securities issued by US non-financial firms (as compared
with about 20 per cent in the UK). But, except for capital gains,
American consumers have not, in aggregate, been adding to those
holdings. In every year since 1958, they have sold more shares than
they have purchased.[1]

Dominance of Intermediation

Table 5.1, which excludes capital gains on equities, shows how new
claims of non-financial firms are distributed directly between
foreign holders, government holdings, personal direct holdings, and
financial institutions. Since 1950 a consistent pattern has emerged in
which 80 per cent of claims are taken up by financial institutions.

As in the UK, indirect ownership means that people accumulate
wealth by means of the investment vehicles and claims issued by
financial institutions. By choosing to transfer to them the task of
meeting their own financial needs, households give over to intermediaries the job of meeting the financial needs of the wealth
creators in the community. This delegation gives the financial
markets a unique position and influence over the accumulation of

Table 5.1 Takeup of New Funds Raised in US Financial Markets by
Non-financial Sector, 1951–1983 (% of total)

	Foreigners	Government	Persons	Financial institutions	Total
1951–60	2.9	2.1	18.0	77.0	100
1961–70	2.6	2.3	4.7	90.4	100
1971–80	7.4	3.1	11.1	78.4	100
1981–83	5.6	2.9	10.5	81.0	100

Source: Friedman, B.M. (1984) 'Financial Intermediation in the United States',
National Bureau of Economic Research Working Paper, No. 1451,
September.

national wealth, and is the basis of government concern about the
safety and soundness of financial institutions and their financial
stewardship. Possible conflicts of interest, self-dealing, insider
trading and other abuses of trust which may arise are tackled much
differently in the United States than is the case in the UK.

Safety

Claims issued by financial intermediaries have risk, liquidity and
convenience characteristics which distinguish them sharply from the
assets upon which they are based. Special attention is given to banks
and savings institutions as custodians of the bulk of the liquid savings of the United States. That interest is interwoven with public
concern for the safety of the payments systems since the majority of
transactions occur through those institutions, and they are the main
route for monetary policy. Because of these functions, a government 'safety net' covers the deposit liabilities of banks and other
depository institutions, a result due to restrictions upon branching
by banks. Individual depositors can be insured fully up to $100,000,
as compared with the 75 per cent insurance cover up to a maximum
of £7,500 provided in the UK.

In both countries the aim is not so much to recompense people
after the failure of a bank but to bolster confidence and thus prevent
the occurrence of the event. To this end, the insurance is supplemented by liquidity support and supervision of the institutions'
activities, the latter designed to prevent undue reliance upon the
public support system. If successful, there are spillovers from

depositors to the banks themselves, since the institutions are able to raise funds at lower perceived riskiness. Differences have arisen between the UK and the US in the form of regulation and the way of handling these commercial advantages.

Large and Small Banks

When comparisons are made between the US and UK financial systems, it is usual to lavish attention on the historical differences in structure, and admittedly a wide gulf remains between the two. As compared with the 648 banks in the UK, there are 15,380 commercial banks in the US. Altogether nearly 40,000 institutions contribute to the US money supply (which includes savings banks and credit unions). Perhaps the majority of these are regional consumer and small business institutions. But it is no longer accurate to depict the US as a country of stand alone or unit banks: in 1981, 6,859 commercial banks (46 per cent of the total) operated 38,353 branches. When making comparisons with the UK, it must be remembered that only 22 of the 648 banks in the UK operate extensive branch networks. Scottish and Irish banks have strong regional links. If building societies are counted as part of the banking system, the importance of regional branching only increases.

The majority of banking assets in both countries are controlled by bank holding companies. There are in all 6,146 bank holding companies in the US, and the largest 345 companies control 70 per cent of the assets of all US commercial banks. Table 5.2 gives details for 1984 of the 10 largest bank holding companies in the United States. By the formation of bank holding companies, which may own a number of banks, these large banks have been able to get around the restrictions upon branching to some extent and expand their operations across state boundaries.

Use of the holding company arrangement also enables banking firms to conduct a range of 'non-banking' activities within the holding company but outside of the bank, through fully or partly owned subsidiaries. The largest US bank holding companies have non-banking offices operating as finance companies, agents for credit-related insurance, mortgage bankers (brokers originating and servicing mortgage loans passed on to other institutions), leasors, and issuers of traveller's cheques, to name the most popular activities. Through use of the holding company device, British

Table 5.2 Ten Largest US Bank Holding Companies, 1984

	Domestic Assets ($)	Domestic Deposits ($)	Banks	Branches	Non-bank offices*
Citicorp	106.0	42.7	42	375	525
Bank America Corp	92.1	65.0	22	1,224	238
Chase Manhattan Corp	49.6	28.9	15	373	240
Manufacturers Hanover Corp	54.1	22.1	16	236	126
Chemical New York Corp	38.4	22.1	11	310	177
J P Morgan & Co	44.9	14.9	10	12	51
First Interstate Bancorp	42.5	31.3	34	995	54
Security Pacific Corp	40.0	23.6	12	666	583
Bankers Trust NY Corp	34.9	9.1	10	14	88
First Chicago Corp	31.8	14.5	15	24	80

Source: Federal Reserve Bank of Chicago.

Note: * Non-bank offices are as of year-end 1983.

banks are financial 'department stores' of impressive dimensions, offering to customers a full range of insurance activities, unit trusts, and investment management services. American banks have been legally constrained from following this route as fully as banks in Britain for a number of reasons.

Conflicts of Interest

One conflict is concern about the link between the bank and its subsidiaries. Legally there is a separation between the two, but in practice a bank cannot be wholly insulated from its affiliates, and there are commercial advantages in the bank having the public perceive them as related. This being the case, competitive advantage may accrue to the subsidiaries as well as to the bank, with spillovers from the public safety net to the activities of the group as a whole.

There are the usual laws on trustee operations and insider trading, reinforced by a physical separation of trust and commercial banking records and staff ('Chinese walls'). Regulators in the US go further by making the range of activities in the holding company a matter for determination by the Federal Reserve System. Amongst those activities which cannot be undertaken by affiliates of banks are the underwriting of securities issues, real estate development, sale and underwriting of insurance and equity positions in non-financial activities.

Many of the financial services provided by British banks are viewed in the United States as giving rise to conflicts of interest and an excessive concentration of power. There are worries that the granting of a loan will be made conditional, implicitly or explicitly, upon purchase of insurance and other services of affiliated companies; that affiliates will receive preferential financing over their competitors; that securities may be sold to the public to bail out improvident loans; that 'inside' credit information and personal files may be used for marketing forays by associated companies. Banks are prevented from being linked with non-financial enterprises and using deposits raised under the protection of government deposit insurance to fund commercial operations.

In the UK there is a growing feeling in some circles that delegation by households to financial intermediaries has resulted in large, impersonal institutions, unresponsive to individual needs and preferences. In the US, fear of 'money trusts' and an anti-bigness sentiment has underpinned a desire that the 'regulatory system should encourage a degree of diversity among institutions, large and small, specialised and generalised, "retail" or "wholesale" oriented.'[2] Such sentiments have produced a financial system in which some of the world's largest banks, insurers and securities firms compete alongside thousands of regionally-based and local institutions. The rules have encouraged and produced a large number of financial firms. Table 5.3 shows over 50,000 in operation in 1984.

An unconcentrated financial structure has been sought after, and, it would seem, achieved. The 10 largest holding companies have 24 per cent of bank assets; the 10 largest savings associations have 17 per cent of the assets of associations; the 5 largest savings banks hold 18 per cent of all deposits of savings banks; and the 10 largest finance companies make 31 per cent of consumer credit loans. While these figures may be higher than expected in view of the large number of institutions involved, they are much lower than in the UK. The 6 London clearing banks (even excluding their subsidiaries) hold 56 per cent of domestic currency deposits,while the 10 largest building societies have 74 per cent of societies' assets.

Table 5.3   Financial Institutions in the United States

	Number of Institutions	1984 Assets ($ billion)
Commercial banks (1983)	15,380	2,275.8
Savings institutions (thrifts)		
Savings associations (1984)	3,391	902.4
Savings banks (1984)	602	288.1
Credit unions (1981)	21,930	115.9
Life insurance companies (1984)	2,124	717.5
General insurance companies (1983)	3,474	249.1
Finance companies (1981)	2,775	287.9
Securities firms (1979)	4,697	62.0
Private pension funds	n.a.	623.3
Government pension funds	n.a.	351.8
Mutual fund investment companies	n.a.	161.2
Money market mutual funds	n.a.	209.7

Source: Federal Reserve Board.

Regulation of Financial Services[3]

A number of concerns relating to safety and conflicts of interests due to delegation have thus overlapped with historical preoccupations about preventing 'money trusts' from shaping the provision of financial services in the US. There are three basic building blocks of the present system. One is a separation of banking and commerce. A second involves geographic restrictions upon branching by insurance companies and most banks and savings institutions. The third is a legal 'compartmentalisation' of the provision of financial services, on a functional basis, into banking and other depository institutions, insurance companies and securities firms. Each group is subject to separate rules; each has its separate regulators: banks and savings institutions distinguished by deposit insurance and subject to dual federal–state supervision (by different bodies), insurance companies under state legislation, and securities operations subject to the Securities and Exchange Commission.

These three blocks have some origins which date back to the last century, but they were firmly cemented into place in the 1930s. In the wake of the Great Crash of 1929 and the collapse of 9,000 banks, the emphasis switched to safety. Banks and savings institutions were to be made safe and kept safe. So as to protect banks and thrifts from themselves, the competitive bidding for deposits was made subject to ceilings (regulation *Q*). For banks to remain as banks, they had to divest themselves of links with securities firms. Later legislation to control the activities of bank holding companies reinforced these themes.

While the system was far from static, the overall framework was held reasonably in place until the 1980s. In the space of a few years in the early 1980s, these three planks have been eroded significantly, and there has been much talk of a financial services revolution. The separation of commerce and banking has broken down; commercial enterprises have become financial 'department stores', and opened banks. New technology has allowed financial firms to operate nationwide. Compartmentalisation has gone: banks have lost their monopoly of transactions services; securities firms have become banks; and life insurance companies have linked up with securities dealers.

5.2   Sources of Change in the US and UK

When examining the forces of change in the United States, one should not lose sight of the many similarities between developments there and in the UK (and some other countries). In both countries the segmentation between the 'retail' and 'wholesale' parts of the capital market has diminished, banks have lost their monopoly in the provision of payments services, there has been a blurring of the distinctions between banks and other depository institutions, a move towards the widespread payment of interest on monetary assets, and a diversification of savings institutions into other financial services. Thus we must enquire into the factors that have prompted these common experiences.

Switch to Retail Banking

After almost two decades of being out of fashion, banks everywhere in the 1980s have 'rediscovered' retail banking and the provision of personal financial services. A number of factors can be cited for the switch of strategy. Changes in the flow of funds have favoured the household sector, creating a source of funds which institutions have fought over. Retail deposits are seen to be more stable, with recent instability and 'deposit runs' arising from large, footloose corporate depositors.

Profit margins in corporate banking have also been eroded; large firms lend deposits to each other and issue their own commercial paper. Faced with the difficulties of international bank lending and short of capital, banks have been attracted to 'off-balance sheet' activities such as insurance broking, investment banking and portfolio management services which generate fees but, because they do not involve deposit-taking and the making of loans, do not dilute existing capital. This has contributed to pressures for liberalisation in the provision of financial services.

Deregulation

Deregulation has been important in both countries. In the UK exchange controls have been abolished, banking controls and hire purchase controls lifted, and a liberalisation of the Trustee Banks has occurred. Major changes to banks and savings institutions occurred in the US with the Depository Institutions and Monetary Control Act of 1980 and the Garn–St Germain Act of 1982. The 1980 Act began a phasing out process of interest-rate ceilings, and permitted banks and savings institutions to offer interest-bearing transactions accounts, thereby ending the exclusive role of commercial banks in the provision of payments services. The 1980 Act also allowed the savings institutions to enter consumer lending and hold commercial paper, and the 1982 Act continued by allowing them to enter commercial banking in a limited way. It also telescoped the phasing out of interest-rate ceilings by ordering the creation 'within two months' of a new deposit instrument (called 'money market accounts') suitable for banks and thrifts to meet the competition from securities firms.

In order to understand this regulatory upheaval we need to examine the technological, competitive and economic factors which coalesced in the late 1970s.

Technology

The general implications of technology were discussed in Chapter 4. Technology played its part in the rekindling of banks' interest in retail banking. For many years, catering for the day-to-day banking business of households and small firms was labour intensive. Developments in computer- and paper-handling procedures have greatly lowered those costs, and allowed banks to be in a position to offer higher interest on deposits, calculated on a daily basis. But, in lowering costs of intermediation, technological developments, such as ATMs (Automatic Teller Machines) and EFTs (Electronic Fund Transfer systems), have brought down barriers to entry and made it easier for other enterprises to compete for personal financial services. Many of the revolutionary products, such as the cash management account and Universal Life insurance policies (both discussed later), would not have been possible without the capacity of computer-based technology to tailor these products to the particular needs of individual customers.

Nevertheless, the role of technology as a vehicle for change in the financial system can be misunderstood. A large variety of products and combinations of services are technically possible, yet may never actually occur. (For example, despite the oft-repeated prophecy of a cashless society, currency is still used in about 90 per cent of all transactions.) Demand, as well as supply, must enter the story. Technology provided the capacity for financial innovation in the United States to take place, but not the incentive for customers to take advantage of the new facilities. The cash management account, which even competitors concede to be the most brilliant and successful financial product of the decade, ran at a loss for two years after its introduction in 1977 and was initially regarded as a 'dog' in the industry. Changes in the underlying environment provided the stimulus for that judgment to change.

Changed Financial Environment

Double digit inflation and interest rates were late in coming to the US. Their arrival in 1979 had a profound impact. While yields on Treasury Bills rose above 10 per cent p.a., and in some months approached 20 per cent p.a., banks and thrifts were constrained by interest-rate ceilings to offer 5 to 5¼ per cent p.a. Life insurance companies offered packages in which the savings element was based on fixed interest securities acquired when interest rates were low. There was created a gap which was too large not to be filled.

Securities firms did so. *Money market mutual funds* are a textbook example of a financial innovation designed to fill a niche. They enabled institutions on behalf of individuals to carry out a 'size intermediation' function, aggregating people's retail-sized deposits so as to take advantage of the higher interest rates in wholesale markets. The great appeal of the funds lies in the market interest rates, low minimum subscription ($1,000), ready redeemability and relatively low risk. Monies collected together are invested in diversified pools of large denomination money market instruments such as Treasury bills, commercial paper and negotiable certificates of deposit, all with relatively short maturities and negligible default risk. Interest rates on those funds are simply market rates minus a small management fee, and computers perform the almost continuous calculations needed for ascertaining the immediate redemption value of the underlying portfolio.

It was a short step from their invention of the money market mutual fund for the securities firm Merrill Lynch to invent the *cash management account* which combines the funds and traditional stock brokerage accounts. To the 'cash' account is tied an automatic overdraft privilege; a chequebook with a conventional commercial bank; and a credit card, usable in automatic teller machines at various banks and other locations. Every Monday excess balances are swept automatically into the customer's choice of three money market mutual funds or into an insured savings account. When cheques are drawn, balances are automatically removed from the funds or savings account in a prearranged sequence. In effect, cheques are written against portfolios of marketable securities.

As at January 1985, Merrill Lynch had 1.1 million CMA accounts with total balances of around $70 million. Merrill Lynch is by far the largest sponsoring company of money market mutual funds, as well as conventional mutual funds (unit trusts). Building on these innovations, it has developed into a major financial conglomerate, diversifying into real estate, insurance, international merchant banking, and bank deposit brokerage.

Introduced in 1970, the funds were little used until 1979. By the end of 1979, the total funds exceeded $50 billion and by the end of 1981 they exceeded $180 billion. Table 5.4 shows that during 1981 the growth of the money market mutual funds rivalled that of pension funds, as households cashed in life policies and withdrew balances from savings accounts. Regulations designed to protect banks and thrifts from excessive competition amongst themselves prevented them from competing with the money funds. This fact spurred the legislators into action.

From the viewpoint of the evolution of the US financial system

Table 5.4 Annual Change in Financial Assets of Households, USA ($ billion)

Year	Savings associations	Savings banks	Commercial banks	Credit unions	Life insurance reserves	Pension fund reserves	Credit and equity instruments	Money market fund shares	Total†
1960	7.6	1.4	2.7	0.5	3.2	8.3	6.2		31.6
1965	8.5	3.6	14.9	1.0	4.8	12.1	2.8		55.1
1970	11.0	4.4	27.0	1.2	5.5	18.4	−1.2		75.1
1971	28.0	9.9	28.1	1.7	6.3	21.1	−8.9		98.3
1972	32.7	10.2	29.0	2.5	6.9	22.6	6.0		122.2
1973	20.2	4.7	35.3	3.6	7.6	25.4	32.0		142.7
1974	16.1	3.1	34.1	2.6	6.7	29.6	36.6	2.4	138.5
1975	42.8	11.2	24.6	5.4	8.7	34.9	27.0	1.3	162.8
1976	50.6	13.0	37.9	6.0	8.4	44.0	23.9	0.0	199.5
1977	51.0	11.1	37.8	7.7	11.5	54.6	27.8	0.2	223.0
1978	44.9	8.6	40.4	6.4	12.0	61.8	56.2	6.9	259.7
1979	39.3	3.4	31.4	4.4	10.7	84.3	52.9	34.4	277.7
1980	42.1	7.5	67.7	8.3	9.7	106.5	28.4	29.2	307.4
1981	14.3	3.0	45.9	3.1	9.2	107.9	12.6	107.5	343.5
1982	39.8	5.3	64.2	11.2	7.2	143.0	43.6	24.7	349.5
1983	110.1	15.3	64.7	15.8	8.0	146.0	83.9	44.1	411.2
1984	112.4	7.8	96.0	12.1	5.2	128.1	84.7	47.2	516.7
1985*	51.6	7.6	58.5	19.4	7.9	152.9	176.7	−2.2	517.2

Sources: Federal Home Loan Bank Board; Federal Reserve Board; US League of Savings Institutions.
Notes: * Preliminary
† Includes checkable deposits and currency not classified elsewhere.

and subsequent developments, the importance of money market mutual funds as a catalyst is difficult to overstate, for a number of reasons:

(1) By offering short-term repositories for savings and also transactions balances (or very close substitutes for them), they forced the legislators to allow banks to provide interest on transactions accounts.

(2) They eroded the earlier segmentation between the relatively unregulated wholesale and closely regulated retail sectors of the capital market, demonstrating that, given the opportunity, individuals were not unsophisticated in their investment habits.

(3) They broke down the barriers, erected in 1933, between investment banking and commercial banking, sparking off the present 'boundary war' between the previously segmented banks, savings institutions, insurance companies, securities dealers and financial conglomerates.

In the UK, the gap between wholesale rates of interest and retail bank deposit rates was due more to the discriminatory pricing practices of the banks than to any regulatory inertia. While the gap was smaller and thus took longer to fill, the process of change in the 1980s was similar nonetheless. Unit Trust managers teamed up with merchant bankers to offer cheque account facilities with market-related interest rates. Building societies and the smaller banks followed suit. This concerted attack upon the major banks' retail deposit base saw them introduce local equivalents of US money market acounts to compete with the transactions acounts offered, for the first time, by a range of other institutions.

Where do matters go from here? In the UK, diversification is proceeding apace, as the building societies get wider powers and securities firms link up with banks and other institutions. Opinion in the US is more circumspect. It is said by some commentators that as inflation is brought under control, many of the forces and pressures for change will subside. If Congress reaffirms the tripartite approach of major financial services, the merger movement now occurring, it is argued, will surely slow down. As the mood for experimentation passes, traditional patterns of specialisation are expected to reassert themselves.[4]

In order to provide some perspective on developments there, and by reflection on trends in the UK, we first assess US markets for personal financial services against the characteristics identified in Chapter 2, and then go on to look at the adaptability of US institutions. Our examination suggests that the changes in the US do have some fundamental origins, and the chapter concludes by looking at various ways of organising the provision of financial services.

5.3   Competition in Financial Markets

There are some special characteristics of financial services, noted in Chapter 2, which distinguish them from 'ordinary' products:

(1) the customer–firm interaction inherent in services;
(2) the two-way process of information flows;
(3) the safety sought after because the exchanges take place over time;
(4) the trust needed because of delegated monitoring;
(5) the basic substitutability of financial services;
(6) the inability to patent services.

Substitutability of Services

To repeat a basic point made in Chapter 2, most financial services, despite their apparent diversity, are directed to three ends: (i) transactions and payment services; (ii) wealth accumulation and consumption transformation; and (iii) financial security. Institutions have discovered how easily financial services can be substituted towards these ends. Securities houses, which sold vehicles for longer-term savings, found that one of their basic products, the mutual fund, could be modified, repriced and allied to payment services. Banks and thrifts responded with new instruments which provide a better avenue for medium-term savings, while offering limited chequing facilities (like the high-interest cheque accounts in the UK).

As a result, the American consumer now has the choice of a number of ways of obtaining transactions services. A conventional cheque account with a bank can still be used. But cheque clearance and money transmission in the US remains slow and cumbersome, and charges for running a cheque account are still high by British standards (annual charges of $36, per cheque costs of 13¢ and minimum balances of $1500 to avoid them seem usual). The functions performed by a cheque account can be 'unbundled' and carried out by separate vehicles: a general credit card issued by Visa, Mastercard, American Express or Sears Roebuck (the Discovery card) may serve as the medium of exchange enabling the individual to obtain the goods; a bank cheque deposit or a NOW account at a savings institution may be used for the actual payment; a time deposit or a money market mutual fund may serve as the temporary abode of purchasing power in between receipt of income and payment for the goods. All three may be accessed through securities firms, insurance conglomerates or a retailer.

In a period marked by variable and uncertain interest rates, short-term vehicles for savings which bear interest rates closely related to those in wholesale markets — like the money market funds and accounts — provide a safe and reasonably remunerative avenue for longer-term savings. Thus the new instruments overlapped into the 'investment sector' of the financial markets, and the experience of life offices illustrates perhaps better than any other the substitution process.

For their basic products, insurers combine death cover with avenues for savings which are, in the case of US life offices, akin to a long-term savings account since the majority of funds are invested in fixed interest securities. This pattern of investment exposed the policies to alternative competition when market rates of interest rose in the late 1970s. Consumers looked to write term insurance policies with life offices and undertake savings themselves by investing in money market mutual funds or in the new deposit instruments.

This 'do-it-yourself' unbundling of death cover and savings had other advantages to the insured. Additional insurance and especially additional savings provision could be added readily, and the mix of insurance and savings rearranged, without incurring the heavy commissions and high encashment costs of traditional life products. This flexibility could be bought without incurring great inconvenience since many mutual funds firms are allied with or own insurers (Merrill Lynch, American Express). In the flexibility offered, we see the spur for insurers to copy the arrangement, indeed to institutionalise it, by means of the new 'universal life' policies, which allow a choice of a number of investment vehicles and flexibility to speed up or remit premium payments. It also spurred them to begin diversification into other financial services, and especially into securities dealing and the management of mutual funds.

Consumer—Firm Interface

Services cannot be produced until they are consumed, and this fact places the customer—firm interaction at the forefront. Reducing consumers' transport and commuting costs provides an incentive to geographic expansion, while the potential to reduce customers' inconvenience costs encourages firms to diversify the product range.

Expansion of US financial firms in these ways has been restricted by the regulations compartmentalising firms by product and geography. As the population has become more geographically mobile, the potential has increased too for *existing* producers of the services to lower customers' external costs. Simultaneously, improved technology has made it cheaper for firms to do so, and to find ways around geographical and product barriers. But because the barriers continue to restrict movement, those firms with existing *non-financial* geographical distribution channels (e.g. Sears Roebuck) or with a widely distributed financial product line (Prudential, Merrill Lynch) possess an ability to enter consumer banking. Technological advances have played an important role in facilitating this entry:

> Telecommunications equipment and computers – technologies commonly available to all enterprises, regardless of their business traditions – work to level the field of financial competition. They allow any company from any business tradition to generate and control offers of generic versions of financial services – loans, deposits, credit cards, and insurance are all important examples – to the company's existing customer base. ... Any company with a large number of customers, such as a merchandise retailer or national credit card issuer, is at an immediate advantage, even if it has no tradition of financial services.[5]

Retailers in particular play a role in the provision of financial services which contrasts with the UK, despite the recent entry of Debenhams into securities dealing and Marks and Spencer into credit facilities. Sears Roebuck, the largest of the nationwide retailers, has 300 Financial Service Centres operating out of Sears stores with adjacent booths offering securities investment and mutual funds, real-estate brokerage, insurance and savings banking.

Its subsidiaries include the largest mortgage banker and real-estate broker, the second largest casualty insurance underwriter, and the fourth largest retail money market funds manager. Other retailers like J C Penney, K-Mart and Krogers are operating joint ventures with insurers, securities firms, and savings institutions. Producers of motor vehicles and computers rival banks in some areas of consumer credit and leasing through their 'captive' finance companies.[6] Such developments have sparked much of the talk of a 'financial services revolution', but it is important to keep recent trends in perspective. In some respects it is the banks, not the retailers and captive consumer financiers, which are the 'Johnny-come-lately' in some aspects of personal financial services. Sears began granting consumer credit in 1910, and its insurance subsidiary was formed in 1931. General Motors began making car loans in 1919, Ford in 1928. General Electric Credit was formed in 1932. Their recent growth may be an attempt to re-establish old market shares, competed away by the non-bank offices of the large bank holding companies. Some of this growth undoubtedly reflects declining profitability in retailing and manufacturing: a combination of push and pull.

Safety and Trust

Financial institutions trade in promises, and potential customers will be looking to buy some guarantee of their delivery along with the product. Indicators of reliability which might be used are the size of the institution ('safety in numbers'), its longevity (past survival being used as a guide to future survival), and its reputation (with the firm seeking to trade on its good name by 'branding' tied suppliers). The latter seems to apply particularly to Sears Roebuck and American Express. Both firms have an established reputation and through size, longevity and familiarity are trusted. These characteristics have enabled them to climb over an important barrier to entry into financial services.

Provision of one guarantee, deposit insurance, has historically been limited to banks and thrift institutions. But the 'non-bank bank' loophole has changed all that. Under bank holding company legislation, a bank is defined as an organisation which '(1) accepts deposits that the depositor has a legal right to withdraw on demand, and (2) engages in the business of making commercial loans'. A non-bank bank comes into being when a regular bank forswears one of these activities, and hives off the activity to an affiliate. It is not legally considered a bank under the Act, which puts it beyond the reach of restrictions upon activities undertaken by bank affiliates (e.g. insurance, securities underwriting). Yet the acquiring firm is able to engage in retail banking, with federal deposit insurance and use of the Federal Reserve's clearing mechanisms.

Via this loophole brokerage firms, retailers and commercial enterprises, acquiring 'consumer banks', which do not make commercial loans, can breach the traditional separations of banking from investment banking and commerce. It is the driving edge to the intense competition now evident between banks and non-banking institutions because the functions of banks can now be conducted nationwide by essentially modest alterations to the forms of banking.[7] By the end of 1983 there were 50 unregulated commercial bank holding companies in existence run by mutual fund managers, consumer finance houses, insurance companies, industrial companies and retail chains. Since then, almost 400 further applications for such charters have been filed.

Non-banking enterprises' willingness to seek out and utilise this loophole is a reflection of their keenness to enter banking and thus meet one of the primary financial needs of consumers. But, at the same time, the entry is a vehicle for widening competition and intensifying pressures for banks and thrift institutions to continue their diversification into non-bank financial services. Some of these pressures can be traced directly to the contrasting experiences of institutions to the changed environment of the 1980s.

5.4 Adaptability of Institutions

Many of the people interviewed by this writer in the US expressed the opinion that thrifts and the life insurance companies are the big losers in the new financial environment. As such, marked contrasts exist with these institutions' counterparts in the UK.

Some strong similarities between the experiences of the thrifts, and savings and loans associations in particular, and the life offices comes from four characteristics. First, they entered the new environment with highly specialised balance sheets. Second, the demand for their basic product was eroded by inflation and innovations by competitors. Third, both found that they were subject to 'disintermediation'. Fourth, it would seem to this observer that neither have reconciled the source of their difficulties, and are unsure about where they should go.

Both savings associations and life offices began the decade of the 1970s with basically a single liability and a single asset. In the case of the associations, the liability was a generic savings deposit offering a fixed rate of interest, and the single asset was a home mortgage. With life insurance, there was not so much a single asset as a set of assets having the same characteristics, namely long-term and with a fixed nominal return. Sales of whole of life policies made up 82 per cent of new policies written.

Savings associations have been able to offer attractive instruments on the liabilities side of the balance sheet to compete with the money market funds, but have been less successful in terms of freeing up their assets to match the interest-rate commitments they have undertaken. Regulatory provisions effectively prevented variable-rate mortgages being written until 1981, and since then they have encountered resistance by their customers to variable-rate mortgages. Well-publicised 'runs' in a number of states testify that net worth has declined to levels that would have led to a national crisis in the absence of federal insurance and liquidity support. Losses of $12 billion were sustained in 1981 and 1982, and in 1984, one third of associations were still operating in the red, as they matched market rates of interest on their deposits, while stuck with a portfolio of fixed-rate mortgages.

Here is a clear illustration of the importance of trust in financial contracts. As Table 5.5 shows, UK building societies are equally specialised in their assets, but can make variable-rate loans. Americans are unwilling to cede to their associations the discretionary power to vary rates which Britons are happy to grant to building societies. Most of the adjustable rate mortgages made in the past few years have been written at a relatively low rate of interest for the first year or two (a 'teaser rate'), with the rate then moving higher and tied formally to some index. Interest rate 'caps' are usual, limiting rate adjustments to 5 percentage points over the lifetime of the loan and to one adjustment of no more than 2 percentage points in any year – certainly not flexibility by British standards.

The development of collaterised mortgages has eased the position to some extent, by allowing many associations to move more

Table 5.5 Distribution of Assets of Selected Savings Institutions, end 1983 (% of total assets)

	US savings and loan associations	US savings banks	UK building societies
Mortgages of which:	75.2	50.7	78.5
Mortgage-backed securities	11.1	n.a.	—
Consumer loans	3.1	4.4	n.a.
Commercial and industrial loans	n.a.	2.6	—
Cash and government securities	10.4	20.3	20.1
Corporate bonds and investments	3.0	13.6	—
Fixed assets	1.4	0.9	1.0
Other assets	6.9	7.5	0.4
Total	100.0	100.0	100.0
(million)	$819.168	$179.532	£85.868

Sources: Savings Institutions Source Book, 1984; Building Society Fact Book, 1984.

towards a mortgage banking role, originating and servicing mortgages which are parcelled up and sold off for other institutions to hold. Nevertheless, the associations face fundamental decisions about the extent to which they will remain as intermediaries of a household's fixed-asset accumulation, or will evolve into more diversified forms.

For life offices, the outward signs are less apparent but the decisions facing them are, if anything, just as fundamental. The industry, for its basic products, bundles together protection against 'risks' (e.g. early death, disability) with various forms of long-term asset accumulation. But the sort of wealth accumulation which can be offered depends ultimately on the assets held, and in 1983 over 80 per cent of assets were fixed interest-rate nominal claims. Risks of default and loss can be pooled and diversified but their nominal character cannot be altered. Whether the bonds or mortgages backing life policies can provide the basis for bonuses which take the policy earnings close to a real guarantee for savings accumulated depends on the accuracy of the inflation premium built into nominal rates of interest.

An alternative route to providing policyholders with a real

guarantee is for the offices to hold assets which are claims, directly or indirectly, to real streams of goods and services in the form of share earnings or real estate and property. Regulations, at state level, covering the type of assets in which life offices can invest prevent them pursuing this route as thoroughly as life offices in the UK, as Table 5.6 shows. Thus, to an observer from Britain, the US life offices have so far not addressed the inherent contradiction between the type of long-term guarantees which households need under inflationary conditions and those claims which the offices provide.

For both the associations and life offices the problem was the inflexibility of the intermediation being carried out. Inflexibility arose, not because they were specialised, but because intermediation was being carried out in ways which could not adapt readily to the changed circumstances of the 1980s. Had the associations been able to adjust rates readily, like the UK building societies, which have been a major success story, most of the problems would have been avoided. Life offices were equally mismatched, as compared with UK counterparts, in having a nominal porfolio in an inflationary environment.

But the general lesson is that diversification does reduce risk. The UK building societies demonstrated that it is possible to have flexibility of interest rates with specialisation, but there may arise

Table 5.6 Distribution of Assets of Life Insurance Companies at end 1983

Type of asset	US life companies (% of total)	UK life companies (% of total)
Government securities	11.7	29.2
Corporate securities:		
Bonds	35.4	3.9
Stocks	9.9	40.8
Mortgages	23.1	3.7
Real estate	3.4	17.9
Policy loans	8.3	0.4
Miscellaneous	8.2	4.2

Sources: American Council of Life Insurance *Life Insurance Fact Book; Financial Statistics*, HMSO.

Notes: 1. UK 'corporate stocks' include unit trusts.
2. UK 'real estate' includes only land, property and ground rents in UK.
3. UK assets are valued at market values: US bonds would be at amortised values.

circumstances when that degree of flexibility may not suffice. Diversification of asset and liabilities across types and customers does reduce exposure and allow firms to respond to circumstances which cannot be predicted in advance. Banks, more than other institutional groups, have shown adaptability, largely because of their diversified balance sheet.

For this reason alone, diversification can be expected to continue. Some of the insurers (e.g. Prudential, American General) have become retail conglomerates, providing a wide range of personal financial services. Savings associations were allowed to diversify into consumer credit and commercial lending under the 1980 and 1982 Acts, which served as a precursor of the new legislation for British building societies. A number of the large associations are using the holding company formula. Thanks to their regulating authority, a unitary S&L holding company can engage in virtually any activity – as one commentator has said, from steel processing to cheque processing.[8]

5.5 Evolving Patterns for Financial Enterprises

Will diversification and the 'despecialisation' process in evidence continue, or will traditional 'compartmentalisation' of financial services return? Based on analyses such as M.E. Porter's *Competitive Advantage: Creating and Sustaining Superior Performance* (see Chapter 3), and after studying other industries in the US which have been deregulated or have had a spell of strong competition (like retailing), the consensus is that firms will evolve under free competition into one of three forms:

(i) A nationwide distributor, offering a full line of differentiated products through a broad geographic network (e.g. Citicorp, Bank America, Merrill Lynch, American Express, Prudential-Bache and Sears are evolving in this direction).

(ii) A low-cost, few frills producer, offering one low-cost product, or perhaps a few related products, but with little servicing. (Discount brokers, 'captive' consumer financiers, money market mutual funds, and firms like Dreyfus, may be examples.)

(iii) A speciality firm or 'boutique', offering highly differentiated products and services targeted to particular groups of customers who appreciate the information provided and quality service supplied (ranging from the local banks, savings institutions, insurance agents at one end through to financial boutiques at the other end of the scale).

If retailing provides the appropriate model, a large role can be expected for the speciality firms. While the large department stores and chains, such as Sears, Penney, K-Mart and Woolworth, dominate 'general merchandising', the specialists account for about 80 per cent of sales for all retail trade. Diversity is the rule. In the US, there are no nationwide grocery chains; and mail-order firms, vending machines and franchisees compete with department stores, variety stores and discounters.

But we have outlined some special characteristics of financial services: to reduce customers' transport and inconvenience costs, a supplier of a 'basic' service is going to look to tie secondary service lines to it. Even specialists seem more likely to offer a product range. Financial institutions trade in promises, and customers will be looking to buy some guarantee of future delivery. Safety in numbers is one way of doing so, favouring the large nationwide producer. Because financial needs of consumers can be tied up in many overlapping bundles, a specialist cannot rely upon uniqueness of the product, a point reinforced by the ease with which ideas can be copied. Areas of entrepreneurship which are most readily saleable seem likely to lie in the quality of the financial advice and investment skills. These are the areas in which 'boutiques' seem most likely to flourish.

Those who perceive a diminished role for specialists in the new environment need look only to the consumer finance industry. That was never part of the grand regulatory design of the 1930s and competition in it has not been artificially constrained. There are now few 'independent' finance companies left. Their ranks have been reduced by the growth of the 'captive' companies associated with major motor manufacturers, like General Motors, Ford and Chrysler — essentially the 'no frills' producers — and subsidiaries of the large bank holding companies, like Citicorp and Bank America — essentially the differentiated distributors. Captive automobile lenders have cut rates dramatically recently, using finance as a 'loss leader' to boost flagging sales of cars, and GMAC, Ford and Chrysler alone held 34 per cent of outstanding car loans in 1982. Customers dealing with the nationwide conglomerates are able to establish a credit record which flows onto other products, while the firm is able to build up information useful in dealings conducted in other parts of the empire.

There are, of course, other analogies which can be drawn. The theory of natural evolution suggests that animals with specialised functions and specialised needs have proven to be less adaptable. Diversification of assets and liabilities across types and customers does reduce exposure, and diversification of capital and labour across different activities allows businesses to respond to unpredicted circumstances.

Before looking further into these matters we examine the ideas of some of those who perceive a role for the specialist in terms of the boutique.

Financial Boutiques

Firms providing personal services are said to be passing through an evolutionary process much like firms producing motor cars and other manufactured goods went through earlier. In the first stage, the 'model T era', emphasis is on *mass production* of a standard product line in order to gain economies of scale, e.g. each family with a cheque account and a savings deposit and a whole life insurance policy. Then emphasis switched to *product differentiation* which, with motor cars, saw trimmings and engine options added onto a basic structure. In the case of banking, there has been a proliferation of various types of special purpose accounts. With insurance, there is an almost bewildering proliferation of policies — straight life, limited payment life, modified life, family plan riders, and so on. According to the proponents of boutiques, financial services are still stuck in this second phase, and are awaiting transition to the next stage (Shostack 1984).

In the next *segmentation* phase, the idea is to break up the potential market into groups of consumers with common needs and wants. The firm then organises itself and tailors or packages its services to meet as many of these special needs as is profitable. As an example, insurers target affinity groups like teachers and servicemen, and design special policies for them. The aim is to be 'all things to *some* people'.[9]

Needs vary between consumers according to age, income, location, employment, education and a variety of other socio-economic factors being explored in marketing research. There is a financial life cycle implicit in the life-cycle model of consumption spending and asset formation noted in Chapter 1, and firms are seeking to establish intertemporal relationships with members of particular income groups. Customers are thought of as forming a pyramid. At the base is the 'down market' segment consisting of people with relatively basic financial needs for transactions services, asset accumulation and financial security. Next up is the 'middle' market segment, familiar through usage with all of the bank's transactions-based accounts and savings instruments and likely to have used mutual funds and discount brokers. At the apex is the 'premium' segment of 'high net worth' individuals, seeking the specialised services of 'boutiques'.

Provision of professional advice and asset management services is seen to be the key for high net worth customers. Cigna and Bankers Trust are two examples of American institutions which have sought to target this group. Cigna combines insurance with investment advice, offering services which include advisory and separate accounts, 14 mutual funds and a closed-end bond fund, and fee based financial planning. Bankers Trust ties banking and investment services together, offering transactions services, lending, portfolio management, brokerage, trustee services, financial plans and retirement planning.

Two features are immediately apparent. These 'boutiques' package together a number of financial services and cover at least two of the three basic needs identified in Chapter 2. Second, neither are small institutions: the secret is to appear to be a small company to the client. Here organisational structure is vital. A number of ways of establishing customer–firm links have been tried. 'Renaissance man' supposes that one person can be a master of all trades and look after all of the customer's financial requirements. The concept of 'representative or relationship manager' recognises the need for specialists but retains one individual as the point of contact with the customer. Both overemphasise one person, leaving the client adrift should he or she be absent or leave. Finally, there is the 'Los Alamos' model[10] with customers dealing with the specialists, coordinated through a central hub holding full computerised information about the customer's preferences and needs. This relies upon computer design to allow full and immediate retrieval of relevant information.

There are implications in these ideas and approaches for other firms in the financial industry as improvements in informational technology make it feasible and profitable to move down the income pyramid and tailor financial services to the special needs of consumers.

Financial 'Department Stores'

Existing diversified suppliers of financial services have been built up from a variety of bases:

- Citicorp, Bank America, Manufacturers Hanover, Security Pacific from banking.
- Finance Corporation of America, Great Western from savings and loan associations.
- Prudential-Bache, American General from insurance.
- Merrill Lynch, Hutton from securities activities.
- American Express from traveller's cheques and credit-card operations.
- Household International, Beneficial from consumer finance.
- Sears Roebuck from retailing.

Table 5.7 compares the product lines of *selected* institutions with those of some UK institutional groups.[11]

For other firms seeking to diversify, there are questions about which of these bases provides the best 'primary relationship', what particular financial services are best to link with a particular firm's regular products and how strong the demand is for one-stop shopping.

Market research undertaken in the United States, notably under the auspices of the Federal Reserve Bank of Atlanta,[12] indicates that over 50 per cent of consumers surveyed said that it would be desirable to get all financial services at the one location, and were willing to consolidate banking, savings, loans, insurance, and investments from one provider. When asked what type of one-stop provision is preferred, 40 per cent of the consumers polled preferred an institution offering all types of services under its own name, 31 per cent favoured a Sears-type 'financial services centre', while only 7 per cent seemed to favour the 'boutique', with 23 per cent indicating no preference. Those respondents who preferred that financial services be provided by a single firm were then asked what

Table 5.7 Comparison of Product Lines of Selected Financial Institutions in the USA and UK

	National Bank (USA)	Federal savings and loan	Merrill Lynch	Prudential Bache	Sears	American Express	Clearing bank (UK)	Trustee Savings Bank	Large building society
Chequebook/transactions account	Yes	Yes	Yes	Yes	Yes	Yes	Yes	Yes	Yes
Savings account	Yes	Yes	Yes	Yes	Yes	—	Yes	Yes	Yes
Certificate of deposit	Yes	Yes	Yes	Yes	Yes	Yes	Yes	Yes	Yes
Government insurance	Yes	Yes	Yes	Yes	Yes	—	Yes	Yes	—
Credit cards	Yes	Yes	Yes	Yes	Yes	Yes	Yes	Yes	Yes
Home mortgages	Yes	Yes	—	—	Yes	Yes	Yes	Yes	Yes
Consumer credit loans	Yes	Yes	Yes	—	Yes	—	Yes	Yes	Yes
Commercial loans	Yes	—	Yes	Yes	Yes	Yes	Yes	Yes	—
Investment banking	—	—	Yes	Yes	Yes	Yes	Yes	Yes	—
General insurance broking	—	—	Yes	Yes	Yes	Yes	Yes	Yes	—
Life insurance broking	—	—	Yes	Yes	Yes	Yes	Yes	Yes	—
Insurance underwriting	—	—	Yes	Yes	Yes	Yes	Yes	Yes	—
Mutual funds management	—	—	Yes	Yes	Yes	Yes	Yes	Yes	—
Discount stockbroking	Yes	Yes	Yes	Yes	Yes	Yes	Yes	Yes	—
Investment management/advisor	Yes	Yes	Yes	Yes	Yes	Yes	Yes	Yes	—
Real-estate broking	—	—	Yes	—	Yes	Yes	Yes	—	Yes
Offshore services	Yes	—	Yes	Yes	—	Yes	Yes	Yes	—
Travel agency	—	—	—	—	—	Yes	Yes	Yes	—
Data-processing services	—	Yes	—	—	Yes	—	Yes	Yes	—

Source: Committee on Banking, Finance and Urban Affairs, HR and Annual Reports.

Table 5.8   Type of Institutions Preferred (respondents preferring single financial institution)

	(%)
Commercial bank	51
Savings & loan association	26
Credit union	16
Full-line brokerage firm	4
Discount brokerage firm	*
Insurance company	*
Others	3
	100
Total number of respondents	924

Source: Federal Reserve Bank of Atlanta.
Note: *Less than 0.5 per cent.

type of institution they would like that to be. Table 5.8 gives the answers. Given these replies, it is perhaps not surprising that many insurance companies and securities firms concentrate on being 'wholesalers' of mutual funds and investment packages to trust departments of banks or have looked to agency arrangements and joint ventures.

Can bank-based financial conglomerates like Citicorp be expected eventually to swallow up specialist financial firms? Clearly in the United States the answer depends much on the continuance of geographic and product-line restrictions. In addition, judged from the Atlanta survey, not all services seem to be sought-after from one provider with the same intensity. Cheque deposits, savings accounts, money market accounts, credit cards and mortgages were the most favoured. Life insurance, real-estate brokerage, managed investment funds and tax planning were amongst those least favoured. Table 5.9 gives details. The distinction we suggested earlier between 'convenience' and 'shopping' goods seems apposite, with specialists focusing upon the latter.

But factors other than consumers' preferences will influence the evolution of financial firms. While the experience of the banks relative to savings institutions and life offices in the US illustrates the importance for institutions to have a flexible and diversified

Table 5.9 Types of Financial Services Likely to be Used at
One-Stop Provider

	Total
Chequing	87
Passbook savings	70
Certificates of deposit	53
Money market funds/accounts	44
Credit cards	60
Lines of credit	33
Consumer loans	33
Mortgages	43
Second mortgages	14
Life insurance	28
P&C insurance	36
Real-estate brokerage	18
Tax preparation service	33
Tax and investment	27
Planning and advice	
Stock and bond brokerage	24
Managed investment funds	17
IRA/Keogh accounts	44
Estate planning	21
Settlement and trusts	
Asset management accounts	11
Total number of respondents	1,864

Source: Federal Reserve Bank of Atlanta.

balance sheet, developments in futures markets, interest-rate swaps and mortgages and loan pools now enable diversification of balance sheets at much lower costs than previously. There is much scope for small institutions through joint ventures to share in technological developments. Finally, there are limits to the success of conglomeration, as true for financial as for other firms, if only on managerial grounds. The position on the effects of financial conglomerates is well summarised in a paper written by staff of the Federal Reserve Bank of Chicago:[13]

No obvious pattern emerges ... in the sense that no particular combinations of activities can be clearly shown to be more conducive to the achievements of synergies, or economies of scope, than others. Rather it would appear that there is no obvious superiority – or inferiority – of

financial services companies associated with conglomerates relative to independent companies of the same type. Success or failure appears to be
much more a function of the particular managements and competitive
situations of the individual firms.

The points are taken up again in the final chapter of this book when,
drawing on experience in the US and the UK, we examine some
implications for financial firms and summarise the factors working
for and against financial department stores or 'supermarkets'.

5.6   Concluding Remarks

This chapter began by comparing political and regulatory thinking
in the US with that in the UK. Undeniably, legislation has shaped
the nature and the practices of the US financial system, continues to
do so today, and will do so tomorrow.

Financial regulation imparts to the system a certain immobility,
which is subject to sudden switches as regulations change. While
pacemakers like Merrill Lynch, Sears and Citicorp grab all the
headlines, large numbers of the 50,000 or so financial firms are conducting much the same sort of business as they have done for many
years, albeit with different process technology. Much innovation is
directed at exploiting legal loopholes. As a result, the observer of the
scene has the task of distinguishing 'natural' developments from the
financial mutations caused by, or designed to get round, the
regulatory framework.

While much of the sense of momentum in the US may therefore
be misleading, an almost bewildering variety of new financial
instruments are being thrown up which have marketing potential
elsewhere. Many novel joint ventures and link-ups are being tried
and tested. Different sorts of conglomerates are being formed,
offering contrasting financial packages. Future success or failure of
the financial service centre concept of Sears and others offers
lessons for British retailers.

British institutional groups suffer little in comparison. Building
societies and banks are well ahead in terms of the trust needed for
the design of simple financial contracts, and have benefited from it.
British insurers and unit trusts have long offered more imaginative
and participatory investment vehicles than their US counterparts.
Banks in the UK provide an efficient payments system. A flexible

and responsive regulatory framework has allowed the clearing banks to provide a range of services as wide as any US financial conglomerates.

At the same time, the rigidity and form of regulation in the US comes about because they have explicitly faced up to issues which have not been at the forefront in Britain. Americans are concerned that large bank holding companies will have a financial advantage and stifle competition in non-banking markets. They do not want bank affiliates to have access to customer information for marketing raids into insurance and unit trusts. They wish to ensure that regional identity will not be lost and that community interests have the choice of being served by local firms. These issues are just beginning to surface in Britain, as new legislation addresses conflicts of interest and potential abuses of trust in financial services, and as the future of Britain's last remaining financial specialists and regionally based institutions – the building societies – is determined.

Notes

* This chapter derives from a study tour undertaken with Professor B. Chiplin in 1985 of central banks and financial institutions in Chicago, Atlanta, Washington, Hartford and New York. The author wishes to thank the 33 people interviewed for their cooperation and assistance. Research economists at the Federal Reserve Bank of Chicago and the US League of Savings Institutions kindly helped with the data.

1. Friedman (1984).
2. Volcker (1981).
3. The structure of US regulation of financial institutions is examined in Benston (1984).
4. For a clear statement to this effect, see Lovett (1984).
5. Federal Reserve Bank of New York, Annual Report, p. 14.
6. Pavel and Rosenblum (1985).
7. Federal Reserve Bank of New York, Annual Report, p. 14.
8. Aspinwall (1985).
9. Steffins (1984).
10. Developed by G. Lynn Shostack for Bankers Trust.
11. Some information for the US institutions is derived from Committee on Banking, Finance and Urban Affairs, House of Representatives, April 1984, reproduced in Aspinwall (1985).
12. Bennett (1984).
13. Kaufman, Mote and Rosenblum (1984).

References

Aspinwall, R. (1985) 'Shifting institutional frontiers in financial markets in the United States', Société Universitaire Européenne de Recherches Financières, *SUERF Colloquium*, Cambridge.

Bennett, V. (1984) 'Consumer demand for product deregulation', Federal Reserve Bank of Atlanta, *Economic Review*, May.

Benston, G.J. (1984) *Financial Services: The Changing Institutions and Government Policy*, American Assembly, Columbia University.

Friedman, B.M. (1984) 'Financial Intermediation in the United States', *National Bureau of Economic Research Working Paper*, No. 1451, September.

Kaufman, G.C., Mote, L.R. and Rosenblum, H. (1984) 'Consequences of deregulation for commercial banking', *Journal of Finance*, July.

Lovett, W.A. (1984) 'The revolution in US banking', *Challenge*, November/December.

Pavel, C. and Rosenblum, H. (1985) 'Banks and non-banks: the horse race continues', Federal Reserve Bank of Chicago, *Economic Perspectives*, May/June.

Shostack, G.L. (1984) 'Organizing to serve the affluent market', *ABA Journal of Personal Financial Services*, Vol. 1, No. 1, autumn.

Steffins, J.L. (1984) 'The demand for financial products', in A.W. Sametz (ed.), *The Emerging Financial Industry*, Lexington Books.

Volcker, P.A. (1981) Statement before Committee on Banking, Housing and Urban Affairs, *Federal Reserve Bulletin*, November.

CHAPTER 6

Banking and Deposit Services

M.K. Lewis and D.M. Wright

6.1 Introduction

Until recently the institutions operating in banking and housing finance could be seen as distinct. The clearing banks, and to some extent the Trustee Savings banks and National Girobank, were the providers of cheque accounts and other transactions services. The building societies provided housing finance. Both kinds of institution offered other services and overlapped in respect of savings deposits. Now there is greater competition not only for saving but also in respect of other services. Technological advances have both introduced new services and radically changed the manner in which more traditional services are carried out.

Although the increased competition has served to blur the distinctions between types of institutions and the services they provide, it is useful to divide discussion in this book into two parts. This chapter deals with issues surrounding shorter-term transactions and savings services. The following chapter deals with housing finance and consumer credit. Each may be regarded as addressing two separate markets, though there are obvious links in a number of ways. Savings generated in one may provide the means for funding house purchases observed in the other. A strong demand for housing finance may enable the institutions to offer attractive vehicles for saving. Customers anticipating a future demand for a home mortgage may wish to save with the likely providers, although greater competition in both markets may increasingly sever this traditional link.

In the final section of this chapter we draw on our NIFS survey to examine the views of the institutions themselves about the changing

137

nature of competition, both in terms of the structure of the market place and the conduct of competitors therein. It is important to note at the outset that competition has to be viewed both in terms of that *within* types of institution (building societies, banks, etc) and *between* types of institution. A large building society, for example, may be competing with other large and regional societies in a particular locality in respect of mortgage lending, but also with clearing bank branches. If the larger societies are more likely to provide cheque accounts, say, then competition here is more likely to be directly with clearing banks rather than with other regional building societies.

Our starting point is an analysis, in turn, of the nature of the banks and depository institutions in Britain, the range of deposit and other services provided to persons and the implications of regulatory changes for the institutions' behaviour.

This chapter needs to be read in conjunction with Chapter 4, which examines the application to banking of new technology (ATMs, EFTPOS, home banking), and also Chapter 5, which compares developments in the UK with those in the US and provides a backdrop to the examination of increased competition for deposits in Section 6.3 below.

6.2 Banks and Depository Institutions

In the minds of most members of the general public, the high-street branches of the large banks and building societies are the providers of banking and depository services. Yet there are over 800 institutions supplying deposit facilities to the public — 'monetary sector' institutions, the National Savings Bank, and the building societies — and the British banking system is one of the most complex in the world. Table 6.1 is designed to show some of the many characteristics which make for this complexity.

First, Britain is unique amongst large developed countries in having more deposits and loans denominated in foreign currencies than are denominated in its domestic currency. This comes about because London has a vast offshore (Eurocurrency) system flanking its domestic banking operations. Because of the extent of Eurocurrency business, the majority of deposits (65 per cent in 1983) are held by overseas residents.

Table 6.1 British Banks and Depository Institutions, end 1983

	No. of institutions of which:			Sterling deposits		Foreign currency deposits	
	Total[1]	*Banks*	*LDTs*	*UK residents (£m)*	*Overseas residents (£m)*	*UK residents (£m)*	*Overseas residents (£m)*
London clearing banks	6	6		50.165			
Scottish and Northern Irish banks	7	7		7,928			
Trustee Savings Banks (TSB)	4	—		6,772			
Other retail banks[2]	5	3		2,692			
Retail banks	22	16	—	67,557	6,250	3,243	20,761
Accepting and discount houses	46	26	—	6,035	1,031	1,475	7,248
Other British banks[3]	241	26	200	8,499	4,575	1,945	30,738
American banks	63	47	13	2,107	2,312	2,859	83,166
Japanese banks	25	24	1	702	1,065	1,725	87,069
Other overseas banks	228	133	84	4,370	6,497	3,943	99,014
Consortium banks	23	20	3	205	574	307	8,441
Monetary sector	648	292	301	89,475	22,304	15,497	336,437
National Savings Bank	1	—	—	6,154	—	—	—
Building societies	206	—	—	78,489	n.a	—	—
Total	855	292	301	174,188	22,304	15,497	336,437

Sources: *Bank of England Quarterly Bulletin* and Report and Accounts, 1984 and
      Abstract of Banking Statistics, 1984.
Notes: (1) In addition to recognised banks, licensed deposit-taking institutions and
        exempt institutions, this includes banks incorporated in Channel Islands
        and Isle of Man.
        (2) Cooperative Bank, Yorkshire Bank, Central Trustee Savings Bank,
        National Girobank and Banking Department of Bank of England.
        (3) Includes subsidiaries of London and Scottish clearing banks.

A second distinction is in terms of the ownership of banks. At the
end of 1983, 316 institutions were foreign-owned, of which
American and Japanese institutions, which numbered 63 and 25
respectively, formed the largest national contingents. A further 28
institutions were consortia of overseas and British institutions.
While primarily attracted to London by the Euro-markets, most
overseas banks have an active involvement in the domestic banking
system, and in 1983 they supplied 9 per cent of all deposits of UK
residents with depository institutions.

Third, there is the distinction made by participants in the financial sector − and in banking statistics − between 'retail' and
'wholesale' based institutions. By the adjective 'retail' is meant
the provision of services to individuals and small enterprises, in
contrast to wholesale business where the customers are large companies and government enterprises and the transactions are

individually of large value. There are now few purely retail institutions in the UK: the clearing banks and the TSB straddle both retail and wholesale business, and the building societies bid for funds in the wholesale deposit markets. Nevertheless, there are those institutions like the clearing banks, with activities which are considered by the Bank of England to be primarily 'retail', where 'retail' constitutes having extensive branch networks or direct involvement in the clearing system. Including the savings banks and building societies, which as groups meet either one or both of these criteria, there were 229 retail and 626 wholesale institutions in the UK at the end of 1983.

Finally, institutions can be distinguished by the regulatory authority and controlling legislation. Under the Banking Act of 1979, any institution wishing to take deposits from the public cannot do so unless authorised by the Bank of England either as a 'bank' or as a 'licensed deposit-taker' (LDT). Building societies and the trustee savings banks are exempted, due to separate controlling legislation, along with credit unions, insurance companies, broking houses and deposit-takers too small to worry about. The National Savings Bank, as the successor of the old Post Office Savings Bank, is an arm of the central government as part of the Department for National Savings, concerned with raising small funds from the personal sector for passing on to the Treasury.

Thus the 855 depository institutions comprise:

(i)   292 institutions 'recognised' by the Bank of England as banks under the Banking Act 1979.

(ii) 301 institutions 'licensed' by the Bank as deposit-taking institutions.

(iii) 214 institutions exempted from the provision of the Act, because of special circumstances and separate controlling legislation. These are the National Savings Bank, the Trustee Savings Banks, the National Girobank, the building societies and the Banking Department of the Bank of England.

(iv) 48 of the institutions operating offshore in the Channel Islands or the Isle of Man which are beyond the jurisdiction of the Banking Act, yet opted in 1981 to come within the Bank's monetary sector and comply with monetary control provisions.

For the non-exempt institutions, the distinction between bank and deposit-taker depends on the range of wholesale services undertaken, and only recognised banks are allowed to call themselves banks (although foreign-owned banks can use their own name even if it includes the word 'bank' so long as it is followed by the phrase 'licensed deposit-taking institution'). Otherwise, to be recognised rather than licensed matters little. Both are required to insure their deposits (75 per cent of one deposit up to £10,000), both are able to undertake all types of banking business, and both are now supervised, on safety grounds, by the Bank of England.

Prior to the Banking Act, a depository institution required no licence before it commenced business, and only a select group of banks were supervised informally by the Bank. There were at least five different statutory lists of banks in operation, leading to a widespread and indiscriminate use of banking names. The secondary banking crisis in the mid-1970s highlighted this unsatisfactory situation. Against the background of a collapse of stock-market prices on the scale of that which had occurred on Wall Street in 1929, a deposit 'run' began on the secondary banks which reverberated through the financial system. Finance companies were soon embroiled and at one juncture the Prudential's shares were written down by 10 per cent when its involvement with a finance company was known, and there were rumours about the National Westminster Bank because of losses on property loans. In order to stop the deposit run from spreading, the Bank of England felt compelled to organise support for the fringe banks − the so-called 'lifeboat'. In all, 28 institutions needed support and four of these became, for a time, subsidiaries of the Bank of England. Subsequent investigations revealed much fraud and malpractice amongst the secondary banks, which the rest of the system found themselves underwriting.[1]

This chastening experience (like the Johnson Matthey affair ten years later) brought home the need to overhaul the regulation of banking which in 1979 saw all institutions taking deposits from the public brought under controlling legislation. This legislation effectively converted large numbers of small financiers into banking status, since there is nothing to prevent licensed institutions from providing the same banking services as recognised banks. Perhaps as many as one-sixth of the monetary sector institutions have some presence in retail banking. Most of the monetary sector institutions, however, have a stronger presence in corporate rather than in personal financial services, and in what follows we focus primarily upon the major retail banks shown in Table 6.1, the building societies and the National Savings Bank.

6.3   Competition for Personal Deposits

Building societies are the major success story in terms of the competition for personal deposits. Figure 6.1 compares the personal deposit shares of the building societies, national savings and the monetary sector institutions as in 1970, 1975, 1980 and 1985. Building societies have consistently increased their share which in 1985 stood at 52 per cent as compared with the banks' share of 33 per cent.

Notably, this growth has been achieved despite legislation which has constrained them to be virtually one-asset institutions (home

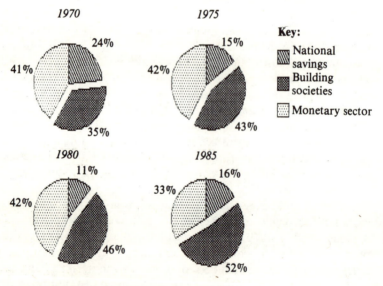

Source: Financial Statistics.

Figure 6.1   Liquid Assets of the UK Personal Sector

mortgages comprise 79 per cent of assets). While cross-country comparisons are hazardous, it is interesting to note that in the UK the building societies and retail banks are roughly equal in size in terms of domestic deposits, whereas in the US the savings and loan associations, which as mutual mortgage lenders are the institutional counterparts of the building societies, have deposits of only about one-third of those of commercial banks. Building societies have also been free of the erosion of profitability and net worth experienced by the US associations during the high-interest-rate phases of the 1980s.

Unlike the savings and loan associations, the building societies have always lent on a variable-rate basis: fixed-rate home mortgage loans hardly exist (and this is true of the banks' lending also). Moreover, unlike the initial 'teaser' rates, interest-rate caps and complicated arrangements for adjusting mortgage rates in the US, the building societies operate a simple procedure: the borrower simply cedes to the society the right to alter rates at its own volition. Customers' capacity to bear the interest-rate risk passed on to them by the institutions is not unlimited, but the societies are further protected by a social welfare system which undertakes to maintain interest repayments for those on social security. In order to 'buy' customers' goodwill, the societies need to appear to be reluctant and unwilling to raise rates, which means they tend to lag market movements. This slowness to react can also work against societies when interest rates generally are falling.

There are, of course, other factors underpinning the success of the building societies *vis-à-vis* banks for, as noted in Chapter 3, the societies have a strong penetration amongst all age groups and income levels. A number of factors have contributed: more convenient opening hours, more congenial offices, a regional identification, a less forbidding attitude to customers, and imaginative marketing of savings schemes. Of these, the first is perhaps the most important. Building society branches are open on Saturday mornings and many societies report that up to 40 per cent or more of their transactions take place on Saturdays. When the bank unions and management agreed to close banks on Saturdays, in the words of a building society spokesman,[2] they handed the building societies two own goals before the game had even started! Rather belatedly, the banks have now sought to correct this problem by opening selected branches on

Saturdays, accompanied by strong advertising, such as National Westminster's 'Satwest' campaign.

The banks' attention has also been upon two other factors: taxation of deposit interest and the linkages (noted in the introduction) from home mortgages to deposit business. For many years the interest paid by the building societies on their deposits ('shares') was subject to a withholding tax, whereas bank interest was paid gross. Under the arrangement, the societies deducted taxation at source and paid-over interest to their depositors (strictly speaking 'shareholders') net of tax, so saving the Inland Revenue the costs of collecting the tax itself. The tax deducted was at a 'composite' rate of 25.25 per cent (the average for taxpayers and non-taxpayers), thus less than the 30 per cent basic rate of personal income tax, resulting in a tax saving for those whose income put them in the basic rate tax bracket or higher. At the same time, there was a tax loss for non-taxpayers whose interest otherwise would not have been subject to tax. Banks long felt that, because the former group outweighs the latter, this arrangement benefited the societies in the competition for taxpayers' deposits, and the banks campaigned strongly for its abolition. Instead, the banks found themselves after April 1985 subject to the withholding tax, and required to pay interest net of tax to most personal depositors.[3] Only the National Savings Bank is now able to cater for non-taxpaying depositors: it offers savings deposits (called investment accounts) on which interest is paid both gross and net of tax, according to the position of the depositor.

Banks gradually began to appreciate that they had lost out badly in the competition for deposits during the 1970s by surrendering the market for mortgage finance to the societies. For all but two years of the 1970s, the banks' sterling balance sheets were subject to monetary constraints, reducing their incentive to enter into direct competition with the societies. But, perhaps more to the point, the banks' hearts lay elsewhere, and they devoted their energies to wholesale and international lending. As earnings declined internationally and risks grew, the banks began to look again at personal financial services. They found that the building societies had both grown rapidly and developed strong intertemporal links with existing and aspiring homebuyers which spilled over to savings deposits. The banks were reluctant to compete for deposits too strongly for risk of cannibalising their own 'cheap' base of current accounts and deposit accounts, and mortgage lending was their preferred way of building up a stronger base of personal customers. When direct monetary controls were lifted in 1980, the banks moved into home lending.

This action in turn probably stimulated the societies to join in the attack upon the clearing banks' deposits which was led by unit trust managers in 1983. The banks had long practised differential pricing between retail deposits and wholesale deposits, offering no interest on cheque accounts and a regulated rate on savings accounts while paying corporate customers rates which closely tracked those paid in the wholesale markets. As interest rates rose and the gap between the two widened, unit trust managers followed the path pioneered by their counterparts in the US, bridging the gap with money market pooled funds and high-interest bank accounts offered in conjunction with merchant banks.[4] Building societies quickly followed this lead by linking up with Scottish and non-clearing banks, offering a combination of a building society high-interest savings account and a cheque account at a bank, with switching arrangements between the two.

This concerted attack upon the clearing banks' remaining 'low-cost' deposit base saw them respond by introducing high-interest cheque accounts (HICAs), beginning with the Midland Bank in February 1984. Like money market deposit accounts in the US, these offer cheque-writing facilities (£200 minimum) and money market rates, subject to a minimum balance requirement (£2,000). (So far, the market 'judgment' would seem to be that British consumers prefer 'do-it-yourself' sweeping arrangements to current accounts than the more formalised cash management account systems in the US.) Until HICAs were introduced, customers wanting market-related interest rates from banks needed about £50,000 on deposit, and a helpful bank manager. There was thus a dramatic reduction in the minimum qualifying balance and in the inconvenience which must be incurred to obtain market-related rates of interest. Indeed, it must be asked how long there will continue to be a meaningful distinction to the banks between the cost of wholesale and retail funds.

From the figures in Figure 6.1, showing a continued decline in the banks' share of personal deposits, it would seem that they still have much ground to catch up. Banks do have a number of potential advantages. Table 6.2 shows them to have a more extensive branch network than the building societies, and a considerable headstart in

Table 6.2　Comparative Statistics of British Banks, 1985

	No. of staff*	No. of branches	No. of ATMs
Barclays	69,100	2,894	807
Lloyds	46,200	2,252	1,672
Midland	46,500	2,278	922
National Westminster	69,300	3,210	1,784
William Glyns*	6,800	324	164
Coutts	1,500	18	—
Bank of Scotland	8,917	546	236
Clydesdale	6,987	391	241
Royal Bank of Scotland*	9,479	549	305
Cooperative Bank	3,604	73	—
National Giro Bank	5,280	22,301	—
Trustee Savings Bank	17,100	1,607	968
Yorkshire Bank	4,226	225	145
Building Societies	61,156	6,927	652

Note: * End 1984.

the number of ATMs installed, although the building societies are investing heavily to make up the gap. Banks differ amongst themselves in the relative importance attached to branches and ATMs. Lloyds in particular has looked to ATMs and machine-run service centres in foyers to counteract the longer opening hours of the societies. Barclays, on the other hand, has led the move to re-open on Saturdays and apparently remains unconvinced that ATMs are a cost-effective way of servicing personal customers.[5] While an ATM cash withdrawal is 65 per cent cheaper than one across the counter, many customers make two or three ATM transactions to withdraw a given sum of money in place of one over-the-counter cheque encashment.[6] A branch, and the opportunity it gives for personal contact, is likely to remain important so long as the intermediation of banks rests so heavily upon a two-way flow of information between them and customers (see Chapter 2). In its plans to be a major force in retail banking in Britain, Citibank perceives the need to 'have a branch within 10 miles of 90 per cent of the British population'.[7]

The clearing banks still offer the widest range of transactions services (e.g. cheques, credit cards, direct debits, standing orders, overseas payments), but face difficulties in pricing those services appropriately. These difficulties arise because many banking services are jointly produced − since banks use the same facilities to provide a variety of services − and jointly consumed. Payments services, for example, involve the banks in jointly servicing two customers, one making the payment and the other being the recipient. Banks' intermediation services (borrowing and lending) can arise only by an act of joint consumption by the loan and deposit customers. Consequently, it may be impossible to allocate the costs of 'output' between the various customers, except in an arbitrary fashion.

In the past, banks have been able to avoid some of these problems by using the interest income gained by lending out the balances left idle by customers in their cheque accounts to offset as much as three-quarters of the costs which the banks identified with money transmission. (In the same way, insurers use investment income on premiums paid in advance to lower underwriting charges on insurance policies.) But competition from other institutions and the introduction of higher interest current acounts (HICAs) has whittled away the amount of funds left interest free in current accounts.

One solution is to raise charges for cheque transfers, cash withdrawals, etc. Indeed, there are many who argue that, under competitive pressures, banks will have to recover fully from explicit charges the cost of transactions services. But the difficulty here is in defining the nature of a transactions 'service'. Many customers regard cash withdrawals, cheque transfers and the holding of funds in a bank deposit as a joint product, and may want to pay for the package as a whole rather than each component separately. Charges have increased, but for over two-thirds of customers the charges are in any case hypothetical since they arrange their affairs so as to meet the minimum, or average, balance qualifications needed to avoid charges. This being the case, we might have expected the qualification limits to have increased sharply but, in fact, the banks have gone in the opposite direction. Encouraged by competition amongst themselves (especially from the Co-op, Trustee Banks and Midland − all seeking to build up their personal base), qualification limits have in fact fallen so that customers only need to stay in credit to avoid charges. This move to 'free banking' effectively shifts the costs of payment services onto borrowers by raising the cost sharply for those current-account holders straying into the 'red', and by forcing others to use more expensive borrowings against credit cards for temporary accommodation. In this way, the banks are thereby exposing themselves to competition on the lending side, especially when the building societies move further into the provision of consumer credit.

Banks have invested heavily in new technology to reduce cheque-handling costs and are experimenting with EFTPOS (see Chapter 4). Another route being pursued by the banks is in widening joint production; in other words aiming to spread existing costs over a wider range of products, tied to the primary banking product. We now turn to consider the banks and their competitors as overall providers of financial services.

6.4   Range of Financial Services

British banks are financial conglomerates of impressive dimensions ranking high amongst the world's largest banks. They offer a full range of 'banking services', covering retail deposit collection through merchant banking to international syndicated lending. They also offer a wide range of 'other' financial services, including insurance, unit trusts and investment management.

In earlier chapters we suggested that diversification by financial firms is prompted by a number of factors: customers' financial needs and a saving of their search and transport costs; economies of joint production and 'scope'; safety and trust; 'branding' and marketing; and the facilitation of information flows needed for financial contracting. It should also be noted that there is a strong functional similarity between the business of seemingly disparate financial firms which makes the distinction between banking and other financial services somewhat arbitrary. Consider, as an example, banks and general insurers. Banks, at the simplest level, take in deposits, invest them in securities and loans to earn interest and then repay depositors. Insurance companies take in premiums from policyholders, invest premiums in securities to generate investment income and then pay out policyholders. As the insurance companies increasingly live off investment income, the similarities grow.[8]

Unlike banks in the US and in some other countries, British banks have never been subject to formal restrictions upon the type of business undertaken beyond largely self-imposed constraints as to 'proper' activities, reflecting prevailing attitudes. Attitudes are capable of changing more rapidly than laws, and about 20 years ago that happened with the banks, as they entered consumer instalment credit, then credit cards, unit trusts, insurance, merchant banking, international and offshore banking, leasing, factoring, and so on. There have been strong commercial incentives for them to divert new ventures away from their own balance sheets to those of subsidiaries. As holding companies, each of the major clearing banks currently offer around 300 separate product lines. Organisationally, these services may be carried out by the parent bank, through a wholly-owned subsidiary, or through an associated company, as may be seen for each of the 'big four' in Table 6.3.

For some services, the banks remain providers even though the lines are by no means profitable. This point applies particularly to executor and trustee business − the oldest of the banks' subsidiary operations[9] − where loss of goodwill is an important factor explaining banks' continued provision of the services. Investment management services tend to be hampered by the normal practice of each investment management account, each estate, and each trust having its own individual portfolio of stocks. For legal reasons it has not been possible, as in the US, to co-mingle funds into common portfolios, so reducing costs.

Table 6.3 Clearing Bank's Provision of Personal Financial Services

	Barclays	*Lloyds*	*Midland*	*Nat West*
Executor and Trustee	W	P	W	P
Investment management	W	P	W	P
Unit trust management	W	W	W	C
Insurance underwriting	W	W	W	—
Insurance broking	W	W	W	W
Pension fund management	W	P/W	W	P
Tax and financial planning	W	P	W	P
Consumer credit	W	W	W	W
Real estate agency	—	W	—	—
Travel agency	—	—	W	—
Credit card	W	A	A	A
Offshore services	W	W	W	W

Note: Code: P = parent, W = wholly-owned subsidiary, A = associate.

Unit trust management merges in well with the banks' life insurance services, and especially with the growth of unit-linked policies. Use of the branch network as a platform for insurance broking and direct sales of insurance is an extension of earlier arrangements in which branch managers were personal agents for various insurance companies. The insurance function is important from the banks' viewpoint as it is a way of offering financial security. By combining payment services and savings facilities with insurance, the banks are able to cover the three basic financial demands of customers identified in Chapter 2. The banks' penetration into the pension funds market has, however, been relatively small. It appears also that their specialist vehicles set up for pension funds investment have not really developed as strong a reputation, or performed as well, as those of other providers.

In respect of tax and financial planning, banks act as full taxation agents for customers, completing the tax return, computing the tax liability or refund and settling up with Inland Revenue. They also advise customers on how to rearrange affairs so as to minimise liability for capital gains tax, and the use of covenants. Allied to this service, the banks provide through their trust sections, financial plans on how to rearrange customers' investments and activities so as to save on estate and probate duties.

Credit cards have been a success area for the banks. Cards are the fastest growing form of non-cash payment in Britain, and Britain is probably third behind US and Canada in terms of penetration of credit-card use. Visa turnover has grown from £76 million in 1972 to £4,130 million in 1984. Access turnover has grown from £25 million in 1972 to £3,995 million in 1984. Visa has 215,000 outless. Access has 218,000 outlets. Banks benefit from being owners of the management companies, saving in terms of money transmission costs and from being able to divert small personal overdraft business into this avenue.

Other personal services provided by some or all of the banks through subsidiaries include consumer instalment credit (which the banks and their subsidiaries dominate), offshore banking and money management, travel agency (Midland) and real-estate agency and surveying (Lloyds). In terms of business services the list is long indeed and includes leasing, factoring, new issues and underwriting, futures dealing, interest-rate swaps, export finance, property investment and management, management buyouts, business advice, accountancy services, and computer services.

Despite providing all these services, it must be pointed out that until recently the banks' diverse activities had essentially been seen as separate concerns with little presentation of them as an integrated range of services. It has been estimated, for example, that none of the banks' insurance subsidiaries has achieved a penetration of more than 5 per cent of the customer base available to them (Green 1985). A survey in 1985 of banks' current account customers revealed that about one-half of them would prefer *not* to obtain insurance, estate-agency services and a home mortgage from a bank.[10]

During the 1970s the clearing banks, relative to their depository competitors, had most of the fields discussed above to themselves. Now the position has changed dramatically. Only the National Savings Bank has retained its original specialist function of providing savings facilities at post offices for large numbers of people; it has over 20 million active accounts. The bank does not make loans or allow overdrafts – all funds are either placed in government securities or passed on directly to the government – and there are no personal cheque accounts offered to customers (but giro facilities are available at all post offices). There are two types of account, ordinary and investment, and in line with its aim of catering for less wealthy customers, an upper limit of £50,000 is placed on its attractive investment account. A range of longer-term savings certificates, some guaranteeing tax-free real returns, is provided through the Department of National Savings, of which the National Savings Bank is a part.

From 'penny savings banks' required to hold only government securities, the Trustee Savings Banks have become fully-fledged banks. Until recently the banks were organised on a regional basis, but from 1983 they merged into one bank for England and Wales, one for Scotland, one for Northern Ireland, and one for the Channel Islands, along with a central servicing and cheque clearing bank. These banks, through the development of the TSB group, have diversified into consumer and commercial loans, and are now the third biggest issuer of credit cards through Trustcard, with a cardholder base of 2.14 million, the seventh largest unit trust manager, and have a growing presence in life insurance through TSB Trust Company.

Table 6.4 compares some of the major product lines available from the four large London clearing bank groups, the TSB group, and the two largest building societies (which would rank amongst the world's 100 largest 'banks'). The extent of the diversification by

Table 6.4 Comparison of Product Lines of Selected Financial Institutions

	Clearing bank	TSB	Large building society
Chequebook account	Yes	Yes	Yes[a]
Savings account	Yes	Yes	Yes
Certificate of deposit	Yes	Yes	Yes
Credit cards	Yes	Yes	Yes[a]
Traveller's cheques	Yes	Yes	Yes
Home mortgages	Yes	Yes	Yes
Personal loans	Yes	Yes	Yes[a]
Commercial loans	Yes	Yes	—
Leasing	Yes	Yes	—
Factoring	Yes	—	—
Merchant banking	Yes	—	—
General insurance broking	Yes	Yes	Yes[b]
Life insurance broking	Yes	Yes	Yes
Insurance underwriting	Yes	Yes	—
Pension fund management	Yes	Yes	—
Unit trust management	Yes	Yes	—
Share broking agency	Yes	Yes	—
Real estate agency	Yes	—	Yes
Real estate valuation	Yes	—	Yes
Housebuilding and renovation	—	—	Yes
Tax and financial planning	Yes	Yes	—
Investment management	Yes	Yes	—
Offshore services	Yes	Yes	—
Travel agency	Yes	—	—
Data processing	Yes	Yes	—

Note: (a) Provided in conjunction with a bank.
(b) Limited to home mortgage-related insurance.

the TSB group is apparent, as is the breadth of services of the banks compared with the building societies (and, indeed, with US financial conglomerates – see Table 5.7 above).

Nevertheless, despite their own perceptions as being constrained by legislation in the competition for personal financial services, the building societies have managed to find some ways around the handicaps. In combination with non-clearing banks, the societies offer chequebooks, credit cards and unsecured loans. The societies have met their customers' desire for consumer credit by lending generously against housing valuations (called 'over-financing' by the Bank of England and discussed further in Chapter 7). They issue certificates of deposit and bid for wholesale deposits. Agency arrangements enable them to offer real-estate valuations and broking, and housing-related general and life insurance. It is interesting to observe just how much insurance business can be squeezed into the housing-related description. Although such developments have occurred through 'bending' the current rules, the regulatory changes which have recently taken place and others which are in the offing are likely to intensify competition in the market still further.

6.5 Regulation and Deregulation

Major steps have been taken to deregulate banks and depository institutions since 1979 (Lewis and Chiplin 1985). A system of exchange controls, in place since the Second World War, was swept away overnight. Controls over bank lending were removed, along with reserve ratio requirements for monetary control purposes. Setting of the Bank Rate, the main weapon of the Bank of England for over 120 years, was abandoned in 1980, leaving open market operations as virtually the sole remaining monetary instrument. A commitment to market forces saw official regulation of consumer instalment credit lifted in 1982. The phased diversification of the Trustee Savings Banks has continued. With the banks freed from direct controls, the building societies have pushed for liberalisation of their governing rules.

But these developments have been flanked by a tightening of prudential controls, beginning with the Banking Act of 1979.

The Banking Act

With the Act, the authorities sought to introduce:

(i) A coordinated system of chartering depository institutions, clarifying which institutions were entitled to be regarded as banks.

(ii) Machinery to monitor and control the risks which banks might assume in the more competitive environment: a need made all too apparent by the orgy of property lending which preceded the 'secondary banking crisis' of 1974.

The first objective complied with the EEC's 1977 directive on 'credit' institutions, but the Act took a different path by focusing upon deposits, and the protection of depositors, requiring licensing either as a bank or a deposit-taker for institutions accepting deposits from the public (unless they are exempted). Not all applicants receive licences. Of the original 614 applications in 1979 from existing deposit-takers, 11 were refused licences and were unable to continue in business. In the five years since then a further 12 institutions have had their licences revoked on the grounds of inadequate capital, insufficient liquidity, imprudence, or failure to supply the Bank of England with adequate information.

Both recognised banks and LDTs contribute equally to the statistics collected by the Bank of England for monitoring risks and exposures of institutions, and the Bank has generally had the aim of treating both sets of institutions equally in the accompanying arrangements for prudential supervision. In a banking system as complex as that in Britain, with the different mix between institutions in retail/wholesale/international business conducted, a quest for equity may be akin to the search for the holy grail. Rather than lay down overall reserve and capital ratios, the Bank has developed guidelines for capital and liquidity needs which take into account the type of assets and the maturity of balance sheets.[11] However, these merely encapsulate jointly agreed upon methods of measuring the risks involved. How much risk should be assumed is a matter of judgment for the institution's management to decide, in consultation with the supervisor, and taking into account the characteristics of the particular business. There are no on-site or surprise examinations of institutions' books and operations rooms, as are made in the US. Rather, in carrying out an arm's length consultation process, the Bank of England supervisor behaves more like the archetypal village priest, relying extensively on the confessional (encouraging banks to bare their souls), personal knowledge ('to know the man is to know his balance sheet'), cultivating a community spirit and with it peer group pressure, and resorting occasionally to the threat of ultimate arbitration in a higher court.

Following the Bank of England's forced takeover of Johnson Matthey's banking operations in 1984, this informal, and trusting, approach to banking supervision has come under close scrutiny.[12] Johnson Matthey's situation stemmed mainly from a failure of management control. Amongst changes mooted, some involving amendments to the Banking Act, is the desire for the Bank to consult in future with a firm's auditors as well as management, and to have the information supplied to it vetted by independent bodies. A dropping of the somewhat arbitrary distinction between banks and LDTs is also on the agenda. At present is would be difficult for large retail-based institutions like the building societies to qualify under the Act as banks rather than LDTs (should their present exemption status be changed).

Attention is also being given to the regulatory and other implications of the continued spread of banks into other financial fields. Particular impetus for this examination comes from the 'Big Bang' on the Stock Exchange. Prior to spring 1986, more than 20 banks had announced links with jobbing and broking firms as a first step to the full ownership allowed under new Stock Exchange rules, and these include three of the 'big four' clearing banks. It is at this juncture not clear how quickly the new competitive environment for wholesale-sized securities dealing will spread through to retail business, but it can be expected that low-cost, few-frills 'discount brokerage' facilities for securities sales and purchases by retail customers will eventuate, as they have in the US.

There is a recognition amongst the regulatory authorities that integrated financial services groups embracing deposit-taking, stockbroking, insurance, unit trusts, and so on, pose special problems for investor protection, policyholder protection and depositor protection.[13] As we noted in earlier chapters, the problems extend beyond this to issues such as competitive fairness, concentrations of financial power, and tied-in sales. Already, two banking groups (Barclays and TSB) are reported to have run into trouble with customers for high-powered cross-selling of insurance through their direct salesforce (Plender 1985).

The authorities are looking to facilitate cooperation amongst the separate regulatory agencies which exist already and which are also to be formed under the Financial Services Bill. An interdepartmental machinery is being set up to share information and coordinate the responses of the separate regulators. At the same time, the Bank of England is moving the focus of its depositor protection and supervisory interests from the banks to the holding company or 'group' activities.

It was never intended that the deposit protection scheme would supplant an individual's obligation to make his own assessment of an institution's safety, and with a maximum compensation of £7,500 it clearly does not do so. Nevertheless, it is probably fair to say that members of the general public expect the Bank of England to provide them with a fuller measure of protection than that. Its intervention in the secondary banking crisis and with Johnson Matthey has established precedents which it finds difficult to shirk. The Bank itself now admits that this responsibility extends to the group:

> Companies within a banking group are frequently identified in the market with the parent bank. Difficulties in a group company – particularly in one undertaking a banking or financial business – will reflect upon the parent, which will in consequence be likely to see a need to support it to the fullest extent which its own resources allow, in order to protect its own standing in the market. (*Annual Report* 1985)

Accordingly, the Bank in March 1986 served notice to the institutions that it will be supervising them on a consolidated basis, assessing capital requirements, liquidity needs and risk exposures in terms of group rather than bank activities.[14]

Trustee Savings Banks

Currently the TSB forms part of the monetary sector, but is subject to control by the Treasury. New legislation, in the process of becoming law, will bring it within the scope of the Banking Act and the supervision outlined above. The Act will also give the TSB powers to introduce equity funding and extend the already wide range of services.

The Trustee Savings Banks began almost 200 years ago with the concept of a people's bank, run by the people for the benefit of the people. A more commercially-oriented approach was introduced in the 1960s and the later concentration of affairs into larger organisational units following the Page Report of 1973 saw a rapid expansion of financial services. The addition of equity funding, by increasing the capital base and clarifying the issue of ownership, will allow further expansion in the provision of loans, instalment credit, credit cards, life and general insurance and the management of unit trusts. With the Bank of England's move to consolidated supervision, the ability of the TSB group to diversify further is strengthened by its relatively low level of gearing and lending in comparison with the clearing banks. In addition, the expansion which has already taken place has produced an experienced market-oriented set of managers.

This process is only just beginning in the building societies, which remain mutual not-for-profit organisations. At present it is not certain which direction the main thrust of TSB developments will take, but further incursions into the more profitable sectors of housing finance and consumer credit may be expected. The possibility for the development of joint ventures between the TSB and other financial institutions remains open as currently little development has taken place here. However, the TSB Group does own United Dominions Trust which enables loans secured on customers' houses to be made.

Building Societies

The Building Societies Act 1962 is clear in two respects. The societies are mutual, non-profit organisations. They are restricted to the one function of raising funds from members so as to make home mortgage loans. Diversification into other areas of personal financial services is thereby prohibited.

This charter has been stretched by the managements of the societies about as far as it can. After a considerable process of public discussion over at least five years, a new Building Societies Act has been passed, based upon the set of proposals contained in the Green Paper *Building Societies: A New Framework*, published in July 1984.

The major changes in the Act as regards new activities are set out in Table 6.5. In general, the proposals relax considerably the original charter. But it is not intended that the societies become fully fledged financial 'supermarkets'. Limits are proposed upon the extension of powers where conflicts of interests may arise, where there may be a high risk to the house financing function, and where the societies' traditional role as low-risk repositories for personal savings is impaired. At least 90 per cent of assets would still be used for home mortgages, and it is recommended that new activities which involve a degree of risk be conducted through subsidiaries so as not to threaten the survival of the society itself nor to bring it within the ambit of legislation relevant to the new activity (other ac-

Table 6.5   The Major Changes to the Powers of Societies contained in the
Building Societies Act 1986

Changes Concerning:	*Comment*
1. Unsecured lending	– Agreed for personal loans for furniture and fittings – Restricted to larger societies and to 15% of non-first mortgage lending – To be limited to £5,000 per individual
2. Housing provision	– Proposed new power to allow ownership, development of residential property – Likely to be restricted to societies with £3m free reserves and to be a small proportion of assets
3. Integrated house buying	– Proposed that societies offer this service – Danger of interest conflicts, especially with respect to estate-agency work – Conveyancing service restricted to non-customers
4. Agency services	– Proposal to allow societies to act as agents for other organisations to improve utilisation of branches
5. Financial services	– Development of services related to stocks and shares will be on a longer time scale
6. Insurance broking	– There will be an extension of current services
7. Formation of subsidiaries	– Should be ability to own equity interest in subsidiaries
8. Money transmission	– Proposal that societies can offer full personal banking and money transmission services if they wish
9. Joint ventures	– Proposal to allow societies to become involved in joint venture provision of services already legally permissible

10. Money raising	– At least 80% should be from individual members; 20% from money markets; 40% with approval of Building Societies Commission

Source: *Building Societies – A New Framework*, HMSO, 1984; and Building Societies Act 1986.

tivities could be carried out in-house). Whilst the expectation is that most societies will continue as mutual institutions, there is scope for demutualisation, but the route is likely to be tortuous.[15]

Although not covered by the new Act, the Government announced in May 1986 that building societies would be allowed to set up subsidiaries which could offer pension savings schemes (but not underwriting facilities) enabling participants to buy pension annuities. The subsidiary would need to operate as a unit trust authorised under the financial services legislation, but such activities could not commence until the passing of the new Social Security Act, which is scheduled to come into force in 1988.

Being granted the power to undertake an activity does not necessarily mean that it is prudent to rush out and do it. Whilst the reaction of the industry itself via the Building Societies' Association (BSA)[16] and of consumer interests via the Office of Fair Trading (OFT)[17] has generally been favourable, there are reservations about a number of areas.

The first of these is the issue of conflicts of interest and other abuses of trust. The OFT in particular is concerned that the societies should not lock consumers into using in-house conveyancing, real estate and insurance services, nor make the use of such services a precondition for the granting of a loan. It has had occasion in the past (with the Halifax) to object to the tie-in of insurance services, and has required undertakings from the societies that insurance-agency requirements will be relaxed. Cross-subsidisation of services and predatory pricing may also be a problem. The OFT has recommended that where building societies offer a range of services, there should be *transparency* in billing, i.e. costs of different services should be itemised so that the consumer could decide whether to go elsewhere for a particular service. *De facto* locking-in may still remain, but more passive customers may prefer the convenience so offered. An alternative view is that these kinds of services should not be provided in-house by societies but through contractual joint ventures in the market place. The Building Societies Act contains safeguards to avoid some of the problems associated with the tying in of associated services. Moreover, the Act also contains restrictions on the ability of societies to offer conveyancing services to their own customers.

This last point introduces the second area of reservation, namely whether societies are equipped for diversification. At one level, the degree of in-house expertise places limits on prudent entry into new areas. At a more general level, the need arises for societies to undertake strategic planning in order to assess their competitive strengths. Small local societies must not eschew their regional identity and personalised services. The large national societies seem likely to follow each other into what are already in many cases highly competitive markets. Returns may be very small, but if they stay out, existing areas of activity may decline because of the knock-on effect of not producing an integrated range of services. Possible solutions to this problem involve a divergence of activities by societies, so that each specialises in a different area; further mergers amongst the national societies to reduce duplication of services; entry into markets by less direct means such as through joint ventures; or concentration of activities on areas close to housing, where their expertise is centred. (The Abbey National Building Society has forcefully stressed this last view, although it is strongly in favour of links with estate agencies and insurance companies.)

Third, just as building societies are seeking to enter new areas, other institutions are entering markets which have been traditionally the preserve of building societies, for example the provision of housing finance by UK and US banks and, more recently, moves to reintroduce Saturday opening. Moreover, the advent of new technology, especially ATMs and EFTPOS, poses serious questions as to the continued cost-effectiveness of large branch networks, for both building societies and banks. There is also the danger that the introduction of money transmission services on their own account could lose societies the current benefits of 'free-riding' on the clearing bank system, in which in effect they hold the balances and the banks do the work.

All three reservations point to the value of joint ventures for the majority of societies. Agency services provide opportunities to better utilise branch networks, lower risks from entry into new areas, reduce the time spent on the 'learning curve', and increase fee income directly. Joint ventures have a firm grounding in the academic literature on corporate strategy[18] (and indeed in the theory of natural evolution itself)[19] in which organisations that are interdependent seek cooperative rather than competitive solutions. In this case a cooperative arrangement provides the benefits of an integrated service without the problems of excess competition should large numbers of societies enter new markets on their own account.

Probable agency services which could be provided are: collection of payments for the gas and electricity industries; insurance broking services; management of property investments, branch outlets for Scottish and overseas banks wishing to enter the English banking market; servicing of mortgages for other institutions. The latter is a possibility where insurance companies or pension funds wish to diversify their portfolio. As will be seen in Chapter 7, this approach offers an alternative means of providing housing finance where it becomes increasingly difficult to attract sufficient funds at the right price from the traditional source of individual savers, and is one implication of the wider developments now occurring in terms of secondary markets and the vertical 'de-integration' of financial services.

6.6 Future Competition

So far we have highlighted developments in the products offered by banking and deposit institutions. Now we look at the changing structure of the institutions in the market place and how these changes relate to expected changes in behaviour.

The position of high concentration and small numbers in retail banking was reached amongst British banks somewhat sooner than has been the case for building societies. Table 6.6 shows that the number of building societies has been falling for almost a century. The trend continues as the societies' managers attempt to fulfil strategies of becoming national or regional competitors. In consequence, the average size of a society in real terms has trebled since 1975.

It is not just size alone that has implications for the behaviour of the industry, but also the extent of variations in size and market power. Although there were some 167 building societies in existence

Table 6.6 The Growth of Building Societies

Year	No. of societies	Total assets at current prices (£m)	Total assets at 1983 prices (£m)	Average size of Society in teal terms (£m) (1983 prices)
1890	2,795	na	na	na
1900	2,286	60	na	na
1910	1,723	76	na	na
1920	1,271	87	800	0.63
1930	1,026	371	6,000	5.85
1940	952	756	9,000	9.45
1950	819	1,256	13,000	15.87
1960	726	3,166	22,000	30.30
1970	481	10,819	49,000	101.87
1975	382	24,204	57,000	149.21
1980	273	53,793	67,000	245.42
1981	253	61,815	69,000	272.73
1982	227	73,033	77,000	339.21
1983	206	85,869	85,869	416.84
1984	190	102,688	97,519	513.26
1985	167	121,000	109,601	656.29

Source: BSA Bulletin, various issues.
Note: Adjusted on basis of Building Housing Cost Index.

at the end of 1985, almost nine-tenths of activity is attributable to just 20 societies. Moreover, the ten biggest societies account for over three-quarters of assets, five for over half of assets and the two largest societies for well over one-third of assets. These proportions have all shown a continuing upward trend over the last 30 years, although the calculations ignore competition from banks and other institutions.

These movements are the result of both entry and exit by building societies. As a result of the rules governing the creation of societies, only 18 which have entered the industry since 1964 are entirely new. Much more significant has been exit, either by means of a union or mainly by a transfer of engagement − a transfer from one society to another of membership and assets. Unlike a union, transfers of engagement do not require a special resolution on the part of the transferring society. The lack of effective control by members over this type of merger has received widespread criticism.

The mergers amongst building societies have for the most part involved smaller societies transferring their engagements to larger ones, rather than ones of a similar size. At the other end of the scale, mergers between societies in the 'largest 20' bracket are unusual. When they do occur, the object is often to merge societies with different regional strengths so as to obtain national coverage. While mergers between societies with overlapping branch networks are not unknown, increasing competition in the market place must lead to greater pressure for them as a cost-effective way of rationalising branch networks. One society 'going it alone' on closing branches would merely lose many of its customers to other institutions.

In terms of diversification of services, all building societies cannot be expected to have the resources to compete directly across all product areas with the main clearing banks. Whilst appropriate for some of the largest societies, such action would be unwise for others better advised to pursue a more selective strategy based on their regional or local strengths.

Questions about competition and diversification were put to the directors and chief executives of banks and building societies as part of the questionnaire survey undertaken in 1985 by the Nottingham Institute of Financial Studies, and we draw upon this and the earlier discussion in Chapter 3. Banks and building societies were asked where they expect future competition to come from, and where they themselves expect to diversify into over the next five years. Of importance, also, is the means by which societies and banks envisage that these changes will come about.

Deregulation is expected to increase diversification by both building societies and banks. As may be seen from Table 6.7, both types of institutions already display a marked degree of diversification. However, when their respective positions in five years' time are considered, clear differences emerge. Substantially more movement is anticipated by building societies than is the case for the banks, notably into insurance broking, banking, estate agency and stockbroking. In the case of the banks, stockbroking is seen to be the main area for expansion and is already occurring on a wide scale.

Competition is expected to increase sharply over the next five years. For the building societies, this competition is seen as coming from other building societies and the banks (see Figure 3.5). In view

Table 6.7   Attitudes to Diversification (%)

(i) *Building societies*	NOW		IN FIVE YEARS	
	Major activity	Others	Major activity	Others
Banking	7.3	14.6	13.2	28.9
Housing finance	100.0	1.2	100.0	2.6
Life insurance and pensions	7.3	26.8	9.2	39.5
Non-life insurance	3.7	37.8	5.3	47.4
Insurance broking	7.3	13.4	11.8	39.5
Stockbroking	1.2	1.2	3.9	13.2
Estate agency	1.2	2.4	0	26.3
Retailing	1.2	1.2	0	2.6
Computing	2.4	12.2	1.3	11.8
Others (please specify type)	4.9	2.4	3.9	10.5

Base number of respondents = 82

(ii) *Banks*				
Banking	100.0	0	100.0	0
Housing finance	16.2	27.0	14.3	34.3
Life insurance and pensions	10.8	10.8	8.6	17.1
Non-life insurance	2.7	8.1	0	17.1
Insurance broking	13.5	16.2	11.4	22.9
Stockbroking	5.4	13.5	11.4	31.4
Estate agency	2.7	10.8	0	20.0
Retailing	2.7	5.4	0	5.7
Computing	5.4	16.2	0	17.1
Others	8.6	10.8	5.7	11.4

Base number of respondents = 37

of recent moves by societies into the provision of cheque accounts through joint ventures, which are likely to be enhanced by liberalisation of regulation, and the moves by the banks into housing finance and into more competitive savings accounts, the reasons for this expectation seem clear. Life insurance companies, insurance brokers, retail companies and stockbrokers feature also as sources of competition, perhaps a reflection of societies seeing themselves as financial supermarkets of the future.

The banks (see Figure 3.2) clearly considered other banks to be the main source of competition in the future. They do not see the societies posing as large a competitive threat as the societies' view of the banks. Interestingly, stockbrokers figure relatively highly as perceived sources of competition.

Four major strategies to achieve the suspected changes may be discerned: mergers, internal growth, the strategic use of technology, and marketing. Figures 6.2 and 6.3 give the views of building societies and banks respectively about some of these matters.

There are strong indications in the survey, from both building societies and banks, that diversification will be achieved by cooperative ventures, especially *non-merger* links. One qualification must be noted: respondents to the survey were more likely to express the opinion that such arrangements would be a general feature of the sector rather than something they themselves would be engaged in. About half of respondent societies expected to be involved in mergers and/or joint ventures, whereas over three-quarters expected mergers and nine-tenths expected joint ventures between different types of institution to be increasingly significant features of the sector. Societies and banks expect internal growth to be their major strategy, bolstered by aggressive marketing. Advertising was seen as the major marketing tool by societies, with direct

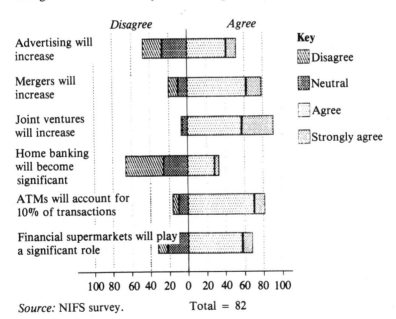

Source: NIFS survey.   Total = 82

Figure 6.2 Building Society Perspectives on Key Issues (%)

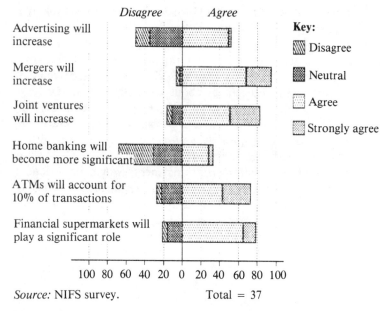

Figure 6.3   Bank Perspectives on Key Issues (%)

marketing less strongly rated. For banks, direct marketing was the preferred route with less than 20 per cent of banks considering that advertising would have a major influence. About one-third of banks saw information technology as being a major strategy, compared with 20 per cent of societies, but for both it was in terms of ATMs rather than home banking.

Both banks and societies have large branch networks and will increasingly need to provide extra value into branches to maintain their viability. In view of the diversifications that societies anticipate making when deregulation permits, along with the emphasis on cooperative ventures and marketing, the suspicion arises that the societies' managers will seek to have them evolve as financial 'supermarkets' for the personal sector, contrary to the intentions of the new legislation.

Banks, on the other hand, seem set to develop securities dealing as their diversification opportunity. A survey[20] conducted in 1966 showed that 53 per cent of all owners of stocks and shares made their transactions through their banks. This trend has been sustained over the intervening 20 years, with the *total level* of activity likely to increase with the interest in individual share ownership renewed recently by the Government's privatisation programme and personal equity schemes. The potential to do so in the form of discount broking would seem to be considerable.

Notes

1. The Bank's role in the crisis is set out in 'The secondary banking crisis and the Bank of England's support operations', *Bank of England Quarterly Bulletin*, June 1978. For another account, see Margaret Reid (1982) *The Secondary Banking Crisis 1973–75*, Macmillan.
2. Walden (1984).
3. The reduction in the basic tax rate from 30 to 29 per cent in the 1986 Budget leaves the composite rate unchanged at 25.25 per cent for 1986/87, because the rate is set in advance. The change is likely to come into force, therefore, in 1987/88.
4. Bateman (1984).
5. Reported in Howcroft and Lavis (1985).
6. Vittas (1984).
7. Reported in *The Banker*, May 1985, p.27.
8. The similarities between banking and insurance are explored in Lewis and Davis (forthcoming, 1987).
9. Hanson (1982).
10. *Banking World*, August 1985.
11. See 'The measurement of capital', *Bank of England Quarterly Bulletin*, September 1980; 'Foreign currency exposure', *Bank of England Quarterly Bulletin*, June 1981; and 'The measurement of liquidity', *Bank of England Quarterly Bulletin*, September 1982.
12. The Bank of England's actions are recorded in *Annual Report*, 1985.
13. Written Answer by Secretary of State for Trade and Industry, *Hansard*, 21 January 1986.
14. 'Consolidated supervision of institutions authorised under the Banking Act 1979', *Bank of England Quarterly Bulletin*, March 1986.
15. A Treasury discussion paper to the Building Societies Bill outlined a variety of routes to decentralisation for discussion at the Bill's report stage. Essentially those proposals involved demanding minimum voting levels by the members of societies asking to decentralise, and the circulation to all members of full details of the implications of a change to company status. For societies' news see Wright *et al.* (1986).
16. Building Societies Association (1985), *The Building Societies Bill – BSA Commentary*, London, BSA, December.
17. Director General of Fair Trading (1984) *Future of Building Societies – Press Release*, 20 November 1984. Also authors' interviews with representatives of OFT.

18. See, for example, Thompson (1967) and Pfeffer and Salancik (1978).
19. 'A nice way to survive', *The Listener*, 17 April 1986.
20. 'How does Britain serve?', A survey for the London Stock Exchange by the British Market Research Bureau, quoted in Hanson (1982).

References

Bateman, P. (1984) 'Money funds and high interest bank accounts', *Planned Savings*, August, pp. 49–53.
Green, K. (1985) 'The banks as life brokers', *Insurance Week*, January 4, pp. 23–26.
Hanson, D.G. (1982) *Service Banking*, Institute of Bankers, London.
Howcroft, B. and Lavis, J. (1985) 'Delivery systems in UK retail branch banking: a strategic perspective', *LUBC Research Paper Series*, No. 14, September.
Lewis, M.K. and Chiplin, B. (1985) 'Deregulation and the competitive pressures on British banks', *Proceedings of a Conference on Bank Structure and Competition*, Federal Reserve Bank of Chicago, pp. 55–71.
Lewis, M.K. and Davis, K.T. (forthcoming, 1987) *Domestic and International Banking*, Philip Allan.
Pfeffer, J. and Salancik, G.R. (1978) *The External Control of Organisations; A Resource Dependence Perspective*, Harper and Row.
Plender, J. (1985) 'UK insurers: indifferent but not immune to the financial services revolution', *Retail Banker International Yearbook*, Lafferty Publications, London, pp. 45–48.
Thompson, J.D. (1967) *Organisations in Action*, McGraw-Hill.
Vittas, D. (1984) 'Pricing policies for ATM transactions', *6th EFMA Convention*, Montreux.
Walden, H. (1984) 'How building societies see their role in the financial services revolution', *The Banker*, March, pp. 33–38.
Wright, D.M., Watkins, T., Price, C. and Hughes, J. (1986) 'The future of building societies', *E.I.U. Special Report 1057*, July.

CHAPTER 7

Housing Finance and Consumer Credit
D.M. Wright

7.1 Introduction

According to a survey carried out for the Building Societies Association (BSA) in 1983, owner-occupancy was the preferred form of housing tenure by 77 per cent of all adults. The Association has estimated that by the year 2000 this level of owner-occupancy may well be achieved. Housing also makes an important contribution to national capital formation (see Chapter 1) and it has been argued that a disproportionate amount of financial lending goes on housing to the detriment of manufacturing and service industry (Lever and Edwards 1980). The housing finance market is therefore a significant and increasingly important feature of the UK economy.

To a great extent, the housing finance market in the UK has hitherto been very closely aligned with that for deposit services. Housing finance has been generally provided by the institutions which collect savings mainly from individuals. In particular, the building societies which have traditionally provided the bulk of funds for house purchase have had to match carefully their cash inflows with cash outflows. The sensitivity of deposit levels to interest-rate changes, unlike mortgage demand, has had serious implications for how societies set their deposit and loan-interest rates. The mutual nature of building societies and their attempts to protect borrowers from the full effects of high interest rates have until recently led to a shortfall between the demand for and supply of mortgage funds.

However, the 1980s have witnessed the development of increased competition in the housing finance market, both between building societies themselves and between building societies and other institutions. These developments have affected the market shares of housing finance institutions, and also the price at which finance is provided and the sources from which funds are derived.

The previous chapter has addressed the nature of competition for savings, which provides the bulk of funds for housing finance. This chapter concentrates on the market for housing finance. The first section addresses the level and nature of demand for such funds. Since the distinction between consumer borrowing for housing and for non-housing activities has become increasingly blurred, as a result of competition and the absence of tax neutrality between various sources, the demand for other forms of borrowing is also discussed. Subsequent sections deal with the supply side of the market, in terms of market shares of suppliers and competition between them. Increasing competition for funds and for borrowers and the lowering of barriers to entry are also having a profound effect on traditional sources of finance and ways in which mortgages are provided. These issues are dealt with in the final section.

7.2   Demand for Housing Finance and Consumer Credit

(i)   *General Trends*

Net advances for housing finance in 1984 amounted to some £16.8bn. In 1985, this figure rose by 8.5 per cent to £18.4bn. Future changes in the level of demand for housing finance have important implications for suppliers in the market. Whilst increased competition may itself help to increase the size of the market, if new entrants help produce a situation where the supply of funds exceeds demand, either the price of finance will fall and/or rationalisation will be required with further impacts on the number and types of suppliers. It is, therefore, important to examine likely developments in the nature and extent of demand for housing and related finance. developments in the nature and extent of demand for housing and related finance.

Demand for housing finance and consumer credit in the future depends upon a complex mixture of factors. Not only are demographic trends important but other developments such as changes in government policy towards council house sales, changes to the taxation regime, increases in living standards and the effects on demand of changes in the way finance is supplied, also have a significant part to play. A Working Group of the Building Societies Association attempted in 1983–84 to estimate levels of demand for the whole housing finance market up to the year 2000. The results of their deliberations, shown in Table 7.1, indicate an expected increase in the total number of loans of about 50 per cent between now and the turn of the century, together with a fourfold increase in funds required measured in current price terms.

Table 7.1 Projections of Demand and Supply of Finance for House Purchase

	Numbers (000s)			Amount (central estimate £m)		
	First-time buyers	Former owner-occupiers	Total	First-time buyers	Former owner-occupiers	Total
1986	640	730	1,270	11,700	15,200	26,900
1991	580	980	1,560	15,200	27,000	42,200
1996	580	1,020	1,600	21,400	48,200	69,600
2000	580	1,240	1,820	28,000	76,800	104,800

Source: Adapted from BSA, 'Housing finance into the 1990s'.
Notes: (1) Assumes average advance is 95% in respect of council house sales component and 85% in respect of other first-time buyers.
(2) Assumes average advance is 60%.

Examining the sources of demand in more detail, the trend for first-time buyers can be divided into former council house tenants and others. Council house sales have decreased as a proportion of total advances, after their initial high level following the passing of the Housing Act 1980. The Housing and Building Control Act 1984 increased the discount provisions and reduced the qualifying tenancy requirements, so providing some upward effect on the demand for housing finance from this source. Market research conducted in 1983 (BSA Bulletin, January 1985) revealed that almost one half of council tenants expected to be owner-occupiers by the mid-1990s. The BSA forecasts indicate that council house sales will fall from about 130,000 in 1986 to stabilise at a level of about 80,000 per annum to the year 2000.

Although the proportion of building society loans to first-time buyers who were previously council tenants (i.e. those *transferring* from council houses to owner-occupancy rather than buying their council house) is currently at its highest level for a decade (20 per cent of all loans), the proportion of loans going to all first-time buyers has continued to decline. In 1970, 61 per cent of mortgages went to first-time buyers, whilst in 1980 the figure was 46 per cent. Some recovery, to 52 per cent, was apparent by 1985, reflecting the effect of council house tenants becoming owner-occupiers. As the size of the population cohorts expected to reach the stage of household formation will decline over the next few years, the number of other first-time buyers is expected to flatten out at about half a million per annum to the year 2000. Changing social factors and generally increasing economic affluence have recently been associated with a growth in household formation, in particular households consisting of one person. Though the number of single-person households increased from one-eighth to one-fifth of all households in the two decades to 1981, this trend appears to be levelling off.

Down-market lending, particularly in respect of pre-1919 terraced properties, has increased steadily since 1970. In 1970, 17 per cent of all loans were on this type of property, whereas by the third quarter of 1985 29 per cent of lending went to this section. Conversely, lending for new houses has fallen from 25 per cent of loans in 1970 to just 11 per cent in the third quarter of 1985.

Overall the share of loans going to all first-time buyers is expected to fall further to about 32 per cent by the turn of the century. It is from current owner-occupiers moving house that most of the demand for housing finance is expected to come (Table 7.1), with a doubling of the number of transactions expected over the next fifteen years. To some extent the increasing importance of owner-occupiers is a reflection of the decline in first-time buyers. But it may also be influenced by the extent to which owner-occupiers increase their borrowing more than they need to in order to finance substantial renovations and home improvements or use mortgage finance as an alternative source of funds to other forms of borrowing in order to finance consumption expenditure. Borrowing specifically for home improvement rose from 13 per cent of all building society advances in 1970 to 30 per cent in 1982. By the year 2000 the BSA estimate that this kind of lending will have increased from about £2.5bn currently to £10bn.

(ii)   *Non-House-Purchase Borrowing*

According to government statistics, net transactions for consumer credit borrowing from banks (including credit cards), finance companies, insurance companies and retailers amounted to about £3.8bn in 1985, some 23 per cent greater than the level in 1984. The market shares of these main suppliers will be discussed in the next section, but an often hidden element of consumer credit borrowing is that part of mortgage funding which does not enter directly into housing finance. Since such borrowing may receive the same kind of interest relief as housing finance, it can have a distorting effect on the nature of competition in the market for consumer credit which ordinarily does not receive such benefits.

Estimates of the extent of 'over-financing' of houses have been made by Drayson (1985). As may be seen from Table 7.2, column 8, the net increase in the stock of house purchase loans has been in excess of the private sector's net expenditure on the sources of supply of housing over the last fifteen years, even when house price increases are taken into account. This 'net cash withdrawal' from the private-sector housing market has been particularly pronounced from 1982 onwards, and demonstrates excess lending by the institutions in the housing finance market so as to enable individuals to fund interest payments on existing borrowing, to repay other borrowings or to maintain consumption levels.

According to Drayson, the reasons behind the recent increase in net cash withdrawals are complex but essentially can be explained as follows. Borrowers may make adjustments either when they move house or by extending or increasing their existing loans. Householders may particularly wish to withdraw cash on moving house in order to obtain consumption benefits from the gains achieved during the period of high inflation in the 1970s. However, householders do not move house that frequently and even when they do, credit rationing may restrict their ability to make adjustments. The gains from high inflation in terms of borrowers' lower gearing ratios may enable net cash withdrawals to be made by borrowers not moving house.

Householders who desire to effect home improvements or acquire other assets or services may simply increase the debt secured on their present property so as to restore gearing to the desired level. As long as such loans are secured against the value of the borrower's property there are no restrictions on the purposes to which such loans are put.

Table 7.2 Estimates of Net Cash Withdrawal from the Private-Sector Housing Market

	Net new loans for house purchase	Value of new private-sector dwellings completed	Value of dwellings purchased from public sector (gross)	Value of private-sector slum clearance etc (net)	Value of improvements to private-sector dwelling stock	Government capital grants to the private sector for housing purposes[a]	Net private-sector expenditure on housing (columns 2 + 3 − 4 + 5 − 6)	Net cash withdrawal (column 1 − column 7)
	1	2	3	4	5	6	7	8
1963	570	560	10	80	100	10	570	—
1964	750	740	10	80	100	20	750	—
1965	700	800	10	90	140	20	840	−140
1966	720	820	10	120	150	20	850	−130
1967	980	850	10	130	200	20	910	70
1968	1,020	990	20	150	270	20	1,120	−100
1969	840	890	20	160	290	20	1,030	−190
1970	1,250	890	20	160	280	20	1,010	240
1971	1,830	1,120	60	200	410	40	1,350	480
1972	2,780	1,410	250	250	470	80	1,800	980
1973	2,830	1,880	240	320	710	150	2,370	460
1974	2,420	1,680	40	290	710	190	1,940	480
1975	3,630	2,020	20	380	940	150	2,460	1,170
1976	3,870	2,210	40	300	1,110	430	2,640	1,230
1977	4,250	2,380	100	300	1,230	580	2,830	1,420
1978	5,410	2,890	260	230	1,380	730	3,570	1,840
1979	6,460	3,400	420	290	2,080	690	4,920	1,540
1980	7,330	3,860	870	240	2,750	800	6,450	880
1981	9,490	3,680	1,130	250	3,300	730	7,130	2,360
1982	14,150	3,730	2,140	180	3,840	1,090	8,430	5,720
1983	14,410	4,780	1,730	90	4,130	1,870	8,680	5,740
1984	16,570	5,540	1,440	100	4,650	2,170	9,360	7,210

Source: Drayson, S.J. (1985) 'The housing finance market: recent growth in perspective', BEQB, March.
Note: (a) Consists principally of local authority home-improvement grants and the housing corporation grant.

The new Building Societies' Act will relax the restriction on unsecured lending, as has been seen in Chapter 6, with consequent implications for future levels of such borrowing.

Even if non-housing borrowing from societies does not qualify for mortgage interest relief (MIR), it is still an attractive source of credit since the gross interest rate is generally below that on alternative sources, and payments may be spread over perhaps twenty years, so reducing monthly outlays. The effective benefit may be seen when the interest rates of building society annuity mortgages, net of tax, are compared with other forms of borrowing. For example, at prevailing interest rates which give rise to an average clearing bank overdraft rate of 17%, and an average personal loan rate of 22.5%, the gross cost of a building society annuity mortgage could be about 15% and the net of tax rate 10.8%. At these levels of interest, credit-card interest rates would be about 27% per annum![1]

There is, therefore, a great incentive for individuals to borrow by means of extending or increasing their mortgage. Given the nature of competition in the market, it is reasonable for the providers of such funds to acquiesce in the wishes of their customers, so that a significant proportion of non-housing-related further advances receive tax relief on the related interest. Whilst this tendency is beneficial to the borrower, it does represent an increasing cost to the nation generally (see Table 7.3) since such tax relief has risen at a rate well above the general level of inflation, representing 3.1% of government revenue in 1978/79 but rising to 4.9% in 1985/86.

Table 7.3   The Cost of Mortgage Interest Relief

Year	£m	% change
1978/79	1,258	—
1979/80	1,450	15.3
1980/81	1,960	35.2
1981/82	2,050	4.6
1982/83	2,150	4.9
1983/84	2,750	27.9
1984/85	3,500	27.3
1985/86	4,750	35.7

Source: Hansard, 31st October 1984, 27th March 1986.

Although higher rate taxpayers do benefit disproportionately from MIR – some 600,000 in 1985 (Johnson 1985) – it could be argued that MIR at the basic tax rate should be maintained if only to preserve fiscal neutrality with business borrowers. However, an asymmetry would remain in that income from business equipment is taxed but imputed income from housing is not. In respect of other consumer credit, it is difficult to provide an economic case for discrimination in favour of borrowing for housing finance. Indeed, prior to 1975, except for the period 1968 to 1971, all personal interest qualified for tax relief. Extending MIR to other borrowing could remove distortions in the market for borrowing by individuals and abolition of the £30,000 ceiling could remove distortions at the lower end of the market caused by a bidding-up of the cost of cheaper dwellings and could be beneficial to first-time buyers. The government, however, seems set on a path of removing the distortion between different types of personal sector borrowing by gradually reducing the real level of MIR benefits (by maintaining the qualification ceiling of £30,000 for mortgages constant in nominal terms in the face of rising prices).

Changes in the nature of MIR can have profound effects upon the balance of mortgage lending. As may be seen from Table 7.4, up to 1982 the share of building society lending taken by annuity mortgages (that is where the capital is repaid in instalments over the life of the loan) was increasingly strengthened such that the societies accounted for approaching three-quarters of loans. However, the

Table 7.4 Building Societies: Types of Mortgage Loans (%)

	Annuity	Endowment	Combination/ Other	Total
1978	67.0	25.0	8.0	100
1979	63.8	26.7	9.5	100
1980	68.6	22.9	8.6	100
1981	74.1	19.6	6.3	100
1982	73.2	19.8	7.0	100
1983	40.7	54.5	4.8	100
1984	38.5	60.2	1.3	100
1985 Q3	42.0	57.0	1.0	100

Source: BSA Bulletin, various issues, derived from BSA or DoE 5% sample survey of building society mortgage completions.

introduction of mortgage interest relief at source (MIRAS) made endowment mortgages (that is, where the capital is repaid at the end of the loan period on the maturity of a life insurance policy taken out at the time of purchase) relatively more attractive and a substantial shift in the relative shares of each type of mortgage is observed from 1983 onwards. In 1985 it appears that the relative shares may be moving in the opposite direction once more. It is noticeable that a number of insurance companies have recently been stressing the advantage of endowment mortgages in their advertising campaigns as a means of improving market share, particularly the Prudential Assurance Group and Abbey Life.

7.3 Suppliers of Housing Finance and Consumer Credit

The discussion in this section begins with an analysis of the general trends in the level of housing finance and consumer credit and the market shares of the suppliers. The second part addresses the behaviour of the main institutions supplying housing finance – the banks and the building societies.

(i) *General Trends*

General trends in the extent and shares of house finance lending and consumer borrowing can be measured either in terms of net advances or balances outstanding, as may be seen in Tables 7.5 and 7.6. Since 1973, the amount of funds advanced for house purchase has increased fourfold, in current price terms.

The building societies are seen to have increasingly dominated the market until 1978 when the banks made vigorous efforts to strengthen their share of the market. The banks' share of net advances peaked in 1982 at 35.9 per cent, with a subsequent retrenchment in 1983 and 1984 and a 'return' in 1985.

Balances outstanding of the Insurance Companies and Pension Funds show an unbroken downward trend over the period shown in Table 7.5. Even on current price terms, their net advances in 1985 were about two-thirds of their level in 1973. Lending behaviour by local authorities and other public-sector sources provides a very small, fluctuating but generally declining share of the market.

The relative share of the consumer credit market (Table 7.6) held

Table 7.5 Shares of the Housing Finance Market (%)

(i) *Net advances*

Year	Building societies	Local authorities	Insurance companies and pension funds	Banks and TSB	Other public sector	Total (%)	Total (£m)
1973	69.1	12.2	6.3	10.7	1.7	100.0	2,893
1974	61.1	22.8	7.7	3.7	4.7	100.0	2,439
1975	74.2	16.6	4.0	1.6	3.6	100.0	3,730
1976	92.1	1.7	2.6	2.0	1.6	100.0	3,928
1977	94.0	0.1	2.7	2.8	0.4	100.0	4,362
1978	94.1	(0.8)	1.4	5.0	0.3	100.0	5,437
1979	81.5	4.5	3.6	9.2	1.2	100.0	6,468
1980	77.1	6.1	4.8	8.0	4.0	100.0	7,423
1981	65.6	2.8	2.8	25.3	3.6	100.0	9,671
1982	57.6	3.9	0.1	35.9	2.5	100.0	14,151
1983	75.5	(2.1)	1.1	24.8	0.7	100.0	14,482
1984	86.7	(1.3)	1.3	13.8	(0.5)	100.0	16,815
1985	77.8	(2.6)	0.6	22.2	2.0	100.0	18,416

(ii) *Balances outstanding*

Year	Building societies	Local authorities	Insurance companies and pension funds	Banks and TSB	Other public sector	Total (%)	Total (£m)
1973	77.2	8.9	6.9	6.2	0.8	100.0	18,956
1974	75.4	10.6	6.9	5.8	1.3	100.0	21,373
1975	75.5	11.5	6.1	5.2	1.7	100.0	25,002
1976	78.0	10.2	5.4	4.8	1.6	100.0	28,856
1977	80.3	8.9	4.8	4.6	1.4	100.0	33,126
1978	82.3	7.5	4.2	4.7	1.3	100.0	38,533
1979	82.2	7.1	4.1	5.3	1.3	100.0	45,001
1980	81.6	7.0	4.0	5.7	1.7	100.0	52,424
1981	79.0	6.3	3.6	9.1	2.0	100.0	62,095
1982	75.0	5.9	2.9	14.1	2.1	100.0	76,246
1983	75.2	4.6	2.6	15.7	1.9	100.0	90,728
1984	76.6	3.6	2.4	16.0	1.4	100.0	108,013
1985	76.5	2.9	2.1	16.5	2.0	100.0	126,843

Source: *Financial Statistics* (Various issues).

by the banks contrasts markedly with their position in housing finance. In a market which has grown two-and-a-half times over the last five years, the banks increased their share to 55 per cent of net advances and 85 per cent of balances outstanding. Credit-card lending accounted for some £850m of net transactions in 1985, being 28 per cent of bank lending and 22 per cent of all consumer credit.

Banks' hold over consumer credit lending results partly from the restrictions upon the building societies which prevent them engaging in unsecured lending. As seen in the previous section, the building societies have competed with the banks by permitting over-financing of houses. The changes contained in the new Building Societies Act, as shown in Chapter 6, will significantly deregulate their lending

Table 7.6   Consumer Credit: Shares by Institutions

(i) *Amounts outstanding*

	Banks[1]	Finance companies	Insurance companies	Retailers	Total	
	(%)	(%)	(%)	(%)	(%)	(£m)
1976	na	na	na	na	na	na
1977	na	na	na	na	na	na
1978	56.8	23.7	2.9	16.6	100.0	8,497
1979	56.7	25.5	2.3	15.5	100.0	10,656
1980	56.1	28.8	2.0	13.1	100.0	13,148
1981	64.6	21.5	2.1	11.8	100.0	14,124
1982	78.6	8.2	2.0	11.2	100.0	16,030
1983	78.2	9.7	1.9	10.2	100.0	18,933
1984	79.0	10.0	1.7	9.3	100.0	22,033
1985	78.2	10.8	11.0[2]		100.0	26,163[2]

(ii) *Net transactions*

	Banks[1]	Finance companies	Insurance companies	Retailers	Total	
	(%)	(%)	(%)	(%)	(%)	(£m)
1976	56.2	14.2	(0.2)	29.8	100.0	473
1977	59.1	24.3	—	16.6	100.0	753
1978	69.1	17.2	0.3	13.4	100.0	1,429
1979	64.6	20.4	0.7	14.3	100.0	1,748
1980	80.3	14.2	1.1	4.4	100.0	1,693
1981	86.6	11.0	1.1	1.3	100.0	2,473
1982	89.5	4.8	0.7	5.0	100.0	2,620
1983	78.7	16.0	1.2	4.1	100.0	3,284
1984	84.0	11.7	0.6	3.7	100.0	3,093
1985	80.0	16.0	4.0[2]		100.0	3,826[2]

Source: *Financial Statistics* (various issues).
Notes: (1) Includes credit-card borrowing.
        (2) Estimates.

powers, although a limit of £5,000 has been made on each unsecured loan.

(ii) *Behaviour of Institutions*

Building Societies   Until the 1980s competition in the housing finance market was heavily influenced by the behaviour of building societies through the Building Societies' Association (BSA) rate cartel. The cartel dates from 1939 and until October 1983 set 'recommended' rates of interest on mortgages and deposits, since which time the rates set have been 'advisory'. The cartel's approach to pricing mortgages and deposits has been to use a variable rate system, reflecting the fluctuating cost of obtaining retail funds. The procedure is as follows.

The starting point was to estimate, in agreement with the government, the desired level of new lending (S_q in Figure 7.1). The level of lending so decided upon was to be financed by mortgage repayments and by shares and deposits attracted from savers. The rate of interest paid to savers (S_{BSA}) was set so as to attract sufficient funds to meet S_q, in the light of rates paid elsewhere, in competing alternatives for the savings of the personal sector. The mortgage rate is then arrived at by adding a margin to cover BSA members'

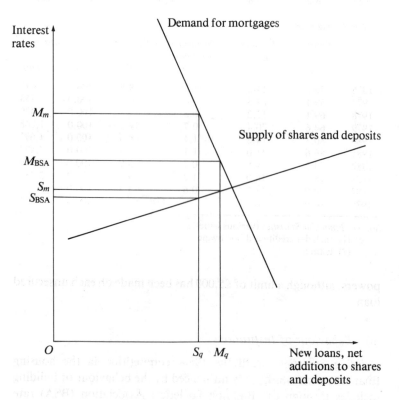

Figure 7.1   The Mortgage Gap

operating expenditures, taxation and an addition to reserves (M_{BSA}).
A mortgage gap (queue) thus occurs, amounting to $M_q - S_q$, being
the extra people who would be willing to borrow at M_{BSA}. In order to
attract sufficient funds to cover this level of lending, societies would
have to pay savers an interest rate of S_m. Hence, the margin of
surplus is seen to be reduced, with a consequent adverse effect on
weaker societies. The alternative of charging M_m for mortgages so as
to clear the market at the present lending level of S_q exists, but was
until recently rejected on the grounds that societies were 'not-for-
profit' institutions. A study by Anderson and Hendry (1984) of
societies' decision-making procedures on loans advanced found
evidence of chronic credit rationing resulting from the views of
management about the level of reserves and surpluses and a relative
lack of emphasis on the movement of other interest rates which had
a direct effect on societies' funding.

Since it was perceived to be important in keeping mortgage
interest rates low and in maintaining equity between borrowers and
savers, the cartel was exempted from the Restrictive Trade Practices
Act 1976, which brought other services within the scope of the anti-
cartel legislation. However, besides the creation of queues already
noted, there are other criticisms of the cartel system (Gough and
Taylor 1979). First, contrary to claims made, it did not produce
lower rates of interest than would otherwise exist. Second, it did not
provide equity between borrowers and savers. Third, it provided no
incentive to improve efficiency. Each of these criticisms requires
some elaboration.

Interest rates may be higher than they otherwise need to be
because of time-lags in their adjustment. For example, in the early
part of 1985, delays in adjustment meant that upward movements in
building society rates coincided with a reduction in the cost of borrowing from the clearing banks. These adjustment lags do raise the
issue of the clarity of signals presented to lenders and borrowers in
the market. Existing lenders and borrowers may not find it worthwhile responding to changes in the rates offered/charged by different institutions because of the costs of adjustments. However, it
is noticeable that a number of institutions have reduced or abolished
their charges for transferring mortgages, so encouraging individuals
to change their source of borrowing.

A lack of equity between borrowers and savers has occurred until
recently as borrowers paid a negative real rate of interest and

benefited also from the capital gain on their house. Lenders, on the other hand, received a negative real rate of interest but no capital gain. Currently the reduction in the level of general inflation coupled with high interest rates means that for the first time for many years, borrowers pay and lenders receive a positive real rate of interest. The operation of the cartel system in the manner shown above served to emphasise the different real rates of return paid/received by borrowers/lenders.

Since the cartel guaranteed a certain margin in the rates charged for lending over those paid to attract funds to the societies, there has generally been no incentive for societies to attempt to reduce operating costs. The cartel system has both enabled the less efficient societies to stay in business and encouraged the more efficient ones to disburse their gains in non-cost-efficient ways. Studies of the existence of economies of scale in building societies (Gough and Taylor 1979; Cooper 1980; Barnes and Dodds 1981; Gough 1982; Gilchrist and Rothwell 1980) have generally found diseconomies at the larger end of the asset spectrum. Societies with larger branch networks have tended to have greater cost ratios (Barnes and Dodds 1983), whilst merger-intensive societies fail to achieve available cost economies (Barnes 1985). From 1975 to 1982 societies' operating expense ratios increased from an average 89p per £100 of mean assets to 130p per £100 of mean assets. (The problem of overbranching has been discussed further in Chapter 6.) Apart from some of the smaller societies, there has been little opportunity for borrowers who do not value non-pecuniary services to exercise their preferred choice.

Over the period since the passing of the Building Societies' Act 1962, a general upward movement in the margin of new mortgages over ordinary share rates of interest can be observed. Throughout the 1960s the average margin was 2.98 per cent, in the 1970s it was 3.51 per cent and in the 1980s the average is 4.7 per cent with the level in 1985 standing at about 5.75 per cent. This tendency to increase mortgage interest rates by a greater amount than ordinary share rates does, however, mask the increasing cost to societies of obtaining retail funds through the proliferation of new types of high-interest-bearing savings accounts.

From October 1983, the strength of the cartel was reduced by the move from recommended to advised rates of interest. Whereas members of the BSA had generally adhered to the recommended rates, it was expected that this would be less so with the advised rates. Initially little difference from the previous regime was observed. However, the changes in the advisory rates made in the late summer of 1984 began to introduce some divergence in the behaviour of societies, but amongst the largest societies price leadership evolved, with follower societies adjusting their rates in the light of those set by competitors so that very quickly the top six societies all offered a mortgage rate in excess of the advised rate. Below this level, a dual market essentially emerged with greater divergence in the behaviour of smaller societies away from the route taken by the larger ones. Although the changes in rates that were introduced occurred more quickly than had generally been the case under the recommended-rate regime, the adjustments in rates did not fully reflect the extent of market interest-rate movements. Similarly, where downward adjustment is required, the continuing need to rely substantially on retail funds for mortgage lending has sustained the absence of full adjustment to market-rate changes and a slowness in response. Hence, overall, the move from recommended to advised rates in itself did not produce substantial changes. Although the Wilson Committee (Wilson 1980), amongst others, had argued for the abandonment of the cartel, it was probably the pressure put on its workings and the side-effects thereof caused by the entry of the banks in a major way into housing finance which provided the major spur for change.

Banks Unlike banks in many other countries, the UK clearing banks had not played a significant role in the housing finance market until the early 1980s. As discussed fully in Chapter 6, one of the major reasons for this late entry was that banks were subjected to quantitative controls on their ability to take deposits and on their freedom to make loans, as part of government monetary policy. With the shift in the 1980s from quantity controls on money to emphasis on the rate of interest, the restrictions on banks were lifted, encouraging them to reassess their attitude towards lending to the personal sector and in particular to housing finance.

The pattern of bank lending on houses has differed from that observed in respect of building societies. For new and secondhand dwellings and for first-time buyers and former owner-occupiers moving, the average bank mortgage is substantially above that for building societies (30 per cent, 39 per cent, 25 per cent and 40 per cent greater respectively in 1985). The tendency has been for banks both to provide larger percentage advances and to lend to the upper end of the market.

After a great surge of lending for housing in 1981 and 1982, the banks effected at least a partial withdrawal from the market in 1983 and 1984, only to be followed by re-entry in late 1984 and 1985. It was at this time also that US banks sought a rapid increase in their market share, providing over one-quarter of bank lending for house purchase in 1984.

The major reasons for the banks slowing down their mortgage lending are as follows. First, the period of rapid lending growth was partly one of adjustment to the new position following a long period where banks had not played a very active part in the market. As banks achieved their target percentages for home mortgages as a proportion of all loans, some slowing down was inevitable. Second, some banks may have felt more inhibited from extending mortgage lending because of pressure on capital ratios. Third, the rapid increase in outstanding bank loans for mortgages meant that capital repayments by existing borrowers depressed *net* new lending for given amounts of *gross* new lending. Fourth, loss of competitiveness by the banks in the market for retail deposits meant that they became net lenders to the personal sector. This deficit position was increasingly funded by relatively expensive short-term wholesale finance and it was prudent to limit this in view of the extent of lending long on mortgages. Fifth, increased demand for credit from industry and commerce meant that some accommodation was required in the form of reduced lending for housing, in order to keep within required liquidity ratios. Sixth, the early surge in bank lending for mortgages had been able to take advantage of their greater speed in making approvals to take customers away from building society mortgage queues. As the queues disappeared, so too did the banks' competitive advantage. Seventh, as building societies responded to the banks' intervention by competing more strongly for business, mortgage rates differentials were pushed down to levels which the banks could not meet with their less competitive structure.

The rapid increase in competition, both between building societies and between societies and the banks, has led to a current position where there are generally considered to be surpluses of funds available for lending and with strong efforts being made by all suppliers to market their services more successfully. As has been shown in Chapter 3, expenditure on advertising by financial institutions has increased rapidly. Moreover, there have been important moves by banks and building societies towards backward vertical integration so as to attract borrowers at earlier stages in the house-purchase process. Of the banks who responded to the NIFS survey of financial institutions, five said they currently had an interest in estate agencies. Lloyds Bank has, for example, through a programme of acquisitions, established the Black Horse Estate Agency network. A further two banks said that they expected to have estate-agency interests by the early 1990s. Building societies have had links with estate agents through agency agreements for a number of years. Three building society respondents to the NIFS survey said they currently had interests in estate agencies. Anticipating the deregulatory effects of the new Building Societies Act, twenty societies (25 per cent of respondents) expected to diversify into estate-agency interests within the next five years. This development by building societies reflects their desire to provide an integrated house-purchase package, which the new Act will make considerably easier except for certain restrictions on their ability to provide conveyancing services.

The breakdown of the BSA cartel and the increasing level of competition in the housing finance market place increasing pressure on both building societies and banks to be more cost efficient. In particular, both institutions are in the process of examining their branch networks, with a view to closing unprofitable outlets and adding value in those which are viable. Building societies are also examining the effectiveness of their agency network. The Abbey National, for example, announced at the end of 1985 that it was terminating the contracts of several hundred of its 3,000 + agency branches and reducing commission rates in certain others.

These developments put pressure on management to act in more commercially aware ways than they may hitherto have been accustomed to. Those which do not respond to the new environmental conditions risk losing their independent existence. Some indication that building society managers are responding to the changing environment is given by the observed reductions in operating expense ratios in 1983 and 1984 (at 126p and 118p per £100 mean assets respectively) after a long period of increases. Part of the threat to societies will come as a continuation of merger activity, part from new entrants into the market, such as US and other overseas financial institutions. Where the management of otherwise potentially attractive building societies is not considered to be of sufficient calibre, either widespread rationalisation may be expected or those wishing to enter the market will seek alternative routes to acquisition of societies. There have been suggestions that US banks have expressed interest in acquiring UK building societies but have been concerned about the quality of management (*Sunday Times*, 14 April, 1985). In such circumstances, some importation of housing finance techniques from other countries may be expected, as will be shown in the next section.

7.4   Alternative Housing Finance Approaches

The familiar way in which people wishing to buy a house obtain funding from a building society, or a bank, is but one way in which, in principle, a house purchase may be financed (Boleat 1984).

In Figure 7.2 five possible routes are shown. The first two options involve those with surplus funds lending directly to those who wish to borrow, either through the family ('grandma') in the personal route, or from the person selling the house. In modern economies these types of finance account for a very small proportion of the house financing market. The contract route is common in France and involves individuals saving for a time at below market rates after which an entitlement to a loan at below market rates is obtained. As the amount of the loan is related to the amount saved, this system is not a very satisfactory means of financing fully the purchase of a house. Under the deposit route, housing finance is provided by the institutions which collect savings, mainly, though not exclusively, from individuals. This is the system prevalent in the UK and features variable mortgage interest rates because deposits too are attracted on this basis. The 'mortgage bank' route usually functions through the use of fixed interest rates. The 'mortgage bank' makes loans to individuals, obtaining its finance by selling mortgage bonds to financial institutions which have collected funds from individuals or companies with surplus financial assets. The financial institutions involved may be either savings or commercial banks or life-insurance companies and pension funds.

The kind of forecasts of increased demand for advances that were

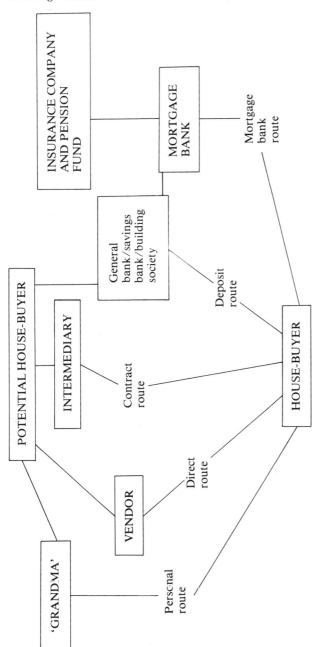

Source: Adapted from Boleat, M. (1984) 'Alternative housing finance systems', *NatWest Bank Review*, August.

Figure 7.2 Routes to Buying a House

shown in Table 7.1 and the fluctuations in cash inflows for different types of institution resulting from interest-rate competition raise the necessity to seek funds from other than the traditional retail sources shown in Chapter 6. Moreover, the nature of mortgage provision is also called into question. Three major developments may be seen to be taking place: the growth of certificates of deposit (CDs); the introduction of secondary mortgage markets; and direct lending to housing finance providers by other financial institutions.

CDs and other wholesale sources of funds involve institutional investors purchasing marketable unsecured securities issued by housing finance institutions. A secondary mortgage market would involve the sale of housing loans to another institution, with the original institution continuing to service the loan. Direct lending to building societies by other financial institutions is currently carried out on a small scale in the UK, but at present building societies have no legal powers to service loans on behalf of others. As they have recently been introduced in the UK and because of their direct parallels with the US, the discussion here will focus upon CDs and secondary mortgage markets.

(i)   *Certificates of Deposit*

CDs have already been issued by banks for some time. Their important introduction by building societies only began after the Finance Act 1983. This Act allowed building societies to pay interest gross of taxation, hence making funds derived from CDs more attractive to institutions such as pension funds.

Initially, the issue of CDs was confined to the larger societies, with Nationwide being the first to issue them. Subsequent legislation has extended the taxation provisions to time deposits, to the smaller societies, and now allows building societies to hold each other's CDs which initially had been prohibited. This last provision was seen as a useful move to enable a secondary market in CDs to develop. From providing £1.039bn of funds in 1984, CDs provided only some £0.717bn in 1985, whereas societies' total wholesale funds increased from £2.23bn to £3.09bn between these two years. Time deposits and negotiable bonds also declined in this period. The major impetus to the building societies' use of wholesale funds occurred in the fourth quarter of 1985 when eight of the largest societies issued floating rate notes (FRNs) on the Eurobond market. The £1.125bn that societies raised in their first quarter in the market suggests a high degree of confidence that this route will provide an increasingly important source of finance. In addition, greater use was made of bank loans, and at the end of 1985 £15m was raised through index-linked bonds.

Apart from its ability to stabilise the level of lending when retail funds inflows are low, wholesale funding has four other advantages which stress their recent increasing use by the providers of housing finance (Phillips 1985). First, judicious timing of their use can enable funds to be raised at a fixed rate in advance of increases in the cost of funds. Second, wholesale funds may be raised for short-term purposes very quickly, thus reducing the lag problem in attracting retail funds following interest-rate changes. Third, although it was initially envisaged that wholesale funds would cost about the same as retail funds in the longer run, experience suggests that wholesale money can be significantly cheaper. Fourth, their use means that marginal funds can be raised without having to increase interest rates on existing deposits. This picture may be expected to continue into the future as increased competition for retail funds both between societies and between societies and banks pushes up interest rates for these funds relative to those for wholesale funds.

(ii) *Secondary Mortgage Market*

The secondary mortgage market is important because it may provide not only an alternative source of new funds for existing players but also a means by which new participants may effect entry.

Essentially, such a market involves the mortgage institution arranging mortgages in the normal way, and then packaging these new loans into amounts of varying sizes which are then sold to an investing institution. The mortgage institution then continues to service the loans for the investor. The secondary mortgage market, therefore, represents a deintegrated approach to the funding of house purchase. Estate agents, for example, have for a long time initiated mortgage business but have not themselves funded the loans. But generally speaking, this has not hitherto been true of the majority of housing finance activity in the UK. The Stow Report of 1979 and, more recently, Boleat (1984) have argued that a secondary mortgage market in Britain would be less efficient than a market where investors purchase CDs and other securities issued by building societies and other providers of housing finance. It might be argued that CDs are less risky than a security backed by a building society mortgage. However, the Bank of Scotland adopted a policy of selling its mortgages in 1984 and Barclays considered such a possibility in 1985. National Home Loans Corporation (NHLC) was formed in 1985 to acquire mortgage loans from various originators, beginning with the Housing Corporation but with intentions to extend its scope to banks, insurance companies and major employers operating staff mortgage schemes.

The USA has a very large secondary mortgage market, which grew from the provision of 8 per cent of housing finance funds in 1970 to 28 per cent in 1982. The mortgage loans market in the USA is illustrated in Table 7.7. The USA equivalent of building societies – savings and loans associations – are seen to originate many more loans than they acquire, and the point is even more true of mortgage banks. 'Mortgage pools', i.e. institutional investors, are seen to be the main purchasers of mortgage loans packages forming the secondary mortgage market. Such a market developed in the USA for three main reasons. First, legislation restricted depository institutions to operating in individual states. A means was therefore required for effecting the transfer of funds from capital-surplus to capital-deficit areas. Second, financial institutions have developed a mismatch between their ability to hold loans and their ability to service (administer) them. Third, and most important, institutional rigidities in the USA financial system meant that savings institutions often had to lend at fixed rates while borrowing at variable ones (see Chapter 5). By the early 1980s the interest cost of savings deposits exceeded the return from lending. Under these conditions, it became attractive for savings institutions to sell loans, since they could earn income not by the difference between lending and borrowing rates for housing finance but rather through fee income derived from originating and servicing loans. Three major governmental organisations have helped stimulate in the USA the secondary mortgage market. These are the Government National Mortgage Association, which provides guaranteed securities backed by mortgages issued by government institutions; the Federal National Mortgage Association, which purchases mortgages for its own portfolio; and the Federal Home Loan Mortgage Corporation, which purchases uninsured loans and then resells them in the form of securities. These agencies, amongst their other roles, provide an

Table 7.7 Mortgage loans in the USA, 1983

Institution	Originations ($m)	(%)	Purchases ($m)	(%)	Sales ($m)	(%)	Net acquisitions ($m)	(%)
Savings associations	81,524	41	32,919	20	50,173	34	64,270	29
Mortgage banks	59,926	30	12,843	7	67,071	45	5,698	4
Commercial banks	42,357	21	3,276	2	13,859	9	31,775	14
Savings banks	10,732	5	2,406	1	2,603	2	10,535	5
Federal agencies	3,180	2	25,347	15	9,646	7	18,881	9
Mortgage pools	—	—	85,949	51	4,044	3	81,905	37
Savings association investment agencies	986	—	5,072	3	—	—	6,057	3
Others	740	—	521	—	719	—	542	—
Total	199,445	100	168,333	100	148,115	100	219,663	100

Source: Boleat, M. (1984) *National Housing Finance Systems: A Comparative Study*, Croom Helm/IUB SSA, Ch.4.

important element of government-backed security for the secondary mortgage market. Since 1981, Savings and Loan Associations were able to make variable rate loans, but these did not become a significant element in mortgage lending until 1984.

A secondary mortgage market may have particular attractions for foreign entrants into the UK housing finance market. Foreign banks may find attractions in holding sterling mortgage assets but may not wish to become involved in servicing (either making or accepting repayments or both) such loans. When the new legislation is passed, building societies will be enabled to undertake servicing functions on behalf of institutions which wish to hold mortgage assets. However, there have been indications that US banks wishing to form links with UK building societies have found unacceptable shortcomings in management calibre. An important development to date has been the announcement in April 1986 by the US-based Salomon Brothers of a scheme which for the first time enables British mortgages to be packaged into securities to be sold to investors in the USA, Japan and Europe. Drawing on its experience in the US secondary mortgage market, Salomon Brothers plans to lend £500m in its first year of operations. Important competitive features of these products are that the mortgages are endowment ones with an interest rate up to $\frac{1}{2}$% below those charged by other suppliers, no arrangement fees, a same-day response to applications and a minimum loan size of £16,000. The use of a direct marketing approach has important cost advantage implications over the more traditional suppliers of housing finance with their substantial investments in extensive branch networks.

There are, however, certain major points which need to be satisfied for a secondary mortgage market to work satisfactorily. We have already noted experience in the US and it would be advantageous if a set of underwriting standards was available which enabled mortgages to be packaged in different ways according to type of property and redemption date. But the major question mark relates to the power to vary interest rates. Essentially, either the originator of the mortgage retains the power to vary rates, or this right is ceded to the purchaser of the loan. Once the originator has sold the loan, it has no incentive to vary interest rates according to market movements. Accordingly, the purchaser may be disadvantaged. If the purchaser gains the right to change interest rates, the borrower will rightly be concerned that the interest rates may be changed in a manner different from that originally anticipated. In the UK, mortgage borrowers have traditionally given lenders the right to vary interest rates, a practice obviously acceptable to borrowers when they know and trust the lending institution. The idea of having interest rates changed at another institution's volition may be less acceptable. A solution to this problem is to initiate loans which carry a rate of interest linked to money market rates (quite probably LIBOR, the London Interbank Offered Rate) free from arbitrary changes by the secondary institution. How often rates are adjusted would need to be clearly established, since money market rates may vary at a frequency unacceptable to borrowers. The Salomon Brothers scheme will involve a floating rate which is set every three months by Salomon after the loans are sold in packages of £100m.

The separation of the mortgage finance provision and servicing businesses represents an interesting new development for financial institutions which may be expected to develop further as the regulatory regime surrounding building societies is relaxed, as US institutions seek entry into the market using familiar techniques, and as traditional mortgage providers continue to feel pressure on their liquidity positions.

7.5 Conclusions

As with many other markets in the financial services sector, that of housing finance is undergoing substantial development. These changes involve the nature of competition between building societies, between building societies and banks and between those more traditional providers of housing finance and new entrants to the market. Moreover, the manner in which housing finance is being and will be provided is changing.

First, there is an increasing trend towards the provision of an integrated house-purchase service. Second, there is a move to the increasing use of wholesale funds to supplement the traditional sources of retail finance. These funds have the advantages of helping to even-out fluctuations in retail inflows and can be less expensive than interest savings accounts. The extent to which building societies will be able to make use of such funds will, however, be circumscribed by the provisions of the new Building Societies Act.

Third, providers of finance for housing through the traditional deposit route are beginning to experience competitive pressure from a secondary mortgage market, being used by foreign institutions to effect entry into housing finance. The nature of the development of housing finance lending in the building societies has until recently produced problems of chronic rationing of funds (Anderson and Hendry 1984), an absence of efficiency improvements resulting from the mergers between societies (Barnes 1983, 1985) and poor choice for investors and borrowers. The developments which are taking place should improve the choice open to investors, reduce if not remove the shortage of mortgage funds, and put pressure on institutions, particularly building societies, to operate efficiently.

Note

1. A recent survey suggests that with wide margins on consumer lending, British banks have the ability to reduce interest rates and offset the low effective cost of mortgage borrowing (*Economist*, 22 March 1986, p. 56). Their reluctance so to do stems partly from their inability to discriminate profitably between consumers, and partly from a lack of complete perception on the part of consumers that the over-financing of house purchase is an available option.

References

Anderson, G.J. and Hendry, D. (1984) 'An econometric model of UK building soceities', *Oxford Bulletin of Economics and Statistics*, Vol. 46, August, pp. 185–210.

Barnes, P.A. (1983) 'The consequences of growth maximisation and expense preference policies of managers: evidence from UK building societies', *Journal of Business Finance and Accounting*, Vol. 10, No. 4, Winter, pp. 521–30.

Barnes, P.A. (1985) 'UK building societies – a study of the gains from merger', *Journal of Business Finance and Accounting*, Vol. 12, No. 1, Spring, pp. 75–92.

Barnes, P.A. and Dodds, J.C. (1981) 'Building society mergers and the size–efficiency relationship – a comment', *Applied Economics*, December, pp. 531–34.

Barnes, P.A. and Dodds, J.C. (1983) 'The structure and performance of the UK building society industry, 1970–1978', *Journal of Business Finance and Accounting*, Spring, Vol. 10, No. 1, pp. 37–56.

Boleat, M. (1984a) 'Alternative housing finance systems', *Nat West Bank Review*, August.

Boleat, M. (1984b) *National Housing Finance Systems: A Comparative Study*, Croom-Helm/IUB SSA.

Cooper, J.C.B. (1980) 'Economics of scale in the UK Building Societies industry', *Investment Analyst*, No. 55, pp. 31–36.

Drayson, S.J. (1985) 'The housing finance market: recent growth in perspective', *Bank of England Quarterly Bulletin*, March, pp. 80–91.

Gilchrist, D. and Rothwell, S. (1980) 'Mergers and medium societies should mean more efficiency', *The Building Societies Gazette*, pp. 20–22.

Gough, T.J. (1982) *The Economics of Building Societies*, Macmillan.

Gough, T.J. and Taylor, T.W. (1979) 'The building societies price cartel, *IEA Hobart Paper*, No. 83.

Johnson, C. (1985) 'Rejig mortgage interest relief', *Lloyds Bank Economic Bulletin*, No. 73, January.

Lever, H. and Edwards, G. (1980) 'How to bank on Britain', *Sunday Times*, 13 January.

Phillips, B. (1985) 'Societies' success in wholesale markets keeps down costs', *Building Societies Gazette*, January, pp. 18–20.

Wilson Committee, '1980 Committee to review the functioning of financial institutions', Cmnd 7937, HMSO.

CHAPTER 8

Personal Investment Markets

R.L. Carter and S.R. Diacon

8.1 Introduction

UK residents can invest their savings in a wide variety of assets. The most important investment for many is the purchase of the family home, with the repayment of a mortgage taking a large part of the annual savings (see Chapter 7). Some invest in their own business enterprises (see Chapter 9), and others prefer to use part of their savings to acquire antiques, gold coins, stamp collections, and similar assets, in part as a hedge against inflation. This chapter is concerned with 'investment' in the financial securities and collective investments shown in Table 8.1.

That table shows a decline in the share of personal wealth placed with deposit-taking institutions (from 41.1 per cent in 1975 to 32.9 per cent in 1984), and placed directly in financial securities (from 23.9 per cent in 1975 to 17.8 per cent in 1984), although the British Telecom share issue in 1984 did reverse the decline in the proportion held in shares. An increasing proportion of gross personal financial wealth (40 per cent in 1984) is held in 'collective investments', some two-thirds of which is equity in insurance and pension funds.

8.2 Choice of Personal Investments

Savers are influenced in making their choices between the different forms of investment by various factors, which may be considered under three headings: reasons for saving; the characteristics of the different forms of investment; and taxation.

Table 8.1 The Distribution of the Gross Financial Wealth of the UK
Personal Sector

	% of gross financial wealth[1]			
	1975	*1978*	*1981*	*1984*
Money (M3)[2]	17.3	14.8	15.1	12.1
National Savings	5.7	5.3	5.5	4.9
Savings bank deposits	2.0	2.1	1.8	—
Building society shares and deposits	16.1	17.1	17.0	15.9
Total: deposit-taking institutions	41.1	39.3	39.4	32.9
Public-sector debt	5.9	4.9	4.6	3.6
UK ordinary and preference shares[3]	16.8	14.0	12.1	13.6
UK debenture and loan stock	1.2	0.8	0.5	0.6
Total: financial securities	23.9	19.7	17.2	17.8
Unit trust and property unit trusts	1.3	1.2	1.0	1.5
Equity in insurance and pension funds	24.8	31.3	34.5	39.9
Total: collective investments	26.1	32.5	35.5	41.4
Others[4]	8.9	8.9	7.9	7.9
Total (£m)	139,892	213,740	333,647	569,850

Source: *Financial Statistics*, November 1985.
Notes: (1) Total assets at 31 December.
      (2) Including notes and coin, and bank deposits.
      (3) Includes shares of investment trust companies.
      (4) Includes members' funds of retail cooperatives; other domestic assets; overseas assets; accruals of taxes, rates and interest; other domestic loans; domestic trade and other credit.

(i) *Reasons for Saving*

How long it will be before savers will plan to convert their savings back into cash, and the risks they are prepared to take in investing them in order to achieve a higher yield, will depend upon the reasons for saving which were discussed in Chapter 1.

When investing short-term savings, the ability to reconvert the

invested funds back into cash speedily and without any risk of
nominal capital loss is a prime consideration, so that bank, building
society and National Savings deposits are normally the first choice
(see Chapter 6). Liquidity is of far less importance for long-term
savings, the saver being more concerned with seeking assets that
offer some protection against the loss of purchasing power, even at
some risk. The three possibilities are: index-linked securities, such
as index-linked National Savings Certificates; fixed interest
securities with an inflation premium built into the nominal interest
rate; and equity-type investments that provide a claim to a real
stream of earnings. During the 1970s and early 1980s long-term fixed
interest rates lagged behind inflation, and there was no guarantee
that an inflation premium built into the interest rate fixed for a
security at inception would be sufficient over the lifetime of the contract. Consequently, the short-term deposit accounts[1] offering near
market rates of interest which have appeared in the last couple of
years may prove in the future to be a better hedge against inflation
than long-term fixed interest investments.

An individual's attitude to risk is partly psychological, and partly
a function of his/her wealth and the reason for saving: the greater
the aversion to risk, the more may the individual be prepared to
trade-off risk against expected yield. This trade-off can be achieved
either by holding some assets with lower but less variable yields, or
by holding a more widely diversified portfolio (but incurring higher
transactions costs).

It may seem worthwhile to expend time and money in searching
for the best terms for the infrequent long-term investment of large
sums. However, as argued in Chapter 2 in relation to shopping and
convenience goods, for the frequent deposit and withdrawal of
small sums, not only may the saver be concerned about liquidity and
the avoidance of significant monetary transactions costs, he may
also value convenience.

(ii)   *The Characteristics of Personal Investments*

Fixed Interest versus Equity Investments   Fixed interest investments can take two principal forms. Firstly, there is the *variable
interest/fixed capital* form where, although the rate of interest
may be varied periodically, the capital sum is guaranteed in money
terms. Examples include bank and building society deposits,

and conventional with-profits life insurance and pension contracts with a guaranteed sum insured to which is added variable bonuses. Secondly, there is the *fixed interest/variable capital* form of investment where a fixed rate of interest is guaranteed until the redemption date of the security when the capital sum falls due for repayment, but during the intervening period the market value of the security will vary inversely to movements in market interest rates: examples are government fixed interest securities and company debenture stocks.

Many National Savings schemes fall between the two. For example, Savings Certificates pay a rate of interest which rises over the lifetime of the certificate. In the case of index-linked Savings Certificates the capital value is maintained in real terms by linking to the Retail Price Index, and a small interest bonus is added annually.

The characteristic of *equity* type investments is that both the value of the capital sum invested and the income derived from it may vary. Examples include ordinary shares, unit trust units, and unit-linked life insurance and pension contracts.

Net Yield Investments differ considerably in the net yield (that is, post-tax income plus capital appreciation/depreciation) which they can generate over their lifetime, and also in the variability of such yields over time.

For many types of investment the net of tax yield in real (i.e. inflation-adjusted) terms can be very difficult to calculate, depending on interest/dividend payments, capital appreciation/depreciation, marginal tax rates, term structure, transactions costs and the rate of inflation. The position is further complicated if the investment takes the form of a regular savings plan (such as some life insurance, and unit trust plans).

Capital appreciation and/or interest income can combine in a number of ways to produce a return on the investment. Fixed interest securities are only partially protected against rises in the price level, while equities offer some possibility of hedging against inflation.

The extent to which taxation can adjust the net of tax yields of different assets is affected by what is known as the asset's fiscal privilege, which determines the extent to which the rate of tax on an asset's yield exceeds the tax that the owner would pay on it if it were added gross to his taxable income. If the degree of fiscal privilege is positive, it means that the real yield is being taxed more lightly than the saver's marginal rate of income tax would lead one to expect. Studies by the Institute of Fiscal Studies (Hills 1984) illustrate the extent to which taxation distorts the net of tax real yield on different financial assets, so that net yields no longer just reflect the degree of risk involved. Over the period 1978–83 life insurance and pension contracts were found to have the highest degree of fiscal privilege, while those assets with the lowest privilege included direct shareholdings, building society deposits and unit trusts.

Liquidity   The liquidity of an asset refers to the ease and speed with which it can be turned into cash without incurring financial penalty.

'Illiquid' assets are those which, if turned into cash at short notice, suffer a fall in expected yield. Premature encashment means that the holder forgoes any future capital gains (net of liquidation costs) and any future increases in real interest income. An extreme case of illiquidity occurs if expected yields on liquidation are negative so that the asset's cash value falls. For long-term assets a crucial factor is the length of time they must be held before their real net market yield exceeds zero. Liquid assets are those which suffer no reduction in expected yields if converted into cash at short notice.

Risk   Risk arises because the future real net of tax yield of almost any type of investment cannot be known in advance with certainty. The only form of investment available to individuals that approaches certainty of yield is index-linked National Savings where the real value of the capital invested is maintained and an additional small annual tax-free interest bonus is guaranteed. All other forms of investment are subject to risk from varying capital value, interest income, future price levels, and changes in future taxation structure and rates.

Since future yields are not known, risk is usually evaluated in relation to an asset's past performance. However, it is not simply the risk from one particular asset that concerns investors holding a portfolio of assets, although the feasibility of so doing is hampered by the transactions costs involved. Unless the returns from the individual assets in the portfolio are perfectly positively correlated, the total collection of assets will be subject to a decreasing level of risk as the number of assets is increased.

(iii) *Taxation*

In choosing a suitable form of investment for their savings, investors should consider both their own personal tax liabilities and the tax treatment of the financial institution involved.

Many savings plans are sold on the basis of 'tax efficiency'. Although income tax relief on life insurance premiums was withdrawn in March 1984, life policies still offer some tax gains, particularly for individuals in the higher tax bands. Also interest paid under some National Savings schemes is tax free; contributions to company superannuation and personal pension plans are fully tax deductible, as are also investments made to provide new finance for companies under the Business Expansion Scheme (see Chapter 9). The Personal Equity Plans proposed in the 1986 Budget will allow individuals to invest up to £200 per month in the shares of British companies quoted on the Stock Exchange with dividends and capital gains being tax-free provided the shares are held for twelve months.

8.3 Fixed Interest versus Equity Investments

If security of capital and liquidity are required, then interest-bearing deposits will best fulfil the saver's needs. Those looking for a fixed income could choose one of the long-dated British government loan stocks, those available through the National Savings Stock Register being particularly suitable for small savers. However, all bear the risk of capital loss should a stock be sold before its redemption date.

The saver who is looking for capital growth must turn to equity investment. Surveys indicate that at most 14 per cent of UK adults hold shares, which is well below the figure for America. Two boosts to share ownership have been the Government's privatisation programme (in particular the British Telecom offer), and an increase in the number of companies providing share option schemes for employees.

The Personal Equity Plans (PEPs) introduced in the 1986 Budget followed policies of a number of other governments in providing tax incentives for personal direct acquisition of shares. In France individuals can each year claim tax relief on an expenditure of up to F.Fr.7,000 for the purchase of shares, which if held for five years can be sold without incurring any tax liability. American taxpayers are allowed to make tax deductible contributions of up to $2,000 per annum in Individual Retirement Schemes which can be invested in shares, with dividends and capital gains accruing free of tax. We can only wait to see whether in Britain PEPs will do much to redress the imbalance between personal and institutional holding of shares. It does seem, however, that institutions will play a major role in the promotion of PEPs and in the selection of share portfolios, not least because there is potential for them to perform a size intermediation function and 'break lots' on large portfolios of shares.

Although the purchase of shares may be somewhat less hazardous for the average saver than starting one's own business, it will always involve a substantial risk of capital loss. That risk can be reduced by portfolio diversification, but because of the relatively high transactions costs (mainly stockbrokers' commissions) involved in the purchase of shares, £20,000 is generally regarded as the very minimum necessary to acquire an adequate spread at reasonable cost. The ending of the Stock Exchange minimum commission scale in October 1986 may lead to the cutting of those costs through the emergence of discount brokers at the retail level, as has happened in America.

The formation of the Unlisted Securities Market in 1980 has made readily available to the public the shares of smaller companies that cannot, or do not wish to, acquire a full Stock Exchange listing. The increases in the prices of some of these shares have been spectacular, but there have been some equally dismal failures.

The riskiest of all investment choices is speculation on the markets for commodities, financial futures, and traded options, even if one has the benefit of expert advice.

8.4   The Role of Collective Investment Schemes

As shown in Table 8.1, investments such as unit trust units, life insurance policies, pension contracts, and investment trust shares, which are alternatively referred to as 'collective' or 'pre-packaged' investments, dominate personal sector financial assets. They enable an individual to participate in equity-type investments while avoiding some of the disadvantages of direct investment by pooling his/her savings with those of others and thereby acquiring an interest in a diversified portfolio of securities or other property. Moreover, the saver can choose amongst the available collective investments to obtain the broad risk/return characteristics desired, whilst leaving the detailed composition and day-to-day management of the fund to professional portfolio managers, and saving on transactions costs. Also, the after-tax return on assets held in a collective fund may be greater than if held individually because of the preferential tax treatment that institutions like life offices and pension funds enjoy, though PEPs (even if handled by an institution in a package-like scheme) should place direct investment on a more equal footing up to the prescribed monthly limit.

All collective investment schemes involve conflicts of interest (the agent/principal problem). These arise because the saver and the fund managers do not necessarily have the same objectives, so that what suits one party may not be the best for the other. This problem occurs both in the management of the fund, and in the behaviour of agents who introduce the saver to the collective. The drawbacks occur particularly when a saver lacks the information and/or expertise to assess the quality of advice he is given by salesmen and the performance of the fund managers. In many cases savers have utilised collective investments precisely because they do not have the time or ability to do it themselves though, as discussed in Chapter 4, changes in technology are reducing those disadvantages. The problem is exacerbated if the complex format of the collective investment makes it difficult to evaluate comparative performance. The types of collective investment schemes are outlined below.

8.5 Unit Trusts

Legally, a unit trust is an open-ended trust fund, divided into units, and administered by a management company which can increase the fund's capital by issuing more units, but also has an obligation to repurchase units from any unitholder who wishes to dispose of all or part of his holding. The fund managers are responsible for day-to-day administration and for managing the investment of the fund, under the aegis of an independent trustee (usually one of the clearing banks or some other major financial institution).

How a Unit Trust Operates

The formation and operation of unit trusts is subject to the control of the Department of Trade and Industry under the Prevention of

Fraud (Investments) Act, 1958, though that will change with the enactment of the Financial Services Bill, as will also the restriction of unit trusts to investing only in securities (mostly ordinary shares, but some trusts specialise in fixed-interest securities). Limits are put on investments in unquoted securities (5 per cent), shares traded on the Unlisted Securities Market (normally 25 per cent), and on investments in any one company.

The charges for administration are set out in each trust deed, but fees are usually 5 per cent on the purchase of new units, plus an annual fee of 0.375 per cent to 1.25 per cent on the value of the fund.

When an investor buys units in a trust he pays an 'offer' price calculated by dividing the value of the existing fund (using Stock Exchange offer prices), plus accrued investment income, dealing expenses and stamp duty, by the number of units issued, and adding the managers' initial charge. Thus the price paid represents the cost of creating new units equal to the value of existing units.

Units are of two basic types. With income units, investment income earned by the fund, less expenses incurred, is available for distribution to the unitholders in proportion to the number of units held, with payments usually made twice a year. With accumulation units the income is reinvested in the unit trust, without an initial management charge being levied, thereby expanding the value of the fund.

Unitholders can sell their units back to the managers at a 'bid' price, calculated like the 'offer' price except that securities are valued at the prices at which they could be sold, less dealing expenses but without a management charge. The bid-offer spread is usually around 6 to 7 per cent. Most unit trusts are valued daily and their prices are published in the newspapers.

Many management groups operate withdrawal plans to provide a regular, fixed income, which involve the sale of units if the income distribution on the units held falls below the fixed amount. The problems arise when units have to be realised at low market prices, so disproportionately reducing the remaining numbers of units qualifying for future income distribution.

Buying and Selling Unit Trusts

Until recently units were sold either directly by the unit trust managers, mainly by means of press advertising, or through intermediaries like banks, accountants, solicitors, stockbrokers, insurance brokers, which may give advice about suitable trusts and their performance, and are remunerated by the payment of commission from the fund managers. The decision by the Prudential in 1985 to sell its unit trusts through its insurance salesforce marked a significant change in practice.

All unit trusts require unitholders to invest a minimum sum ranging from £25 to £2,000 or more, although many fund managers offer regular savings plans with monthly contributions in a few cases as low as £10, giving the advantage of 'pound-cost averaging'.[2] Unitholders wishing to sell all or part of their units need only instruct the fund managers, and normally payment of the sale proceeds will be made within a few days after the return of the registration certificate.

An alternative to investing directly in unit trusts is the purchase of unit-linked life insurances and single premium bonds (see below), and these accounted for one-third of the total value of unit trust funds at the end of 1985.

The Structure of the Unit Trust Market

It was not until after the early 1960s that unit trusts developed rapidly, in terms of both numbers of trusts and sums invested, to become significant competitors for personal savings, as shown in Table 8.2.

Table 8.2   The Growth of the Unit Trust Industry

Year	Number at end of period: Unit trusts	Holdings (millions)	Total funds at end of period (£m)	Sales of units (£m)	Repurchases of units (£m)	Net sales (£m)
1960	51	0.66	201	27	13	13
1963	70	1.05	371	77	18	60
1968	176	2,15	1,482	329	70	258
1978	375	1.95	3,873	530	294	236
1984	766	2.20	15,099	2,920	1,476	1,444
1985	806	2.55	20,307	4,487	1,949	2,538

Source: *Financial Statistics* and the Unit Trust Association.
Note: Unit holdings exclude units allocated to linked life policies which numbered 3.7 million at end 1985.

Although repurchases of units have risen from an annual average of 5.5 per cent of total funds in the 1960s to 9.4 per cent in the 1980s, research conducted for the Unit Trust Association has shown that relatively few unitholders actively trade in units (Corner and Matatko 1984).

In recent years, a third or more of gross sales have been to insurance companies, pension funds, investment trusts, etc., and at the end of 1983 institutions held almost 40 per cent of total unit trust holdings by value.

Most unit trusts are managed by companies forming part of large financial groups, including major banks, life insurance companies and investment groups. Almost all are members of the Unit Trust Association whose rules limit the commissions payable to approved intermediaries. At the end of 1984 the 21 largest management groups, each of which manages several funds with combined funds exceeding £200 million, controlled 78 per cent of the total unit trust funds, though the share of the top six groups has declined.

Types of Unit Trusts

The general trusts seek to provide a balanced mixture of income and capital appreciation for unitholders, but other trusts concentrate on achieving the growth of either income or capital. There are also specialist trusts that limit their investments to certain sectors of the stock market or to particular countries, and thus offer potentially higher rewards to investors but at a far higher risk. In 1985 the first 'managed' or 'fund of funds' trusts were launched, the fund being invested in the range of unit trusts managed by the particular group.

The Investment Performance of Unit Trusts

Any evaluation of the returns to unitholders, both from individual trusts and in comparison with other investment media, is very sensitive to a number of factors, notably the time period under review (as illustrated by the differences in the 1985 and 1986 figures of Table 8.3); movements in security prices and dividends; and for the overseas trusts, foreign exchange rates (e.g. the effect of opposite movements against the pound sterling on the performance of the Australian and Japanese trusts in Table 8.3). Most unitholders treat unit trusts as long-term investments, and Table 8.3 shows that as at

Table 8.3 Percentage Change in the Real Value of an Investment of
£1,000 (offer to bid, income reinvested)

	As at 1 January 1985		As at 1 January 1986	
	Over 5 yrs	Over 10 yrs	Over 5 yrs	Over 10 yrs
Unit trusts				
UK general	87.3	188.4	89.5	105.1
UK growth	78.4	148.7	70.1	99.4
UK equity income	76.6	167.2	105.1	100.6
UK mixed income	64.0	97.9	95.2	58.9
Gilts and fixed income growth	14.5	—	22.9	—
Gilts and fixed income income	7.0	17.2	14.8	16.2
Investment trust units	119.1	189.6	77.5	100.3
Financial and property	79.7	82.4	69.9	88.6
International	79.1	92.5	57.7	58.5
North America	74.8	41.8	53.3	32.1
Europe	38.7	45.3	133.1	114.7
Australia	− 11.6	− 11.4	− 50.3	− 33.2
Japan	166.6	121.0	119.1	378.0
Far Eastern	84.7	112.8	22.3	—
Commodity and energy	3.4	46.8	− 39.6	59.2
Deposits and savings certificates				
Bank deposit	− 5.6	− 41.4	− 2.4	− 30.2
Building society deposit	2.6	− 28.7	6.8	13.6
National Savings certificates	6.4	− 23.1	19.4	25.9
Indices:				
FT Industrual Ordinary	91.1	193.1	107.9	73.0
FT All Share	112.8	333.9	104.0	144.9

Source: Unit Trust Association.
Note: The UK Retail Price (all items) Index was used to deflate the increases in the end of period
  values of the original investment of £1,000.

both January 1985 and 1986 for almost all types of unit trust the
median selling prices of units purchased five or ten years earlier
(with income reinvested) had more than maintained the purchasing
power of an original investment of £1,000. When compared with the
FT indices the median performance of the trusts is less impressive,
though the performance of individual trusts within each of the main
classes varies considerably. For example, in the 12 months to 16
December 1985 the offer price of the top performing UK trust rose
by 92.8 per cent, whereas the worst declined by 5.6 per cent, and
during the same period losses were incurred on all of the Australian

trusts (*Sunday Times*, 29 December 1985). The spread of results over a five-year period is equally wide. Although deposit accounts and Savings Certificates are also shown in Table 8.3, for individual savers net of tax comparisons of those forms of investment *vis-à-vis* unit trusts would be affected significantly by individual circumstances.

Unitholders

A survey in 1984 of 5000 unitholders summarised the profile of the typical unitholder as:

> ... a person rather more than 55 years of age, usually male and often retired, with children who have left home. In general he will not have a high income, especially if in the retirement age bracket. (Corner and Matatko 1984)

Unit trust penetration of the younger age, and higher income groups remains low, though arguably their appeal to both groups is equally small. Investment in unit trusts is a savings instrument appropriate for people who can afford to take some risks, but for whom direct investment in shares (other than investment trust shares) is not attractive.

8.6 Investment Trust Companies

There are some 200 companies recognised by the Inland Revenue as investment trust companies which, like unit trusts, provide for the collective investment of funds subscribed by investors, mainly in the ordinary shares of other companies. Like unit trusts, there are general and specialist investment trusts, but there the similarities end. The differences are:

(1) Investment trusts are public companies with shares which are quoted and traded on the Stock Exchange, and whereas the market prices of unit trusts closely reflect the value of the fund, investment trust shares usually stand at a discount.

(2) They are not 'open funds' in that their share capital is fixed, and their shares cannot be resold to the company.

(3) They can raise additional funds through the issue of preference shares, or by borrowing, thereby gearing-up their capital structure.

(4) They are allowed to advertise only new issues of their shares.
(5) They can invest in the securities of unquoted and unlisted companies, or in land and property.
(6) They do not, when formulating their investment policies, have to provide for the withdrawal of funds by investors.

Buying and Selling Investment Trust Shares

An investor who wishes to acquire shares in an investment trust company can do so either by subscribing to a new issue, or by purchasing shares from existing shareholders. There is no management charge, but both purchases and sales are subject to the normal stock exchange commissions and stamp duty. Savings plans first introduced in 1984 provide for both the reinvestment of dividends through the purchase of additional shares, and the investment of regular monthly contributions of as low as £25. Life insurance and personal pension plans linked to investment trusts are also appearing on the market. The growth of the investments held by investment trusts is shown in Table 8.4.

Table 8.4   Assets of Investment Trust Companies (£m)

Year	Holdings at end of year:	
	UK securities	*Overseas securities*
1960	1,407	563
1963	1,962	878
1968	3,467	2,011
1978	4,163	2,198
1984	7,127	8,124
1985	8,876	8,299

Source: Financial Statistics.

Gearing and Discounts

Most investment trust companies offer the advantages (and disadvantages) of capital gearing, which affects both income and capital values, as can be shown by a simple example. Assume that a trust has been established with an issued share capital of 5 million £1 ordinary shares and £2.5 million 8 per cent debenture stock. Suppose that after 8 years its initial portfolio of investments of £7.5

million doubles in value. However, as shown below, the gearing results in the net asset value (NAV) per share increase by 150%.

	Year 1 (£m)	Year 8 (£m)
Portfolio value	7.5	15.0
Less debenture stock	− 2.5	− 2.5
Assets attributable to ordinary shareholders	5.0	12.5
NAV per share	£ 1	£2.5

There is a similar gearing up of income: assume that the portfolio was invested in equities yielding an unchanged 6 per cent:

	Year 1 (£)	Year 2 (£)
Income from portfolio	450,000	900,000
Less debenture interest @ 8%	200,000	200,000
Gross income attributable to ordinary shareholders	250,000	700,000
Income per share	5p.	14p.

On the other hand, if the value of the portfolio declines, or the rate of gross income falls, the gearing effect works to the disadvantage of the shareholders by accentuating the downward movements.

The market prices of investment trust shares usually stand at less than the share's net asset value for various reasons, such as the possibility that if a trust were liquidated it might not be possible to realise quickly a large portfolio of assets without adversely affecting market prices, and the lack of interest by institutional investors in the shares of those trusts that are not bought and sold in large quantities. The size of the discount, which in the mid-1970s on average exceeded 30 per cent (as against 22 per cent end-March 1986), varies both over time and between trusts, according to such factors as the popularity of different sectors of the stock market; the market's expectations of the future performance of investment trusts; etc.

For the investor, the ability to buy investment trust shares at a discount offers the opportunity for additional reward, not only in terms of its gearing effect on income, but also of capital gain if the discount subsequently narrows. On the other hand, there is the risk that the discount may widen.

The Structure of the Investment Trust Industry

The majority of investment trusts are controlled by management groups that administer several trusts, the management groups themselves being mainly merchant banks and investment companies, and the 21 largest groups account for about half of the total assets.

Individuals account for about 70 per cent of the 450,000 shareholdings, although, like individual shareholdings generally, their share by value has continued to decline from 46 per cent in 1971 to around 30 per cent in 1985. The main shareholders are institutional investors, notably insurance companies and pension funds, but the industry is making efforts to compete for the savings of individuals.

The Performance of Investment Trusts

The prices of investment trust shares are subject to the same sort of influences as unit trusts. Over the five years to end December 1985 the average price of investment trust shares (as measured by the FT-Actuaries Investment Trust index) rose by 168 per cent compared with a 179 per cent rise in the FT-Actuaries All Share index and a 37 per cent increase in UK retail prices; over a ten-year period the comparative figures are 432 per cent, 532 per cent and 157 per cent respectively. Table 8.5 records the average inflation-adjusted performance (with net dividends reinvested at ex-dividend prices). Not only have investors in investment trusts generally been able to secure a real return on their funds over the period concerned, they have also tended to do better than holders of unit trusts, though the figures in Tables 8.3 and 8.5 cannot be compared directly because of the different price bases employed (i.e. offer to bid prices for unit trusts and mid-market to mid-market for investment trusts, so favouring the latter). Like unit trusts, there is a wide spread in the performance of individual trusts even within the same sector.

Table 8.5 Percentage Change in the Real Value of an Investment in
Investment Trusts as at 31 December 1985

Type of investment trust	*Share price total return over:*	
	5 years	*10 years*
Capital and income growth:		
General	107.0	122.6
UK	124.7	179.6
Capital growth:		
General	82.7	144.3
International	100.2	107.7
North America	83.2	103.6
Far East	89.3	117.2
Japan	132.8	144.4
Commodity/energy	− 8.5	34.8
Technology	81.7	115.9
Income growth	131.1	130.9
Smaller companies	91.9	256.5
Special features	101.2	93.5

Source: Association of Investment Trust Companies.
Note: Share price total return is the value of an amount invested at the beginning of
the period, on a mid-market to mid-market basis, assuming that all of the net
dividends received during the period concerned were reinvested in the shares of
the trust at the time the shares were declared ex-dividend.

8.7 Life Insurance Contracts

Life insurance companies provide two basic services: financial protection against the risk of premature death (or, in the case of annuity and pension contracts, unanticipated longevity); and vehicles for personal savings, returning premium contributions with interest (see Chapter 2, p. 31 above). Only term (or temporary) life insurance offers solely the first service; the other life insurance contracts give a mixture of protection and saving in varying proportions.

Life insurance can be used as a form of saving for many purposes, though the long-term, illiquid nature of most life contracts generally only makes them suitable for longer-term savings. They can be used as a means of financing long-term expenditure (e.g. house purchase); providing an inheritance (including provision for tax on capital transfers); and supplementing future income.

Types of Life Insurance Contracts

Life insurance premiums may be paid either in instalments over a number of years (annual premium business), or as a single capital sum (single premium business). Single premium bonds (whether linked or not) generally have relatively short maturity terms of around 3 to 5 years, and include only minimal amounts of life insurance protection. Over the last few years (see Table 8.6) single premium business has increased in importance, with the value of business transacted growing at an annual rate of 40 per cent (1980–84). This trend, particularly in unit-linked contracts, suggests that policyholders are using life insurance increasingly as a tax-efficient method of investing a capital sum and taking advantage of the low marginal tax applying to life office investment income and the 'top-slicing' method of taxing benefits (so that, for example, basic-rate taxpayers obtain their benefits free of income tax).[3]

Benefits may either be fixed at the outset (non-profit policies and guaranteed bonds) or dependent upon the investment performance of the underlying funds (conventional with-profits and unit-linked life policies). The premiums of conventional contracts are placed in a fund and invested as the life office sees fit, normally being spread across a wide portfolio of assets. Under the with-profit policies, bonuses are added to a guaranteed sum at the discretion of the life office's actuary. Premiums of linked contracts are usually used to

Table 8.6 Breakdown of New Individual Life Insurance Written in the UK (£m)

| | Annual premium business | | | Single premium business | |
	Ordinary unlinked	Linked	Industrial (unlinked)	Unlinked	Linked
1974	120	40	73	8	125
1978	244	63	130	74	282
1980	358	142	207	206	325
1982	438	214	226	287	713
1983	830	290	235	200	1,410
1984	685	312	229	290	1,790
1985	570	302	240	145	2,465

Source: Life Insurance in the United Kingdom, Association of British Insurers.

purchase units in a unit trust of the policyholder's choice, often selected from a group of unit trusts managed by a subsidiary of the life office (over 40 life offices now manage unit trusts).

Linked business has risen from 28 per cent of the ordinary life insurance new annual premium income of UK life offices in 1980 to 31 per cent in 1984, and from 61 per cent to 86 per cent of single premium income. This trend signifies a shift in preferences away from low-risk/low-yield contracts towards ones subject to greater risk but higher expected yields and increased liquidity. Also, the individual saver has both some control over the composition of the portfolio and discretion to switch between funds. For further analysis of recent trends, see Diacon (1985) and Diacon and Carter (1984).

Risk/Return Characteristics of Life Contracts

Table 8.7 gives the risk/return characteristics for 10-year with-profits and unit-linked endowment contracts maturing in February 1985, averaged across a number of life offices or linked funds. The total maturity value from a with-profits policy is composed of three factors: a guaranteed sum insured; accumulated reversionary bonuses (which take the form of guaranteed additions to the sum insured once declared); and a terminal bonus, the amount of which depends on the capital value of the life fund at the commencement of the year in which the policy matures. On average, across 62 life offices, the guaranteed sum insured (GSI) makes up 52 per cent of the total maturity value, while the added guaranteed reversionary bonus (RB) brings the share up to 81 per cent.

The ten top performing life offices have typically smaller GSI than average, but only slightly larger reversionary bonuses, so their GSI + RB is around 4 per cent above the average for all offices, while their terminal bonuses are almost double the overall average: it is the non-guaranteed additions that bolster their performance. On the other hand, the poor performers have slightly larger GSI than the average for all offices, but lower reversionary bonuses, so that their GSI + RB is 6.5 per cent below the overall average. Their low terminal bonuses (comprising less than 7 per cent of their total maturity values) downgrade their performance. For the 10 years to February 1985, terminal bonuses accounted for almost 80 per cent of the variation in performance between the 62 life offices examined.

Table 8.7 Risk/Return Characteristics for Life Insurance Contracts

| | *With profits* * *(62 offices)* | | | | *Unit linked* * *(99 funds)* |
	Total maturity value	*GSI*	*RB*	*TB*	*Total maturity value*
Average of top 10 companies (£)	4,998	2,177	1,382	1,439	6,852
Average of bottom 10 companies (£)	3,413	2,240	949	224	3,164
Average of all companies (£)	4,200	2,191	1,220	789	4,981
Standard deviation (£)	519	70	230	456	1,088
Coefficient of variation (%)	12	3	19	58	22

Source: *Planned Savings*, April 1985, United Trade Press Ltd.
Notes: * 10 year endowment policies with benefits payable on 1/2/85 for a male aged
29 years 11 months at outset for a gross premium of £20 per month (including
policy fee).
GSI = Guaranteed sum insured
RB = Reversionary bonus
TB = Terminal bonus

Turning to the unit-linked endowment contracts, these exhibit greater variation in overall performance (with a coefficient of variation of 22 per cent). The top 10 funds outperformed the with-profits policies over the period by 37 per cent (although this feature is largely a consequence of a comparison between the 10 best with-profits *offices* and the top 10 linked individual *funds*). The bottom ten linked funds produced benefits which were 36 per cent below the average for the 99 funds, and only a small part of which would have been guaranteed. In contrast, the worst with-profits policies yielded average benefits of £3,413 which were 19 per cent below the average for the 62 offices, but 93 per cent of which was guaranteed.

Liquidity Characteristics of Life Contracts

Table 8.8 illustrates the liquidity characteristics of with-profits life insurance by comparing the total maturity value paid on a 10-year

Table 8.8 Liquidity Characteristics of Life Insurance Contracts*
             (69 offices)

	Total maturity value after 10 years	*Surrender after 10 years:*	
		15-year policy	*25-year policy*
Average of top 10 companies** (£)	2,180	1,682	1,348
Average of bottom 10 companies** (£)	1,428	1,237	1,052
Average of all companies (£)	1,788	1,406	1,194
Standard deviation (£)	242	212	188
Coefficient of variation (%)	14	15	16

Source: *Planned Savings*, September 1985, United Trade Press Ltd.
Notes: * With-profits endowment policies with benefit payable on 1/7/85 for a male
aged 29 years 11 months at outset for a gross premium of £100 per annum.
** In terms of total maturity value for maturing 10-year endowment.

endowment policy with the surrender values of 15- and 25-year contracts after 10 years. Surrender values are appreciably lower than
the maturity value (for the same premium paid), and decline as the
policy term increases, so that on average, policyholders incur a
penalty of 21 per cent of maturity value by surrendering the 15-year
contract after 10 years (i.e. two-thirds of its maturity term), and of
33 per cent in the case of a 25-year contract (after 40 per cent of its
maturity term). Surrender values for unit-linked contracts are not
reported; they are usually based on the values of the cashed-units (as
indeed are maturity values) so that there would be no appreciable
difference between the three cases discussed above.

8.8 Pensions Contracts

There are three main types of pensions contracts: (i) occupational
(superannuation) pensions schemes; (ii) executive or directors' pensions; and (iii) personal (or self-employed) pensions. As well as

income on retirement, many pension contracts provide a tax-free lump sum on retirement, and widow's and dependants' pensions on death. So long as certain conditions are met, the pension contracts get beneficial taxation treatment including: wholly tax deductible contributions (up to a specific maximum); exemption from corporation and capital gains tax; tax-free lump sum on retirement; and treatment of the pension as earned income for income-tax purposes. Of the three types of pension contracts, superannuation schemes dominate. Contributions are shown in Table 8.9.

Employers paid three-quarters of the total contributions, with the balance paid by employees. There is a considerable diversity of occupational pension schemes, and the performance of such a collective saving is very difficult to evaluate. The Finance Act 1970 lays down maximum benefits (geared to the value of the pensioner's final salary), but many schemes do not provide maximum benefits because of the cost involved for the employer.

Many employers can no longer afford defined benefit schemes, and instead money purchase plans are used to roll-up contributions until retirement date, when the accumulated fund is used to purchase a retirement annuity, so that the pension to be obtained is

Table 8.9 Income and Expenditure of Occupational Pension Schemes, 1983 (£m)

	Employers' contributions	*Employees' contributions*	*Total contributions*
Funded schemes			
Insured schemes	1,687	830	2,517
Self-administered	3,149	728	3,877
Public corporations	1,800	636	2,436
Local authorities	1,031	450	1,481
Total	7,667	2,644	10,311
Notionally funded schemes	1,616	884	2,500
Unfunded schemes Public sector	1,976	224	2,200
Overall total	11,259	3,752	15,011

Source: *Financial Statistics*, April 1985, Table S15.

uncertain. Staff may be able to make additional voluntary contributions, the most common being executive pension plans.

Pension schemes for senior executives provide them with increased pensions, but have a number of other advantages. In particular, they are a tax-efficient alternative to a pay rise; they are more portable; loan facilities on an interest-only basis are normally available; they can be used to reduce corporation tax liability; and the built-up funds can be part invested in the company's business.

Personal (or Self-Employed) Pensions

Personal pension plans are mainly available for self-employed persons, but may also be purchased by those in receipt of non-pensionable income, and those not contracted out of the upper tier of the state pension scheme (i.e. SERPS – the State Earnings-Related Pension Scheme). Changes to the social security system to be introduced in 1988 will allow every employee to take a personal pension, whether or not his employer runs an occupational scheme (*Reform of Social Security*, Cmnd. 9691, 1985). It would seem that only around one-third of those entitled to buy a personal pension actually do so, and of those that do, many do not pay anywhere near the maximum level of 17.5 per cent of net relevant earnings per annum.

Table 8.10   Breakdown of New Personal Pensions Business Written in the UK (£m)

	Annual premium business		Single premium business	
	Unlinked	*Linked*	*Unlinked*	*Linked*
1978	60	23	57	9
1980	61	30	83	13
1982	98	65	174	57
1983	108	73	230	71
1984	173	128	314	106
1985	245	199	391	139

Source: News (Quarterly figures on new life insurance published by Association of British Insurers).

Personal pensions have been growing rapidly, at 35 per cent p.a. for annual premium business 1980—84, and 45 per cent p.a. for single premiums (see Table 8.10). Again the growth has been strongest in unit-linked business.

Until the early 1980s, contributions to personal pension plans were locked up until retirement. Most life offices now offer a loan-back facility so that savers can borrow against the lump sum to be received at retirement either from the insurance company itself or from an outside agency such as a bank.

In the analysis of the performance of 35 with-profit contracts, the average pensioner had an accumulated cash fund of £5,535 from a 10-year personal pension contract (with annual premiums of £240) (see Table 8.11). This was 32 per cent greater than the corresponding amount for the average 10-year with-profit endowment shown in Table 8.7 (with the difference even greater if the endowment had been purchased by a 55-year-old person). A comparison between with-profits and unit-linked contracts shows that over the 10 years to 1985, linked contracts produced the better performance on average, but with much greater variation.

Table 8.11   Risk/Return Characteristics of Personal Pension Contracts*

	Accumulated cash fund	
	With-profits (35 offices)	*Unit-linked (49 funds)*
Average of top 10 companies (£)	6,520	8,204
Average of bottom 10 companies (£)	4,718	4,160
Average of all companies (£)	5,535	5,896
Standard deviation (£)	765	1,488
Coefficient of variation (%)	14	25

Source: *Planned Savings*, November 1985, United Trade Press Ltd.
Note: * Accumulated cash fund available on retirement for man aged 65 on 1/9/85 from 10-year personal pension contract effected in 1975 for £240 p.a.

8.9   The Investment of Life Insurance and Pension Funds

Life insurance and insured pension business can only be transacted by companies authorised by the Department of Trade and Industry to conduct such business in the United Kingdom. At the end of 1984, of the 290 companies so authorised, 218 were specialist life offices and 72 composite companies writing both life- and non-life insurance business. At the end of 1983, the five largest UK life offices controlled around 35 per cent of the total world-wide long-term premium income of British insurance companies, and the largest ten accounted for 51 per cent.

Occupational pension schemes can also be provided by approved exempt Superannuation Funds: in 1984 there were 99 such funds operated for the employees of local authorities, 31 for other public-sector employees, and 4,216 for private-sector employees. The local authority and other public-sector schemes are dominated by large funds; and the private sector too has very large funds, with the top 35 controlling 46 per cent of total assets, leaving the smallest 4,000 funds with only 19 per cent of the total assets.

The investment activities of these funds obviously affect the quality of the savings contracts that they offer. In a wider perspective too, the investment activities of the fund will impinge on the well-being of their contract-holders.

The major objective of fund managers must be to serve the best interests of their clients − as they perceive them. By delegating the responsibility for investing his savings to an agent (i.e. fund manager), the principal (i.e. policyholder or pensioner) creates a potential conflict of interest arising from their different objectives. Even if the principal's objectives could be conveyed to the fund manager, it may not be possible to construct a system of incentives which could guarantee that these objectives would be fulfilled. For these reasons savers may wish to undertake their own investment or may prefer to manage their businesses directly.

In practice, the objectives of individual savers and of fund managers may differ in a number of respects. First, they may have different interpretations of the legal responsibilities of the fund managers. Life offices are required to satisfy the 'reasonable expectations' of with-profits policyholders. Pension trustees must act in the 'best interests' of their beneficiaries. Following the judgment in the dispute between the National Union of Mineworkers and the other trustees of the National Coal Board Pension Fund (April 1984), these 'best interests' must be construed as 'best financial interests' and,

> In the case of a power of investment, as in the present case, the power must be exercised so as to yield the best return for the beneficiaries, judged in relation to the risks of the investments in question. (Sir Robert Megarry)

The NUM's investment strategy had taken a broader interpretation of 'best interests' and had wanted to restrict the fund's assets to UK ones only – particularly to those sectors which, in the Union's view, would help to revive the economy. This judgment has clear implications for the common criticism that life insurance and pension funds have failed to favour the interests of the manufacturing sector and of small firms.

Secondly, fund managers and their clients may have differing risk/return trade-offs. Such problems seem best solved by agreeing a 'risk profile' with the contract-holders, as is done with equity-type contracts with holders of unit-linked policies choosing the type of trust in which they want to invest. Universal life policies, as developed in the US, allow flexibility in a large number of dimensions.

Third, there may be differences in the respective time horizons. Most life and pension contracts represent comparatively long-term liabilities for the fund, and so should be matched by similarly long-term investments. Increasingly, the investment performance of fund managers is being assessed over comparatively short time horizons both by financial journalists and commentators, and by the clients themselves. This 'short-termism' encourages fund managers to compete in terms of quarter-to-quarter performance, even though they are charged with looking after the principal's own interests. There can be no assurance that a favourable past performance even over a number of years will be projected into the future.

Finally, there are issues of the use of inside information, which are addressed in the new regulatory framework.

8.10 The Regulation of Personal Investment Markets

An important element in the regulation of investment markets, as discussed in Chapter 2, is the need to protect investors. It covers such matters as the security of funds placed with institutions; the information given to consumers regarding the terms, risks and prospective rewards offered for savings and loans; and an institution's relationship with, and the rewards offered to, salesmen. Also, there is a need to deal with potential conflicts of interest, such as the agent/principal problem in connection with collective investment schemes mentioned earlier.

Some of those issues in connection with the operations of the main types of institutions involved in the UK's personal investment markets, particularly matters of financial security, are already the subject of supervision by government agencies or self-regulatory bodies under the provisions of such statutes as the Banking, Building Societies and Insurance Companies Acts. Additionally, the following three major regulatory developments are both affecting market organisation and competitive behaviour and extending the protection afforded to investors:

(1) the changes being made to the self-regulatory rules of the Stock Exchange, following a 1983 agreement with the government which in return had withdrawn a reference of the Exchange's rules to the Restrictive Practices Court;
(2) the major changes to the law on the protection of investors proposed in the Financial Services Bill; and
(3) the provisions of the Building Societies Act, discussed in Chapter 7.

The Stock Exchange Deregulation

The main agreed changes to the Stock Exchange's rules provide for:

(a) the introduction of a new competing market system of dealing under which member firms will be able to act in a dual capacity as both brokers and jobbers;
(b) the ending of the minimum commission scale for brokers;
(c) the ownership of Stock Exchange firms by non-member firms; and
(d) the creation of a new gilt-edged market requiring three new, substantially capitalised, categories of member firms – market makers, inter-dealer brokers and money brokers.

Already both British and foreign banks, insurance companies and other financial institutions have acquired interests in stockbroking and jobbing firms, in some cases bringing both together into the same group, and discount broking has appeared in the wholesale market. The potential consequences of the full implementation of all of the ownership and operational changes in October 1986 are such as to have earned the epithet 'the Big Bang'. Whether it will lead to the widespread appearance of retail discount brokers that could substantially cut the costs for individuals of dealing in the stock market remains to be seen.

The Financial Services Bill

The Bill embodies most of the recommendations of the White Paper *Financial Services in the United Kingdom* (Cmnd. 9432), its aim being to institute a system of regulation that:

(a) provides for the consistent treatment of different forms of investment by basing regulation on definitions of 'investments' and 'investment business' (see Chapter 10, p.260 for definitions);

(b) will be the minimum necessary to protect investors, in order to avoid heavy monitoring and enforcement costs, and inhibiting the development of new financial services and products; and

(c) will build upon what is best in self-regulation.

At the time of writing, the Bill is in the Committee stage in Parliament so that important changes may still be made. However, the Government is not willing to concede the principle of self-regulation, and a Securities and Investments Board (SIB) and a Marketing of Investments Board Organising Committee (MIBOC) set up by the Government are establishing the organisational arrangements and the drafting of the detailed rules. The details outlined below reflect the latest proposals as at the end of April 1986 as they affect personal investment markets, other than the taking of deposits.

The System of Self-Regulation

The Bill provides for the government to transfer most of its powers to a Regulatory Agency, which is to be SIB following the combining of the roles of SIB and MIBOC into one Board. The Board's rules and regulations will have to reflect the following basic principles set out in Schedule 6 of the Bill:

(1) The promotion of high standards of integrity and fair dealing in the conduct of investment business, requiring an authorised person to act with due skill, care and diligence, to subordinate his own interests to those of clients, and to pay regard to the circumstances of his clients and to act fairly between them.

(2) The disclosure by authorised persons of interests in, and facts material to, any transaction, and of the capacity in which, and the terms on which, they enter into the transaction.

(3) Provision will have to be made for the protection of clients' property and for the keeping of proper records.

The Board will be empowered to recognise self-regulatory organisations (SROs) set up by persons and firms undertaking certain aspects of investment business. Those SROs will have to have rules and authorisation procedures at least equivalent to those of the Board, and each SRO will regulate only certain investment activities. It seems that there will be six SROs.

Authorisation to Conduct Investment Business

Only authorised persons (including corporate bodies and partnerships) will be allowed to engage in 'investment business'.

The Board will have powers to recognise Investment Exchanges (e.g. the Stock Exchange and the UK Commodity, Financial Futures and Options Exchanges) and Clearing Houses that meet the requirements set out in Schedule 3 of the Bill. However, the members of such bodies will have to be separately authorised.

Apart from the above, there will be seven possible ways in which persons and firms can be authorised. Besides authorisation under the Insurance Companies and the Friendly Societies Acts, and by other EEC member states, the main methods will be direct authorisation by the Board, or by being a member of either a professional body (in the case of professional firms that undertake only a limited amount of investment business) or an SRO recognised by the Board. Firms (including parent companies and their subsidiaries) carrying on more than one type of investment business may, therefore, need to be authorised by the Board or seek membership of more than one SRO. All applicants will have to show that they are 'fit and proper persons' to carry on the type of investment business proposed, which will cover such matters as: the expertise and experience of a firm's controllers, directors and key staff; and compliance with specified minimum capital requirements, including liquid capital resources.

Protection for Investors

The Bill contains various provisions designed to protect investors dealing with authorised persons. First, authorised persons will have to comply with 'conduct of business' rules laid down by the Board, or the SRO, covering those matters set out in Schedule 6 of the Bill (see above). However, the Board intends that there will be some relaxation of the rules when authorised persons are dealing with professional investors who engage in such investment transactions in the course of their normal business. Secondly, clients' money will have to be held in trust. Thirdly, investment businesses will be required to produce regular reports on their activities, including the firm's financial status, which will be monitored. Fourthly, schemes will be arranged to compensate the clients of a firm which cannot meet its obligations. Fifthly, the Board will set up an Ombudsman scheme to deal with investors' complaints.

Collective Investment Schemes

The Prevention of Fraud (Investments) Act, 1958 will be repealed, and unit trusts and the proposed open-ended investment companies will be regulated under the provisions of the new Financial Services Act. Authorised persons will be prohibited from promoting collective investment schemes which are not approved other than to another authorised person or someone whose ordinary business involves the acquisition and disposal of the same kind of property.

Domestic unit trusts will continue to be authorised by the Department of Trade and Industry, but they will be given the same freedom of investment as insurance companies.

Collective investment schemes authorised in another European Community member state will be approved for promotion to the public, as will other overseas schemes, provided that at home they are subject to regulation equivalent to that of the UK.

The Marketing of Investments

The Bill prohibits the making of unsolicited calls for doing investment business, and persons who do so will be unable to enforce any resulting contract. Three exemptions from this provision are:

  (i)   calls on professional investors;
 (ii)   calls made on a person with whom the caller has a written agreement that contemplates such calls; and
 (iii) calls for the sale of life insurance products and unit trusts, both of which will be subject to 'cooling-off' regulations giving the client 14 days to reconsider his decision.

The marketing of life insurance and unit trusts will be subject to a number of other important provisions. Only independent intermediaries who act as impartial advisers to their clients, and the representatives of particular companies, will be allowed to advise on or sell such investment products.

Independent intermediaries will have to take reasonable steps to provide the best possible investment advice to their clients, and if they recommend the products of just a few companies, they must have examined other companies' products and found them less satisfactory. Also, there will be regulations regarding the disclosure to clients of the commission receivable for selling a life policy or unit trust. An independent intermediary that deals with only a particular type of investment product (e.g. a building society that arranges only mortgage-related life policies) will have to make it clear to clients that his range of advice is limited.

A company representative will be responsible only for recommending the best product offered by his company: he will not be allowed to offer the products of other companies, and he must make his status clear. Companies will be responsible for the actions of their representatives, and although there will be no obligation to disclose commissions, the sales incentives paid by companies to their employees will be monitored by the Board to ensure that they are not excessive compared with those paid to independent intermediaries.

Investors will have to be given all the material facts about a recommended life insurance or unit trust before making a decision. The information will have to be readily understandable, manageable in quantity, relevant, either factual or based on realistic assumptions (e.g. projections of with-profit life insurance bonus rates) and, in the case of life policies, state the amount receivable in the event of early surrender. Companies and individuals will have to keep records showing that an adviser had full knowledge of a client's circumstances, and recommended what was best for the client.

A proposal to introduce a system of licensing for all life insurance and unit trust salesmen, whether working for an authorised independent intermediary or company, was abandoned by the government after opposition from both within the industry and from consumer bodies who viewed it as expensive and probably ineffective.

Remaining Issues

There remain many points of detail to be resolved. It is not clear, for example, what will be the position of either occasional 'introducers' of business to life offices or unit trusts, or of employees of financial conglomerates who might refer a client to another part of the group.

The Board would like to see an industry agreement on the maximum level of commissions payable for the different types of life insurance product, though it recognises that such an agreement alone will not eliminate the possibility of a salesman being biased between products carrying different commissions.

Debate also continues regarding the organisation of the bodies that will be recognised as SROs, and their rules. Finally, there is concern regarding the staffing of the Board and the SROs. The success of the self-regulatory system will depend upon those bodies being able to attract a sufficient number of experienced, competent officials capable of monitoring the activities of all of the firms undertaking investment business.

Notes

1. See p.145 above.
2. That is, the average cost of the units purchased will be less than their average prices at the dates of purchase.
3. See Diacon and Carter (1984), pp.114–115.

References

Corner, D.C. and Matatko, J. (1984) *Unitholder Survey 1984*, Unit Trust Association.

Diacon, S.R. (1985) *The UK Insurance Industry: Structure, Development and Market Prospects to 1990*, Staniland Hall Associates.

Diacon, S.R. and Carter, R.L. (1984) *Success in Insurance*, John Murray.

Hills, J. (1984) *Savings and Fiscal Privilege*, Institute for Fiscal Studies.

HMSO (1985) *Financial Services in the United Kingdom. A New Framework for Investor Protection*, Cmnd. 9432.

HMSO (1985) *The Financial Services Bill 1985*.

CHAPTER 9

Entrepreneurial Finance for Small Business

M.R. Binks and J. Coyne

9.1 Introduction

The recent emphasis upon entrepreneurship and new enterprise in the UK has grown alongside rapid changes in the provision of and demand for financial services. In this chapter we investigate two major issues: the problem and factors involved in direct investment by individuals in small business; and the availabilities of capital to individuals wishing to start their own small business. Our main focus is on equity provision and we shall argue that though there have been dramatic changes in the channelling of investments into smaller higher-risk enterprises, there may still be a shortage of equity at a critical point in the development of new firms. While this 'equity gap' due to information asymmetries is demonstrable, it continues to constitute a potentially serious but unquantifiable barrier to employment creation and/or economic development in new firms.

First, we turn to an examination of aspects of personal direct investment in small enterprises.

9.2 Personal Investment in Small Business

A British Market Research survey conducted in March 1983 (BMRB 1983) showed that only 7 per cent of the UK adult population directly owned equities in companies of any kind. Recent research conducted on behalf of the Treasury has suggested that the proportion has risen to 14 per cent, or six million individuals, by 1986 (Treasury 1986), but it appears that the calculation may include a substantial element of double counting and that the true proportion is closer to the 7 per cent level (*Economist*, 10 May 1986, p. 79).

A very small fraction of these holdings will be in small unquoted companies. Individuals will consider an investment in a small company or a new company in exactly the same way as any other investment which they may wish to make. There are three broad principles with which they will be concerned; namely the three R's – RISK – RETURN – RECOVERY. That is to say, they will be concerned with the risk which is inherent in the investment, the rate of return which they will receive along with its timing, and the ease with which they can recover their capital should they require access to the funds involved. Each of these can be examined in a little more detail with respect to investments in new and small companies and in comparison with other forms of investment.

(a)   The Risk

The risk associated with new enterprise will generally be quite high. It is an investment in a relatively unknown quantity; a previously untried combination of product, process and management. It is an exercise in backing judgment – that of the investor in assessing competing projects and that of the business man whose venture is being supported. It is necessary to be sure that the business is well thought out, well planned and has genuinely identified a profitable opportunity. This review process is vital and can be expensive, both in terms of time and money. For this reason the cost of initial assessment and the subsequent costs of monitoring must always be considered alongside the size of the investment and the anticipated returns. These fixed costs are one reason why traditional venture capitalists are not interested in small-scale investments, as will be discussed later.

For the personal investor with a limited budget available, these fixed transactions costs also make it expensive to hold a diversified portfolio of equity stakes in small business. Hence the risk may also be concentrated where the holding is in a single company with whom the investor may have little contact or involvement once the initial investment has been made, and limited control. Indeed, if the investment is made under the Government's Business Expansion Scheme, the close involvement is barred under the terms of that scheme and would lead to a loss of the inherent tax benefits. The

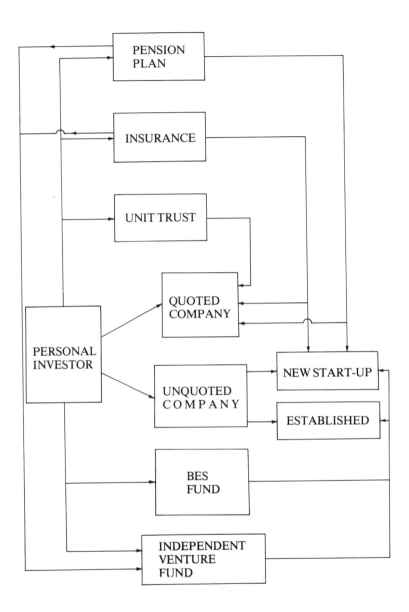

Figure 9.1 Routes for Personal Investments in Enterprise

same factors apply to individual equity holdings in large publicly quoted companies and explain the emergence of financial intermediaries in the form of unit and investment trusts (Chapter 8).

As Figure 9.1 makes clear, the personal investor has a number of choices available ranging from direct investment in quoted or unquoted companies through pooled investment via pension funds, life insurance policies and unit trusts. These intermediaries may themselves invest in either quoted or unquoted firms and operate venture capital funds. In the unquoted sector a stake can be taken in either an established enterprise or a new start-up.

(b) The Return

The individual's personal attitude to risk will be an important determining factor in the choice of investment. The risk-averse investor will generally avoid even consideration of such direct investment in unquoted companies whilst the risk preferrer may be very attracted. However, it is unhelpful to talk about risk in isolation from the financial rewards to be gained from the risky venture. What is an acceptable risk will depend on the probability distribution of possible losses and gains. Not only the expected size but also the timing of the returns will be crucial to the individual's investment decision. Without an active market in the securities the investor needs to take a long-term view of the firm's prospects. Particularly in a new enterprise there is always a period of consolidation and establishment before gains are made, and start-up costs need to be recouped. The potential return through income or capital gains to attract such investment must be high. Other things being equal, the higher the risk the higher the required rate of return. National Savings, bank and building society deposit rates are base-line risk-free returns against which the return on small-firm equity stakes may be compared. Recent advice given to potential entrepreneurs by a leading accounting firm suggests a minimum required return of 20 per cent compound per annum (Peat Marwick and Mitchell 1985a).

(c) The Recovery

Access to the capital invested and the eventual realisation of any capital gain are also important determinants. The essential elements are speed and cost. It is generally difficult to gain immediate access to an investment in an unquoted company. If a share of a small unquoted company is owned by an individual outside the firm, then the funds invested will often be fully committed and can only be released if there is some other investor willing to replace them. If the investment has to be realised in the early years of the company's life, it may not be possible to recover quickly the full value of the sum initially invested. Much, of course, depends on individual circumstances and the growth path of the company involved, but in general the earlier and quicker the recovery required the lower the return (if any) that will be earned. Equity investment in a small business is, therefore, closely akin to individual direct purchase of real assets with the associated problems involved (Chapter 1).

The greatest scope for high-return recovery occurs where the company grows sufficiently to have its shares traded publicly. Until 1980, this meant a full listing on the Stock Exchange with the requirement that the company have a five-year profits record and a substantial amount of equity available for public purchase (at least 25%) to provide an adequate market. The speed and ease of listing has been reduced considerably in recent years, as has the cost, through the establishment of the unlisted securities market (USM) and the over the counter market (OTC). The USM allows firms to go public earlier in their life by diluting stock market requirements; for example, only a three-year profits record is required, and only 10 per cent of the equity needs be made available. The fixed costs of the prospectus and brokers' and underwriters' fees are also generally lower, though the difference in costs is more sensitive to the type of sale and the amount being raised. The OTC market is operated by some dealers who make a market in shares which are not listed on either of the stock markets. The market leader in this field in 1985 — Granvilles — listed some thirty shares in small companies which could be bought and sold through them. The OTC provides possibly the cheapest and quickest way of establishing a market in shares which will enable an equity holder to realise part or all of his investment in a new small company.

The USM was set up in part due to concern voiced by the Wilson Committee in 1979 that a cheaper more efficient means of listing should be developed (Wilson 1979b). The idea has since spread to France where the 'seconde marche' has been established. The USM in mid-1985 listed 300 companies. Since its inception, 376 companies had been quoted on it, and these raised almost £675m on flotation,

45 companies had moved up to the main market and a further 22 had been acquired. During 1985, 99 listings were introduced but there is some evidence of a recent slowdown with only 7 additional listings being added in the first quarter of 1986 compared with 18 in the corresponding period for 1985. (*The Times*, 10 May 1986). Despite this turndown, the USM has undoubtedly been a major success in enabling an early realisation of venture investments in small, new and growing companies.

9.3   The Business Expansion Scheme

Thus the individual wishing to invest in a new enterprise will weigh up the risk, the return and the recovery in deciding whether or not to place an investment with a new or small unlisted company. Risk and illiquidity characteristics are such that few individuals do invest directly in such companies. This paucity of equity funds has been recognised and initiatives directed at the individual have been implemented to try to alleviate the situation. The principal initiative by the Government has been the setting up of the Business Expansion Scheme in 1983 which succeeded the Business Start-Up Scheme. It attracted over 20,000 investors providing over £100m in its first two years of operation. Tax allowances are given on investments made into qualifying companies up to a maximum of £40,000 (1986) of taxable income in any fiscal year. The company need not be entirely new and share holdings in the company must be so distributed that no one individual has more than 30 per cent. Except for bona fide liquidations, the investment must be held for a minimum of five years. The tax advantage can be quite substantial: for an individual paying tax at the marginal rate of 60 per cent, the Government is underwriting 72 per cent of the capital subscribed.

The Business Expansion Scheme itself does not eliminate the search and evaluation costs for an individual. However, the existence of BES Funds, which are approved vehicles for the investment of individual tax-exempted monies, does enable pooling and cost sharing in return for a management fee. The BES scheme did not achieve all the aims of its initiators because of the looseness of the requirements for qualifying companies and the restrictive nature of the conditions attached to involvement. There was an emphasis on asset-backed schemes such as agricultural land (now banned), residential renovation projects, hotel schemes, fine wines and nursing homes. These caused little of the employment creation or economic development for which the scheme was intended but gave greater security to investors. In response to these imperfections, the scheme was further modified in the 1986 Finance Act to exclude ventures with more than 50 per cent tangible asset backing (Finance Act 1986).

9.4 Informational Problems: the Enterprise and Agencies

In the capital market for small firms there are major search costs involved in simply identifying the potential market participants. Thus if the individual does wish to invest in a new enterprise, and wishes to do it directly, a major difficulty is actually finding an appropriate company in which to invest. By the same token, a small company seeking new funds or an entrepreneur requiring start-up capital needs to obtain information about potential investors. Even where there is a supply of funds on one side, and a demand for funds on the other, bringing these two sides together may not be easy. For this reason the conventional sources of small business capital have been the commercial banks, and frequently new companies start with equity provided by the owner managers supported by external loan finance. Evidence also suggests that the majority of owner managers in small firms resist external equity participation. One of the surveys undertaken for the Wilson Committee indicated that 60 per cent of firms took this view (Wilson 1979a). Further, since the small firm will have a small number of equity holders, their identity and characteristics are likely to be of importance to the managers. Thus there are additional search and information costs which have to be met by the firm in identifying and vetting potential investors.

Such information requirements suggest that there may be a case for the establishment of an information exchange of the type that exists in the labour market in the form of job centres and private placement agencies. In the small firms sector this need has been recognised by the formation of local enterprise agencies. The London Enterprise Agency provides one example of the concept in action.

The London Enterprise Agency: A Small Business Marriage Bureau

The London Enterprise Agency has pioneered the application of the 'marriage bureau' concept to the problem of identifying both potential lenders and borrowers in the capital market for small firms. The Agency provides a focus and a clearing house which brings together would-be backers and seekers of capital. The introduction of the scheme was prompted by its observance of an apparent information/equity gap. In its view it was virtually impossible to raise sums of less than £100,000 and absolutely impossible to raise sums of less than £50,000 from conventional venture capital providers, due to the cost of evaluating a company (in the order of £15,000–20,000) and then monitoring its performance (£5,000 per annum).

The Agency publishes a bulletin which presents proposals from individuals seeking investments in their venture, and also provides a means of directly introducing the parties. The introductions often take place at a monthly meeting where proposers get 20–30 minutes to outline their scheme to an audience of potential backers; about half of the proposals find funders. Half an hour cannot permit full consideration, but it does provide a cost-effective filter for plans worthy of later assessment. In the Bulletin of May 1985 there were some 70 proposals and in only a handful was the required investment greater than £50,000. Thus the scheme is primarily concerned with the market for small-scale equity.

Such a marriage bureau does perform a valuable function in reducing the search costs involved in identifying potential market participants, but it does little to deal with the other costs involved in appraising the business and monitoring performance. These costs remain high and pose difficulties for entrepreneurs seeking to found or expand their own businesses. We now turn, therefore, to an examination of the problems of raising finance.

9.5 Obtaining Entrepreneurial Finance

Obtaining the required finance in an appropriate form is one of the major tasks facing the would-be entrepreneur. Whilst the product has to be good, the management sound and the market well researched before a firm will have a chance of success, the acid test of these proposals is very often the scrutiny which they receive when capital is being raised. A full business plan will be required for presentation to potential backers which should include the background of the founder and his 'track record', alongside details of the product, premises, production process, targeted market, projected sales, competitor analysis, profit projections, cash-flow projections and sensitivity analysis. The potential backer will wish to know the best possible outcome and the worst. The business plan should identify the level of finance required to meet all the major areas of the business including its launch, the cost of equipment and premises, the working capital requirements and the flexibility required to cover temporary deviations from the plan. The purpose for which funds are needed will determine the type of financing sought; the cash-flow projection should show both the maximum amounts required and their expected incidence throughout the duration of the project.

The type of finance obtained may be critical to the success of the venture. There are two broad sources of capital: (a) internal – provided by the founder or owner; and (b) external – supplied by outside backers, whether individuals or institutions. The outside backers tend to be commercial banks, specialist venture capital companies, individuals, either alone or through BES funds, and government and local authorities. In addition, funds can be generated through lease and hire purchase of equipment and premises through trade credit, and through factoring (the discounting of invoices to get cash early). In evaluating external finance, a major consideration is always whether to use loan or equity. With a loan the interest repayments have to meet a fixed schedule and the repayment of loans ranks first in any liquidation; the lender usually seeks security or a floating charge over assets. Equity gives the holder a right to share in the net worth of the company, and founders of new firms often prefer loans so as to keep the equity to themselves, even though this decision increases the financial burden on the company in the establishment phase.

Because of this self-rationing, individual founders experience difficulty in raising the start-up capital, and there are currently no incentives equivalent to the BES to tax-exempt individuals for their own business. Information asymmetries mean that risks are invariably perceived as greater by the outside backer than by the individual entrepreneur, who may thus be faced with apparently unreasonable demands for security on loans provided. There may also be an additional element of 'moral hazard' in some cases where the banks are unable to influence outcomes or monitor effectively, and the Wilson Committee's small firms survey found evidence of required ratios of secured assets to loans extended in excess of 2:1. These problems are, of course, not peculiar to the finance of new enterprise. They arise when there is a separation of savings from the accumulation of wealth, and found reflection in Keynes's distinction between 'entrepreneurs' and 'lenders' risk (see Chapter 2, p. 36).

The Loan Guarantee Scheme was designed to offset these risk problems by encouraging banks to lend to firms which lacked adequate security by providing a government-backed guarantee. The banks can lend up to £75,000 with 70 per cent of the sum covered by the Loan Guarantee so that in the event of failure the banks only have 30 per cent of the loan exposed. The first scheme was established in June 1981 for three years. It was then extended to the end of 1985; 15,000 guarantees had been issued and over £500m loaned. Unfortunately, nearly one in three of the firms supported had failed within the first twelve months and the overall scheme was showing a deficit of £75m. The fund is supported by an interest-rate premium which was expected to cover the cost of any losses, an expectation which was not met. The premium was raised in an attempt to achieve a self-funding scheme, but this curtailed the operation to such an extent that the surcharge was halved in the 1986 Finance Act. Although risks have so far proved to be high, and both the banks and the Government have expressed concern at the cost of the scheme, a perceived need from the small business sector has seen its operation extended until a further review in 1989.

9.6 UK Policy Towards Small Firm Finance

The emphasis in the UK in the early 1980s upon the need to promote external equity participation in small and new firms to enable growth and development dates back, at least, to the 1931 Macmillan Committee on Finance and Industry. It indicated a difficulty facing small and medium-sized firms when attempting to raise long-term capital in sums which did not justify a public issue. This 'Macmillan Gap' referred to amounts below £200,000 (1930 prices).

In an attempt to close this gap the Industrial and Commercial Finance Corporation Ltd (ICFC) was formed in 1945 which, in 1984, was subsumed within 'Investors In Industry' (3*i*). In 1959 the Radcliffe Committee (Report on the Working of the Monetary System) argued that the finance shortfall indicated by Macmillan had been covered by the ICFC, and that any shortcoming in the supply of finance referred primarily to that available for technical innovation. Part of the response to this omission involved the creation of Technical Development Capital Ltd which became a subsidiary of ICFC; TDC was seen as a prominent supplier of high-risk capital to begin to fill what could be termed the 'innovation gap' (Radcliffe Committee 1959).

Following the lead of the Bolton Committee of 1971, the Committee to Review the Functioning of Financial Institutions in 1979 (Wilson 1979b) switched the emphasis to the need for additional securities markets, encouraging the 'over the counter' (OTC) market in securities of small firms provided by licensed dealers outside the Stock Exchange, and sowing the seeds for the establishment of the unlisted securities market (USM) in 1980.

The Committee's suggestion of tax-deductible investment in new and small firms found reflection later in the Business Start-Up and Business Expansion Schemes.

Much of this institutional response was designed to make good a shortfall in the supply of equity capital, attributed to a decline in funding from families and close friends (the 'Aunt Agathas'). The extent to which this decline was caused by more progressive taxation or the growth of much safer alternative investment opportunities is difficult to ascertain. Given the expansion of sources of equity capital and more particularly the growth in number and size of the venture and development capital outlets, it seems unlikely that an equity supply problem would still exist in the UK. There are three main reasons, however, for believing that a shortfall still exists.

First, there is the evidence that the majority of small firms resent and resist the prospect of external equity participation (Wilson 1979b and Binks and Vale 1984). This trend may gradually be reversed as owner-managers learn that such events do not necessarily imply any dilution of control. Whilst a claimed shortfall exists for this reason, however, it is created through choice by small firms themselves, not the suppliers of funds.

Second, the fixed information costs in processing, evaluating and

monitoring investments mean that small and new firms find it difficult to raise finance. A firm which lacks appropriate equity funding and which fails to attract sufficient loan finance, of course,
never exists. Many firms come into existence and finance their early
growth through an overdraft facility. This is quite appropriate as a
source of working capital, but its use for capital formation can
handicap a potential 'high flier'. Rapid growth brings with it the
need to fund increasing working capital requirements due to the
time lag between the costs of producing goods and the receipts from
their sale.

If the firm's overdraft facility and collateral is already committed, then there is a shortfall of working capital and the firm appears
to be overtrading. As indicated, the rapid-growth firm is necessarily
more vulnerable to this event; an inappropriate financial structure
on start-up and early expansion simply raises the probability of
restriction or closure.

Third, the 'type' of new entrepreneur varies with the economic
climate. New entrepreneurs consist of those 'pulled' by innovative
ideas and those 'pushed' by unemployment elsewhere. Declining
industries provide a source of owner-managers who are 'pushed'
rather than 'pulled' and it is unlikely that these entrepreneurs will be
aided by access to new sources of private external equity provision.

9.7 Entrepreneurial Finance in the United States

To a large extent, institutional private and public initiatives and
trends in the UK are similar to those occurring earlier in the USA. It
is not appropriate here to attempt a comprehensive comparison of
the economic, social, cultural and historical backgrounds of the UK
and USA in an attempt to explain differences in personal financial
services, attitudes to entrepreneurship, risk, etc. It is, however,
useful to consider certain key developments in the USA which com-
plement our earlier discussion of other personal financial markets.
In the United States encouragement has been given to the small
firm, both non-financial and financial (Chapter 5). The particular
needs and problems of new and small businesses have been
acknowledged and catered for in a more coherent and consistent
way than has been the case in the UK. The Small Business
Administration (SBA) was established in 1953 to nurture the small

firm sector. It recognises the need for loan guarantees, and offers a variety of loan programmes. The SBA licences, regulates and provides financial assistance to privately owned and operated Small Business Investment Companies (SBICs). The aim is to provide equity directly or in the form of 'pseudo-equity', for example unsecured loans. While these companies may, because of the fixed information costs, fail to accommodate the newest and smallest, they provide a source of equity which had, until the 1980s, had no similar counterpart in the UK.

Aside from the SBA's role as a provider of equity finance, the USA had a highly developed OTC market at the time (1979) that the Wilson Committee was recommending the introduction of such markets in the UK. The Committee's observations serve as a useful indication of the nature and scope of the US OTC organisation in contrast to the embryonic developments in the UK.

> The activities of both Stock Exchange member firms and licensed dealers fall well short of the situation in the US, where the over-the-counter market is much larger and more organised. It has been estimated that the shares of about 90 per cent of the approximately 33,000 companies traded in the US are dealt with on the OTC market rather than on the New York, American or regional stock exchanges. (Wilson 1979b)

Despite the existence of a more established and coordinated system to meet the needs of small firms in the USA, there has still been a change in emphasis towards the need for improved financial flows of equity provision. The formidable growth potential of high-technology firms provoked a swift response in the US to provide venture and development capital. This trend emerged in the UK a few years later, though the response was in some respects quite different.

9.8 The Venture Capital Market

One of the fastest growing parts of the UK financial sector has been the venture capital industry. As recently as 1980 there were very few true venture capital firms and a very fragmented and small market. The major participant in the market was the ICFC, now 'Investors in Industry'. Since 1980 there has been a rapid growth in the number of lenders, the type of business being done and the volume of funds committed. Many of the ideas and much of the impetus have come from the United States where the venture industry is much more deeply integrated into the financial scene. The transatlantic transfer has been through the involvement of US-based venture capital companies becoming established in the UK and through the arrival of US personnel. At the same time, there has been a greater degree of portfolio diversification amongst financial institutions to include a venture element, particularly amongst the insurance companies and the pension funds. The major commercial banks have also established 'in-house' venture capital arms.

Venture capital is a term which is often applied to two forms of financing, that for unquoted companies and new start-ups, and that which is part of the later development of the company, often called development capital. It is difficult to distinguish in the statistics on the UK market what the proportions of investments are in each of these categories. Thus the two are treated together here. The three key characteristics of venture capital are that it involves actual or potential equity participation; that the investment is long term (usually a minimum horizon of five years); and that there is generally some degree of continuing involvement with the management team. The involvement is often a very useful way by which the financial acumen of the company can be strengthened and the investment safeguarded. One of the major criticisms made in a recent survey of small firms was the poor degree of financial expertise which companies contained (Robson Rhodes 1983). In many respects the degree of involvement is one of the most important features which distinguishes venture financing from conventional forms of passive investment.

A common objective of venture capital providers is to realise a gain through the appreciation in value of the equity which they hold in a company; participation in dividends is generally secondary. For this reason the venture investors are usually looking for prospects of growth, preferably a quick pick-up onto the growth path, and an early opportunity to have a marketable share through a listing of some kind (full, OTC, or USM). In other respects the venture capitalists are quite different and have varying backgrounds, attitudes to investment decisions, and preferred areas of lending. The market has become more competitive with over 120 specialist venture capital institutions now operating, with the consequence that the potential entrepreneur can 'shop around' for funding for a project.

The venture capital institutions generally fall into two broad categories – independents and captives. The latter are specialist venture capital arms of larger financial groups such as Barclays Development Capital in the Barclays Bank Group and County Bank with the National Westminster Bank. There are now over 50 established independent funds which between them raised over £600 million between 1980 and 1984, with over half that sum occurring in the two later years (Venture Economics 1985). Table 9.1 provides information on the sources of capital for these independent funds in the years 1982–84. Of the total of nearly £200 million in 1984, some 55 per cent came from pension funds and insurance companies. Both the absolute and relative involvement of both types of institution have increased significantly since 1982 as they have sought ways of improving the return of their portfolios. In addition, as noted earlier, venture capital investments may require a longer-term horizon to be taken than with the purchase of equity stakes in established quoted companies. Given the nature of their liabilities, pension funds and life insurance companies are more able to take a long-term view.

As Table 9.1 also shows, BES funds have helped to encourage the

Table 9.1 UK Venture Capital Industry: Sources of Capital for Independent Funds

Source	% of total capital raised		
	1982	1983	1984
Pension funds	27.4	30.6	40.2
Private individuals (BES)	11.1	39.8	19.4
Insurance companies	6.9	9.2	14.7
Foreign institutions	16.6	9.0	9.8
Industrial corporations	—	—	8.6
Investment trusts	—	—	2.8
Banks	15.6	7.4	1.3
Government/local authorities	10.3	—	0.4
Academic institutions	4.5	—	0.2
Other	7.6	1.3	2.6
	100%	100%	100%
Total capital raised	£39.9m	£112.0m	£193.2m

Source: European Venture Capital Association, 1985.

personal investor and in 1984 over 19 per cent of the capital raised by independent venture funds was through the BES scheme. The expansion of the BES funds through 1985 has enabled continued growth in the venture industry, while the decline in the banks as providers of funds to independents is not evidence of withdrawal from the market so much as a diversion of available funds to their own captive in-house funds.

Certain areas of business have tended at various times to be more attractive to venture funds than others, such as computers and biotechnology in terms of product group, and for management buyouts in terms of type of project, but further generalisations are not appropriate. About 40 per cent of investments are in consumer or computer-related areas and about one-third of investments are in new ventures as opposed to refinancing or management buyouts.

The UK venture capital market has developed and grown quickly. Two factors have been important in encouraging its growth: (a) the stimulus to entrepreneurship and its general rehabilitation within the UK; and (b) the establishment of the USM, offering an early exit to investors. An additional impetus has been provided through the tax exemptions offered in the BES scheme. Nevertheless, the UK venture capital market, both relatively and absolutely, does not match that of the US. In 1984, US independent venture firms raised

Table 9.2 Total Size of Venture Capital Funds Available in the European Community (December 1984)

	Local currency (millions)		Rate	ECU (millions)
Belgium	BF	4.323	44.9762	96
Denmark	DK	765	7.9855	96
France	FF	1.116	6.83034	163
Germany	DM	700	2.23139	314
Greece	DRs	2.000	91.0190	22
Ireland	£	35	0.715379	49
Italy	Lit	235.000	1,368.84	172
Luxembourg	LF	496	44.9762	11
Netherlands	DFls	1.865	2.51938	740
United Kingdom	£	2.264	0.610479	3.708
				5.371

Source: European Venture Capital Association, 1985.

over \$3.2 bn (£2.3 bn) compared with the £193 mn raised by independents in the UK. However, it has been estimated that total venture funds available by the end of 1984 in the UK, including all pension funds and captive institutions, amounted to £2.3 billion (Peat Marwick and Mitchell 1985). Comparative figures for the rest of the European Community are given in Table 9.2. Thus, the UK has by far the largest amount of funds available for specific investment in venture capital. There are major differences in the economic and legal regimes between the countries which can account for some of these differences, but it is still clear why the development of the UK venture capital market is the envy of other European countries.

The venture capital market offers two advantages for the personal investor/prospective new firm proprietor. There are a number of funds into which investments can be made which allow risk pooling and professional management, and there are a number of alternative providers of funds which can be approached for support for any particular new venture. The rapidity with which it has grown in the UK is a significant element in the changing pattern of personal financial services. It also reflects the increasing demand for higher-risk investments in smaller enterprises, which is mainly due to the correspondingly higher potential return, but possibly also because of a growing appreciation of the need for young dynamic firms, in particular, to proliferate and prosper in the UK.

The economic contribution of the venture capital institutions is clearly large and expanding, but where there is a shortage, it is of viable projects, not funds. The information costs of appraisal and monitoring still remain for small but potential high-growth firms. Thus, they may still face difficulties in expanding to a size sufficiently large to benefit from this relatively new source of institutional risk capital.

9.9 Conclusion

This chapter has considered the question of entrepreneurial finance for small business from both sides of the market as it impinges on the individual: the opportunities and issues involved in personal direct investment in small business; and, on the demand side, the issues facing individuals seeking funds to create or expand their own businesses.

As the examples provided in this chapter have been chosen to indicate, the increasing attention given to new and small firms is a characteristic of central government, local authorities and financial institutions. While their objectives may differ, there is a considerable degree of consensus as to the 'type' of firm which they wish to encourage; most of the objectives are best achieved through rapid growth or 'high flier' firms. For central and local government these are most likely to create employment. For private investors using institutional channels, these are most likely to create considerable capital appreciation which may be realised when the company's shares are traded on the OTC or USM markets.

It has been argued, however, that despite the variety of initiatives implemented by the Government and institutions, a fundamental difficulty remains in obtaining external equity funds in small amounts. In general, small, potentially rapid-growth firms are most vulnerable to the constraint on expansion which this difficulty might impose. While the main source of the problem lies in the inherent costs of evaluating, monitoring and undertaking such small investment, the implications of its effects are clear. Such firms may never grow to a size where the benefits of new venture capital provisions are accessible.

The number which, in the absence of this problem, would have provided sound investment propositions for venture and development capital can only be discovered if the information asymmetries could be removed. It is, by definition, impossible to observe the number of 'high fliers' which never flew!

References

Binks, M.R. and Vale, P.A. (1984) Nottingham University Small Firms Unit, Paper 6, mimeo.

Bolton, J.E. (1971) *Small Firms: Report of the Commission of Inquiry on Small Firms*, HMSO, Cmnd 4811.

British Market Research Bureau (1983) *Building Societies and the Savings Market*, Building Societies Association, June.

Macmillan Committee (1931) *Report of the Committee on Finance and Industry*, HMSO, Cmnd 3897.

Peat Marwick and Mitchell (1985a) *Starting Up Your Own Business*, June.

Peat Marwick and Mitchell (1985b) for the European Venture Capital Association Conference Proceedings 1985.

Radcliffe Committee (1959) *Report of the Committee on the Working of the Monetary System*, HMSO, Cmnd 827.

Robson Rhodes (1983) *A Study of Some Early Claims under the Small Business Loan Guarantee Scheme*, Department of Industry.

Treasury (1986) *Economic Progress Report*, No. 183, March–April.

Venture Economics (1985) *Venture Capital Journal*, July.

Wilson Committee (1979a) Committee to Review the Functioning of Financial Institutions, *Studies of Small Firms Financing*, Research Report No. 3.

Wilson Committee (1979b) Committee to Review the Functioning of Financial Institutions, *The Financing of Small Firms*, Cmnd 7503, HMSO.

CHAPTER 10

Markets, Regulation, and the Financial Firm

R.L. Carter, B. Chiplin and M.K. Lewis

10.1 Changes in Markets

Change has been rapid in financial and capital markets in a wide range of countries over the past two decades. Five broad trends listed below are of particular consequence, and the interplay between them has produced a marked increase in competition. The trends are:

(i) *'Institutionalisation'* A growth in financial intermediation has resulted in 'financial deepening'. Institutions such as pension funds and life offices dominate share markets. Wholesale banking finances more of corporate and international investment.

(ii) *'Liberalisation'* Markets in most countries have been liberalised by the release or relaxation of exchange controls. Price fixing and interest-rate controls have broken down, direct controls over consumer credit and finance have been removed, and there has been a switch to market-based methods of monetary control.

(iii) *'Integration'* Markets have been integrated domestically by the development of new instruments such as money market funds which straddle previously segmented sectors. Markets have been integrated internationally by the rise of international banking and the development of offshore currency centres.

(iv) *'Innovation'* Financial innovation has been rapid in terms of markets, e.g. Eurocurrency and Eurobond markets, secondary asset markets swap and futures markets), instruments (cash management accounts, variable rate lending, leveraged buyouts) and technologies (ATMs, data processing).

(v) *'Universality'* The traditional segmented and differentiated institutional groupings have given way to more diversified and 'universal' structures, embracing the provision of a wide range of retail and wholesale financing functions. Large financial conglomerates have been formed to organise this provision.

Institutionalisation

These general trends in capital and financial markets are clearly evident in the markets which meet consumers' needs for financial services. Individuals have certain needs in respect of transaction services, wealth accumulation and financial security, and they seek the assistance of financial intermediaries to help them satisfy these needs. Intermediation is the central market process involved in the financial system, and in its simplest form acts as a channel for funds from those with excess income to those who wish to borrow. The suppliers of personal financial services principally comprise banks, building societies, life insurance companies, insurance brokers, stockbrokers, pension funds and unit trusts. Savings by the personal sector in the UK represent the major source of the flow of funds to these intermediaries. Over the last decade the personal sector has been the only one which has consistently been in financial surplus and which has chosen predominantly to place this surplus in financial assets rather than directly owning the corresponding real assets. As noted in Chapter 1, the savings of households have increasingly been in the form of savings committed to long-term savings and investment vehicles, along with loan repayments, and the recent figures suggest that there has been discretionary dissaving.

Liberalisation

Deregulation has played an important part in liberalising financial markets, especially those for consumer credit, housing finance and deposit services. Changes to trading rules and pricing practices on the Stock Exchange seem likely to stimulate greater competition for personal 'investment' services. Nevertheless, many developments have been in anticipation of, rather than as a result of, deregulation, such as the 'bending' of rules by building societies to extend consumer credit and offer insurance. The trend in several countries is for governments to remove, or at least relax, those regulations which primarily constrain competition between institutions, but to strengthen controls, including self-regulation, aimed at protecting consumers. Major changes in regulations in the UK across a broad front have been, or are in the process of being, introduced, and we devote Section 10.2 to a specific analysis of this issue.

Integration

Personal financial markets are not yet integrated internationally. Because of the importance of confidence, trust and information flows in financial contracts, the extent to which they will be integrated by direct consumer–firm links is likely to be limited. As a consequence, differences in the cost of consumer credit and housing

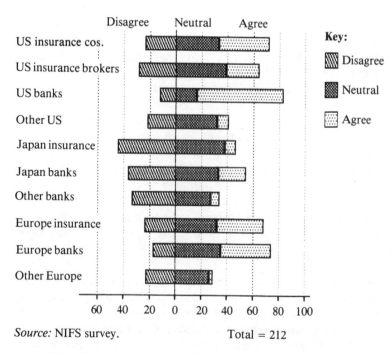

Source: NIFS survey.   Total = 212

Figure 10.1. Foreign Companies will be a Significant Force

finance between countries remain to be eliminated indirectly by market institutions. The present development of secondary markets may facilitate this process. While personal financial markets are thus predominantly national, they are not the sole province of national intermediaries. Banks and other institutions attracted to London's international banking, securities and insurance markets have a presence in the domestic retail markets, and are expected to increase that presence in the future.

Figure 10.1 reports the results of our enquiries into the likely impact of foreign-owned firms on the personal market. US banks stand out as being the only group which is seen as having a significant impact by a majority of respondents (67 per cent). US and European insurance companies, and European banks are seen as important by around one-third of respondents. Japanese companies are not seen as playing a major role, with just over 20 per cent of respondents seeing Japanese banks as significant. This view is perhaps a little surprising given that whereas in 1970 eight of the world's ten largest banks were either British or American, by 1985 there were only two American banks and no British banks amongst the top ten. Seven of these top ten positions were held by Japanese banks (*Economist*, 3 May, 1986, p. 116).

Innovation

Financial innovations have integrated domestic markets in personal financial services. In particular, innovations in cash management techniques, introduced in both the UK and USA by securities firms, have broken down the previously segmented retail and wholesale deposit markets and, at the same time, brought the deposit market closer to that for investments. Financial innovations can be classified into four main types: cash management, investment contracts, market structure and institutional organisation (Silber 1983). Some of the most important were listed in Table 1.2, and examined in following chapters. The innovations in cash management, which relate to the consumer's need for transaction services, include money market funds, cash management schemes, debit cards, automated clearing houses, automatic teller machines, point-of-sale terminals and home banking. In terms of investment contracts, which relate to the needs of wealth accumulation and financial security, innovations have encompassed extensions and enhancements to unit-linked policies, universal life insurance policies, portable and personal pensions, the personal equity plan announced in the 1986 Budget, and integrated house purchase services with housing finance.

Universality

Market structure changes are seen as concerning electronic market trading, discount brokerage, the development of secondary markets, increased securitisation and the impact of the 'Big Bang' and investor protection (discussed below). Institutional organisation refers to the scope and delineation of the financial firm including mergers, joint ventures and the role of the 'financial supermarket' (see Section 10.3). As was discussed in Chapter 2, these innovations are being introduced by a wide variety of financial institutions. The new products straddle a number of previously distinct market segments and all of the major financial institutions are extending from their traditional base. This diversification process has been spurred on by the 'Big Bang' which is seeing the formation of a large number of financial groups integrating banking, securities dealing, insurance and investment services. Only the building societies, as a group, remain as the last bastion of financial specialisation in the UK, and their move towards a more 'universal' structure is well in train.

The Diversity of Trends

New information technology has played an important role in hastening along these trends; sometimes facilitating desired changes, and at other times initiating them. There is no doubt that the financial services sector is undergoing a rapid technological transformation which is breaking down traditional barriers between institutions and leading to new and newly packaged products, and new marketing and distribution methods. A fundamental catalyst for change has to be seen also in the efforts of individuals, businesses, financial institutions and markets to adapt to the historically high rates of inflation of the 1970s and early 1980s which both created fundamental problems for some institutions and presented new opportunities for others. These rates brought in their wake a trend towards securitisation, i.e. an increased use of capital market-type instruments as a source of finance, and a significant increase in the volume of trading which is not unconnected with the reduced per unit transaction costs brought about by new technology.

We are not yet able to see the full implications of computer technology for financial services, and thus the extent to which it may reverse the trends to 'institutionalisation' and 'conglomeration'. Indeed, such developments, we contend, raise the question of to what extent it is meaningful to talk of clear trends in personal financial markets. In terms of 'institutionalisation', we note that financial institutions, like all firms, owe their existence to economies of scale and scope, in their case in portfolio management and the processing of information. These economies are neither continuous nor unchanging, depending on the state of technology and the range of markets.

The innovations which have taken place in cash management and investment contracts can be viewed from an alternative angle in terms of their impact on risk transferability, liquidity, and equity generation. Risk-transferring innovations have been most prevalent on wholesale markets and allow economic agents to transfer the price or credit risk involved in financial positions. Currency swaps, interest-rate swaps and futures contracts are recent growth areas, which may filter through to retail transactions. Cash management programmes and money market funds have all had the effect of increasing the liquidity of market-based instruments. The extension of personal share ownership, the growth of stock option schemes, management buyouts funded largely by loan capital, and the proposed personal equity plan have all acted to enhance interest in the role of individuals in equity markets.

In other respects, also, we think that it may be a mistake to look for pronounced trends in personal financial markets. A recent examination of emerging trends in the structure of financial services in the United States (Carlson 1984) identified, in addition to deregulation, the following six basic trends:

- Consolidation
- Conglomeration
- Unbundling
- Repackaging
- Automation
- Networking

This perhaps illustrates the point we wish to make: that the best description of the factors at work in personal financial markets is one of diversity, and that it would be wrong to look for uniform developments common to all of those markets.

There are, we believe, good reasons in terms of economic theory for expecting to observe diversity. Financial services are directed towards a number of basic needs of consumers, but the mix of transactions services, wealth accumulation, and financial security demanded will range from individual to individual. People have different attitudes to confidence, trust and safety, and contribute unequally to the flow of information. For firms to meet these specific needs adequately, it would be desirable to provide a fully customised set of services to each customer. But financial firms, like other firms, must balance this demand for product variety with the achievement of economies of scale in the production of services, which demands some standardisation and prepackaging. Each firm must determine this trade-off and thus decide the 'optimum product differentiation' (Lancaster 1975, 1979; Spence 1976).

Financial services are ideally suited for the application of information technology, and developments in it have altered, perhaps in fundamental ways, the trade-off between variety and productive efficiency. Diversity can now be satisfied at a much lower and continually falling cost. Cash management systems preprogrammed to individual risk-return preferences and universal life insurance policies are obvious examples which have revolutionised personal financial services in the United States (Chapter 5). They hold a portent of future possibilities in personal financial markets generally.

Unbundling, repackaging, networking, conglomeration, and automation can all be expected as firms grapple with the implications for them of the new technology. Adding to this changes in consumer tastes, growth of secondary and hedging markets, and rapid variations in the macroeconomic environment, diversity clearly has implications for how firms organise themselves for change, considered in Section 10.3 Heightened competition in financial markets, different 'cross-industry' tie-ups, and the variety of ways in which firms are repositioning themselves have implications also for the regulation of financial services, considered in the following section.

10.2   The Regulation of Financial Services

Legislative controls are both a part of the environment within which industries and markets operate and a response by government to the political pressures arising from the changing economic, social, legal and technological conditions which are a part of that environment. Thus differences in the national structures of financial markets, and the modes of marketing financial services, can be attributed at least in part to differences in regulatory systems and rules: as explained in Chapter 5, the exclusion of American banks from non-banking-related insurance business is a case in point. It is not surprising, therefore, that there is a widespread belief that one of the forces for change in financial markets is the revision of the regulatory systems under way in many countries. So in the case of Britain, the survey of financial institutions conducted by the Nottingham Institute of Financial Studies revealed that 56 per cent of respondents agreed that future UK legislation will increase competition and decrease regulation in the UK personal financial services market. Also, one-third believed that EEC regulations will constrain the growth of their companies, whereas almost a quarter were of the opinion that they will assist growth.

The belief of the majority of the respondents that changes in UK regulation will increase competition is well founded. Since the 1971 White Paper on *Competition and Credit Control*, the government has been moving in the direction of dismantling statutory regulations, and encouraging self-regulatory bodies to modify their rules, which hamper competition between institutions, including the relaxation of restrictions on the functions which particular institutions can undertake (e.g. the Building Societies Act). However, it would be wrong to view regulatory changes as always initiating market changes: at times governments and self-regulatory bodies largely have to amend the rules to meet new market conditions brought about by other forces, such as technology, as discussed in Section 10.1. In other words, regulatory changes may merely legalise a change towards more competitive behaviour that has already occurred.

In the case of regulations primarily concerned with consumer protection, instead of deregulation the trend is for governments to strengthen the legislation not only due to pressure from consumer movements but also in the UK and other parts of the EEC due to the harmonisation of supervisory laws within the Community.

UK Regulation of Financial Services

It has long been recognised that the protection of investors and other consumers of financial services presents somewhat different issues to the protection of consumers of goods and other tangible assets (see Gower 1982). Consequently, in Britain not only have persons and firms engaged in supplying financial services been subject to the general laws controlling the formation and operations of trading organisations (i.e. the Companies, Partnership and Friendly Societies Acts, the law of agency, etc.), and to the various statutes which regulate monopolies, mergers, restrictive practices, and other aspects of competitive behaviour, in many, though not all, cases they have also been the subject of the following:

(i) special rules for the supervision by government agencies and/or self-regulatory bodies operating within a statutory framework of particular types of institutions (e.g. banks, building societies, insurance companies, insurance brokers, etc.) and activities (e.g. dealing in securities); and

(ii) the rules of professional organisations which regulate the activities of their members (e.g. The Stock Exchange and Lloyd's) or of self-regulatory organisations set up by professional bodies to regulate the activities of their members or persons dealing with them, such as the Panel on Takeovers and Mergers.

Details of the regulation of building societies, banks and other licensed deposit-takers can be found in Chapters 6 and 7. Consumer protection legislation applying to insurance business falls under two headings. First, insurance companies conducting any class of insurance business in the UK are subject to supervision by the Department of Trade and Industry (DTI) under the provisions of the Insurance Companies Act, 1982, designed to control entry to and exit from the market, to ensure that minimum standards of solvency are observed, and to control certain aspects of behaviour, including the selling of insurance.[1] Secondly, if despite those controls an authorised insurance company gets into financial difficulties, under the provisions of the Policyholders Protection Act, 1975, other companies carrying on the same class of business are required to contribute to a levy to safeguard the financial interests of the company's UK private policyholders. The Lloyd's market has its own policyholder compensation arrangements under the self-regulatory system provided for in the Lloyd's Acts, 1971–1982.

Individuals and firms wishing to call themselves 'insurance brokers' are required to comply with the registration requirements of the Insurance Brokers Registration Council under the provisions of the Insurance Brokers (Registration) Act, 1977. That does not prevent other persons acting as insurance intermediaries, but all intermediaries who wish to conduct 'investment business' will be controlled by the forthcoming Financial Services Act.

Both the trustees and the management companies of unit trusts must comply with capital and other regulations laid down by the DTI in order to obtain approval. The regulations under the Prevention of Fraud (Investments) Act, 1958, controlling the marketing of unit trusts are being replaced by the Financial Services Bill.

The Influence of the European Economic Community

Britain's membership of the EEC has necessitated substantial changes being made to its supervisory laws as progress has been made towards the creation of common European markets in financial services. For example, the Directives on the Freedoms of Establishment for Insurance required major changes to the Insurance Companies Act regarding the authorisation of companies to transact insurance business in Great Britain and Northern Ireland (including provisions preventing the authorisation of new composite companies writing both life and non-life insurance business); the admission of 'Community insurers' to the UK market; and the capitalisation and solvency of insurance companies. Likewise, the implementation of the Directive on Undertakings for Collective Investment in Transferable Securities will expose UK unit trusts to competition from similar European institutions. Traditionally, the UK government has adopted a less restrictive approach to the supervision of financial institutions than most Continental European countries. For example, the British approach to the protection of insurance policyholders has been to concentrate on financial controls to reduce the risk of insolvency, and then to leave matters of premium rating, product design and investment policy to the commercial judgment of insurers so that consumers have the choice of a range of competing products. The Germans, on the other hand, argue that uniformity of policy conditions, terms and premium rates improves market transparency for consumers and thereby promotes responsible competition between insurers (Finsinger *et al.* 1985). Agreements on the harmonisation of laws to achieve progress towards a common market have to accommodate such differences of approach, so that for Britain part of the cost of participating in the European Community is an obligation sometimes to adopt more restrictive regulations.

Problems Posed by Developments in Financial Services

The market changes discussed in Section 10.1 have exposed various weaknesses in UK consumer protection legislation. For example, the formation of new integrated financial services groups raises such problems as:

(1) If, say, the banking division of a conglomerate runs into financial difficulties, it may seek the loan of funds perhaps from the life insurance division to help it through its (hopefully) temporary problems: that could not only jeopardise the interests of the life policyholders but, at worst, it may lead to the collapse of the whole organisation.

(2) Information regarding clients in one part of the organisation may be made available to other parts for marketing purposes, leading to possible conflicts of interest in relation to clients and unfair disadvantages *vis-à-vis* competitors.

(3) There is a danger that a bank or other lending institution engaged also in insurance business may make the granting of a loan conditional on obtaining the borrower's insurances.

Likewise, differences in the regulations applying to different types of service and product may result in unfair competition, and they may also inhibit developments which would be beneficial to both consumers and the general economy. Consequently, in 1981 Professor L.C.B. Gower was asked to undertake a complete review of the legislation for the protection of investors.

He recognised that there is often a conflict between investor protection and market efficiency, and therefore argued that regulation should be reduced to the minimum necessary to protect 'reasonable people from being made fools of' (Gower 1984; para. 1.16). He considered too that though some parts of the security industry are over-regulated, others are insufficiently regulated or not regulated at all, so that substantial legislative changes are necessary to provide for the consistent regulatory treatment of different forms of investment.

Gower examined the relative advantages of self-regulation of industries and markets by those working in them as against government regulation (Gower 1982). In large measure the advantages and disadvantages of one are largely the converse of the other. For example, self-regulatory bodies are flexible and able to deal with infringements of the spirit of their rules, but enforcement over non-members is difficult and the public interest is not always paramount. Government regulation, on the other hand, tends to suffer from inflexibility, though a regulatory agency has legal powers of enforcement. He concluded that the two types of regulation should not be regarded as antithetical but complementary, and recommended a system whereby day-to-day regulation would be undertaken by self-regulatory agencies (ultimately paid for by investors), subject to basic policy, overall surveillance and the residual regulation of investment business being undertaken by a government agency – so being paid for by the taxpayer (Gower 1984, Appendix III).

The Government accepted Gower's principal recommendations and set out its proposals for legislative reform in the 1985 White Paper *Financial Services in the United Kingdom* (Cmnd. 9432), which formed the basis for the Financial Services Bill.

The Financial Services Bill

The Bill is an important step towards market-based rather than institution-based regulation in that it deals with all types of 'investment business' (see below). Other types of financial services, however, will continue to be regulated by different agencies under existing separate legislation, such as deposit-taking activities under the provisions of the Banking Act, 1979; insurance business under the Insurance Companies and the Lloyd's Acts; and the activities of friendly societies under the Friendly Societies Acts, though the regulation of certain aspects of investment-type life insurance will fall within the provisions of the Financial Services Bill.

The objective of the Bill is to provide a system of investor protection that will encourage market competition, efficiency and innovation and inspire the confidence of investors. It sets out to remove present inconsistencies in the treatment of different forms of investment business by basing regulation on 'investments' and 'investment business' as defined in Schedule 1 of the Bill. 'Investments' cover a wide variety of financial assets including company shares and loan stocks, government and public securities, share warrants and certificates, unit trusts, options, futures, and investment-type long-term (i.e. life) insurance contracts. 'Investment business' covers dealing in (other than for one's own account), arranging deals in, advising on, and managing investments; and establishing collective investment schemes. Consequently, as explained in Chapter 8, common marketing and investment regulations will be introduced for life insurance contracts, unit trusts and other forms of collective investments, so removing the distortions to competition arising from the present separate, differing regulations.

The problem, however, of the regulation of the integrated financial services group remains. As explained already, the Government's powers to change the regulatory system are circumscribed by its EEC obligations: the 1979 Life Insurance Freedom of Establishment Directive, for example, requires insurance companies to transact only insurance business. Therefore, the development of financial conglomerates will have to be within the framework of a holding company form of organisation with the subsidiaries subject to separate supervisory regulation, though that alone does not remove the risk of cross-infection. In viewing the situation in 1984 the Governor of the Bank of England said that consideration would have to be given:

> ... to the preservation of the independence of the separate managements, and the erection of barriers preventing cross-infection through exposure to the same risks ... Where there is more than one supervisory authority, as with banking and insurance, this will clearly require co-operation between the officials concerned. (*Bank of England Quarterly Bulletin*, June 1984)

The government response, as noted in Chapter 6 (p. 155), has been to set up interdepartmental arrangements for the separate government regulators to share information and coordinate responses, and the Bank of England proposes to supervise banking holding groups on a consolidated basis.

Besides the proposals relating to the marketing of collective investments outlined in Chapter 8, the Financial Services Bill also deals with some of the other problems arising from the integration of financial institutions. The Government accepted that reliance could not be placed on arrangements to prevent the flow of client information between different parts of an integrated group and instead preferred to rely on the duties of disclosure, fair dealing and the use of skill and care applicable to all investment businesses to safeguard the interests of investors. Doubts have been cast on whether the rules framed to deal with the conflicts of interest arising from the introduction of the dual capacity on the Stock Exchange will be workable (*The Times*, April 23, 1985), and it is hard to believe that persons engaged in investment business will not sometimes use available information for their own rather than their clients' interests. Moreover, a freedom to pass information between the different parts of an integrated group has important competitive implications too.

Finally, on the subject of competition, the Bill provides for the rules, regulations, guidance and arrangements of recognised self-regulatory organisations, investment exchanges and clearing houses to be exempt from the provision of the Fair Trading Act 1973, the Restrictive Practices Act 1976 and the Competition Act 1980. But the SROs will have to be vetted by the Director of Fair Trading who, if he considers that they restrict competition to a significant extent, will report to the Secretary of State accordingly.

10.3 Diversification and the Financial Firm

So strong have been the competitive forces upon financial markets, from a variety of sources, that it is tempting (as noted in the introductory chapter) to speak of a spontaneous outbreak of competition. Despite the increased competition, there is considerable optimism amongst many financial firms as to their growth prospects. We asked firms to estimate the growth of the real value of their assets over five years up to 1990. The results are shown for the three major institutional types of banks, building societies and life insurance companies in Figure 10.2. Life insurance companies are the most optimistic with 32 per cent of respondents expecting their real asset value to have more than doubled by 1990, and 51 per cent

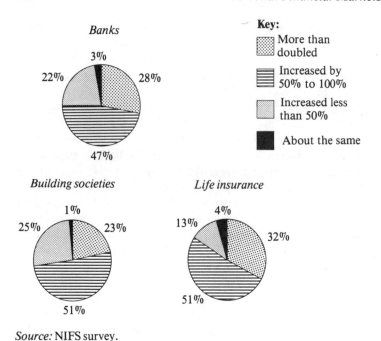

Source: NIFS survey.

Figure 10.2   Expected Growth of Real Assets over Five Years

expecting it to have increased by between 50 per cent and 100 per cent. The figures for banks are 28 per cent and 47 per cent respectively; and for building societies 23 per cent and 51 per cent.

In looking at their growth prospects, we asked financial institutions to consider the importance of alternative strategies available for achieving this growth. The responses are recorded in Figure 10.3. Internal growth was the most significant, being seen as important or very important by over 80 per cent of respondents. Advertising (75 per cent) and direct marketing (73 per cent) were close behind. There were differences between institutional types, of which the most notable were the high emphasis placed on advertising by building societies and the importance of direct marketing by life insurance companies. Acquisition or merger was seen as important or very important by 45 per cent of respondents, but interestingly, some 53 per cent placed joint ventures in the same category.

We asked institutions their opinion as to whether diversification

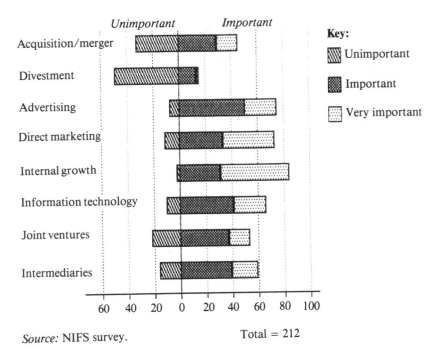

Source: NIFS survey.   Total = 212

Figure 10.3 Strategies for Growth of Financial Institutions

by different types of institution would be a major factor in the market for personal financial services. The results are shown in Figure 10.4. It is evident that banks and building societies are seen as major movers, but retail stores also figure significantly with 54 per cent of respondents seeing their diversification as a major influence. Diversification by life insurance companies is also expected to be important. But only a minority perceive diversification by non-life companies, insurance brokers, stockbrokers, estate agents and computer companies as having a major influence upon personal financial markets. Even if there are clear advantages to be gained from combining activities, these may be achievable through joint venture and other forms of cooperation and do not necessarily require the amalgamation of companies.

As might be expected with industries opened to greater competition, the first entrants are those firms whose entry and exit costs are

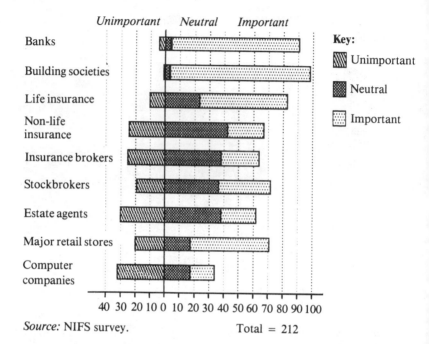

Source: NIFS survey.   Total = 212

Figure 10.4 Diversification by Institution

lowest. These are most likely to be other financial firms, rather than those without experience in the provision of financial services. For the former, entry and exit can be on a limited scale by adding to or substracting from an existing range, given the inherent substitutability of financial services noted in Chapter 2.

This does raise the question of how permanent the trends are away from traditional patterns of specialisation in the provision of financial services, and what is the appropriate form for organising widened product ranges. These are matters upon which we surveyed British financial institutions as part of the NIFS survey.

Whether internal transactions are relatively more efficient than market ones has long been seen as a major determinant of the nature of the firm (Coase 1937). As recorded in Figure 10.5, 79 per cent of the respondents to our questionnaire agreed or strongly agreed with the view that mergers between different types of financial institutions will significantly increase over the next five years, which

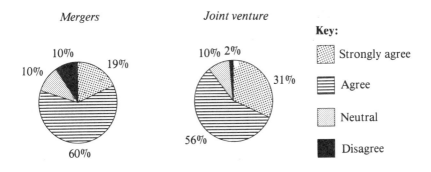

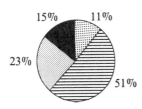

Figure 10.5

implies a belief in the gains available to large organisations. However, 87 per cent agreed or strongly agreed with the statement that links other than by merger, e.g. joint venture, will significantly increase over the next five years.

We concur with the significance that our respondents place upon joint ventures, for a number of reasons. Joint ventures offer means of achieving economies of scale and scope without resort to merger and the formation of large-scale enterprises. The joint venture route enables a sharing of costs, and benefits, of rapidly changing technology. In a changing market environment, joint ventures enable firms to experiment at low cost with additional product lines, since few know in advance what combinations of products and mix of services will succeed, and product life cycles in financial services are often short. The existence of joint ventures provides financial firms with the same 'make or buy' choice open to firms in other activities.

Joint ventures are already of considerable significance in the UK. Links between unit trust managers and merchant banks and between building societies and non-clearing banks have seen the major banks lose their monopoly of cheque provision in England. Building societies offer credit cards, insurance services and real-estate services in cooperation with other institutions, and an expansion of such arrangements can be expected following the passage of the Building Societies Act. Joint ventures have been announced between insurance companies and US banks to provide home mortgages.

Nevertheless, there are those who see that the future lies with the giant firm in terms of financial conglomerates, or 'supermarkets'. Notably, only 15 per cent of our respondents disagreed with the statement that financial supermarkets will play a significant role in the marketing of personal financial services, while 62 per cent agreed (Figure 10.5).

While it is difficult to escape from common usage, the description 'financial supermarket' is in many ways a poor one since it implies self-service and supply of products from a variety of 'manufacturers'. Despite the growth of ATMs and machine-operated service foyers, most financial products involve some 'customisation' and are often highly information specific, although these characteristics apply more so to 'shopping' than to 'convenience' goods. Nor is 'financial conglomerate' a good description. It has 'cross-industry' connotations inappropriate when traditional industry boundaries in finance are being eroded by regulatory and technological developments. Conglomeration can also imply merely ownership of financial services firms, without any tying-in of services, in order to exploit those opportunities for portfolio diversification which are not open to shareholders in their private portfolios. Financial 'department store' is a term which perhaps best describes the integration of services and the opportunities to realise economies of scope.

Based on our examination of the characteristics of markets for personal financial services and our observations of developments in the UK and US, we offer some comments on the future of financial 'department stores'. They are summarised as follows:

Arguments For Financial 'Department Stores'

From the viewpoint of the customer:

(1) Offering a range of services provides the convenience of one-stop shopping and reduces customers' travelling costs.

(2) By 'branding' and 'good housekeeping awards' a known and trusted supplier can reduce consumers' search costs. Ownership and control of the supplier ensures quality control.

(3) Dealing with a large diversified firm provides 'safety in numbers' and continuity of the intertemporal relationships.

From the viewpoint of the financial firm:

(4) There may be economies in assessing the credit standing and monitoring the accounts of households which consume many services.

(5) Technological improvements have increased the role of multipurpose capital equipment in producing financial services – computerised record-keeping and telecommunications links with customers and markets. Diversification permits the cost to be spread across additional product lines.

(6) As ATM usage has grown, branch networks and distribution systems have excess capacity, and diversification is a way of putting this to use – an example of an economy of scope.

(7) Economies of marketing and advertising may be realised when offering a set of related services to actual and potential customers.

(8) Diversification allows flexibility in resource use across numerous activities and protection of the balance sheet in the face of unexpected changes in the environment.

Arguments Against Financial 'Department Stores'

To begin with, we list some reasons to be sceptical about the permanence of the diversification trend:

(1) The particular circumstances of the first half of the 1980s offered opportunities for unit trust managers and other firms to provide transactions services as the rise in market interest

rates exposed the price discriminatory pricing by banks of retail deposits. As banks have been forced by competition to offer market related rates, the attractiveness of the alternative suppliers' products have dwindled.

(2) Many of the moves to conglomeration are defensive. Much of what is hailed as new in technologically-based financial services is little more than 'spicing and repackaging' of products of other firms. Since no-one really knows what combination of services is going to work, everyone who is big enough is setting up a number of experiments in order to establish a minimum presence in most areas. Firms are positioning so that they can jump onto a bandwagon.

In addition there are some attitudes of consumers:

(3) UK clearing banks have long provided through their subsidiaries, and have had on offer in branches, an extensive array of financial services. Their penetration of their customer base is low for most product lines (5 to 10 per cent at most). Many bank customers surveyed in a Banking World Poll in 1985 said that they prefer to obtain insurance, real estate and even mortgages from specialist suppliers.[2]

(4) Consumers also seek diversification. Many may wish to spread future lending prospects across a number of potential suppliers. Or, they may separate their transactions plus borrowing package from their investment package.

(5) Reinforcing this is the 'do-it-yourself' financial movement. In the past consumers have put funds into banks, savings institutions, unit trusts and life offices with often little interest or control over the investment of this money, and the mix of return and safety. They are now being encouraged by government schemes into investing in or establishing their own enterprise and acquiring shares directly. These attitudes may carry over to financial intermediation, leading many to 'mix and match' and seek out specialist firms.

From the viewpoint of firms, the following factors may limit the tendency to conglomeration:

(6) Benefits of diversification can be obtained outside of the firm. Technology and market arrangements have adapted so

as to dramatically alter pooling costs. Most of the major developments in computerised payment facilities have involved sharing. Joint ventures allow firms to widen product lines, and thus geographic reach, to the convenience of consumers, while retaining specialised skills. Developments in futures markets, interest-rate swaps and mortgages and commercial loan pools now enable diversification of balance sheets at much lower cost than previously.

(7) Cultural and remuneration differences exist between the various providers of financial services. Staff in banks and building societies are normally salaried, whereas insurance salesmen and securities brokers are on commissions. Merchant bankers and securities dealers are used to a free-wheeling independent mode of operation. If various parts of the group operate independently, potentiality for 'synergy' is lost. Frequently it seems that the combination of the parts is less than the sum of components, and diversification is an expensive way to buy another firm's mailing list.

(8) There are limits to the success of conglomeration, as true for financial as for other firms, if only on managerial grounds. How many products can agents be expected to have knowledge of? Can branch staff in British banks really explain all of the 300 products offered to customers? How much can chief executives of diversified organisations grasp? Financial institutions, like firms in general, exist largely because they can process and use information efficiently, but are ultimately constrained in size by the 'span of control' in assimilating and acting upon the information. For such reasons, many industrial conglomerates set up 20 years ago are currently being divested.

This last point is an appropriate one on which to close. Developments in financial markets, and the services and products they offer, in Britain, the United States and other countries, are frequently referred to as a 'revolution in financial services'. Certainly advances in information technology, the potentiality for joint ventures, the 'deintegration' of financial services, and the 'despecialisation' of financial functions all point to a considerable diversity in the future provision of personal financial services. At the same time, our study leads us to believe that:

    (a) in many respects so far there has been more talk and experimentation, with institutions positioning themselves to take advantage of the opportunities which might occur, than there has been substantial action;

    (b) the developments to date, at least in the UK, would be better described as evolutionary rather than revolutionary, and one is led to recall the old saying 'the more things change the more they stay the same'.

Perhaps this should not be surprising. Fundamental changes affecting all types of suppliers of financial services are occurring that no market participant can afford to ignore. But there are also important outward signs of continuity, for change in financial markets is much more a story of the adaptation of existing firms than it is one of the birth of new ones. Ultimately the financial firm, like any other, depends for its success on the people who work for it, their communications with customers, and their ability to formulate and respond to new ideas − factors common to all times.

Notes

1. The provisions of the Insurance Companies Act, 1982, cover:

    (i) the minimum financial and other conditions for the entry of new UK and foreign incorporated insurance companies to the market, and the authorisation by the DTI of existing companies to write additional classes of insurance;

    (ii) continuing solvency requirements for authorised insurers:

    (iii) obligations on companies to notify to the DTI changes in owners, controllers, and managers who must be 'fit and proper' persons;

    (iv) the provision of annual accounting and other statistical returns to the DTI;

    (v) the valuation of assets and, for life insurance, an annual actuarial valuation of the life fund assets and liabilities;

    (vi) regulations relating to the marketing of insurances;

    (vii) the powers of the DTI to intervene in the affairs of a company or to withdraw authorisation; and

    (viii) the winding-up of insurance companies.

2. See p. 151 above.

References

Carlson, R. (1984) 'The evolving life insurance industry', in A.W. Sametz (ed.) *The Emerging Financial Industry*, Lexington Books.

Coase, R.H. (1937) 'The nature of the firm', *Economica*, New Series, Vol. IV, pp. 386–405.

Finsinger, J., Hammond, E. and Tapp, J. (1985) *Insurance: Competition or Regulation?* Institute of Fiscal Studies.

Gower, L.C.B. (1982) *Review of Investor Protection: A Discussion Document*, HMSO.

Gower, L.C.B. (1984) *Report on the Review of Investor Protection*, Cmnd. 9125, HMSO.

HMSO (1985) *Financial Services in the United Kingdom: A New Framework for Investor Protection*, Cmnd. 9432.

HMSO (1985) *The Financial Services Bill 1985*.

Lancaster, K. (1975) 'Socially optimal product differentiation', *American Economic Review*, Vol. 6.

Lancaster, K. (1979) *Variety, Equity and Efficiency*, Columbia University Press.

Silber, W.L. (1983) 'The process of financial innovation', *American Economic Review and Proceedings*, Vol. 73, May, pp. 89–95.

Spence, A.M. (1976) 'Produce differentiation and welfare', *American Economic Review Papers and Proceedings*, Vol. 66, May.

Author Index

272

Subject Index

Abbey Life, 63, 69, 177
Abbey National, 61, 92, 160, 185
Access, 29, 97, 150
Advertising, 57–67
Allied Dunbar, 63, 69
American Express, 119, 121, 126, 130
American General, 126, 130
Automatic teller machines (ATMs), 37, 45, 80–81, 83, 91–95, 96, 101, 146, 165–166
Automatic clearing systems, 90, 91

Bank America, 126, 127, 130
Bank of England, 140–141, 153, 154, 155, 156, 260
Bank of Scotland, 46, 88, 99, 100, 190
Bank holding companies, 34, 42, 108–109, 121–122, 149, 155–156, 260
Bankers Trust, 129
Banking Act 1979, 20, 140, 141, 153–156, 259
Banks:
  UK, 20, 30–31, 56–58, 137–167, 178, 183–186, 235, 237, 242, 262–264
  US, 108–113, 118–119, 121–122, 130
Barclaycard, 29

Barclays Bank, 91, 146, 155, 190, 243
Beneficial Finance, 130
'Big Bang', see Stock Exchange
Bolton Committee, 239
Branching: 34
  by banks, 143–146, 166
  by building societies, 143, 166
  restrictions on in the US, 108, 110, 120
BP, 97
Building Societies' Association, 159, 169, 171, 172, 179
Building societies, 20, 59–63, 125, 134, 142–148, 151–153, 157–167, 169–170, 176, 177, 179–183, 188–189, 262–264
  cartel, 61, 179–183, 185
Building Societies Act 1962, 157, 182
Building Societies Act 1986, 59, 157–161, 175, 178–179, 193
Business expansion scheme, 230, 234–235, 239

Cash dispensers, see ATMs
Cash management accounts, 43, 45, 115–118
Certificates of deposit, 115, 188–189, 190
Chase Manhattan, 101

274